The Sporting
Urban Voltaire

The Sporting Urban Voltaire

JACK MCLEAN

FOREWORD BY HAZEL IRVINE

cheers!

Jack McLean

Neil Wilson Publishing • Glasgow • Scotland

© Jack McLean, 1994

Published by Neil Wilson Publishing Ltd
309 The Pentagon Centre
36 Washington Street
GLASGOW G3 8AZ
Tel: 041-221-1117
Fax: 041-221-5363

The moral right of the author has been asserted.

A catalogue record for this book is available from the British Library.
ISBN 1-897784-25-2

Typeset in 11 on 12pt Perpetua by Face to Face Design Services, Glasgow
Printed in Scotland by Scotprint Ltd, Musselburgh

Dedicated to Eddie Rodger
my sports editor

CONTENTS

FOREWORD

JACK McLEAN is many things. He's witty, well meaning although at times his political correctness is askew. He's idiosyncratic, he's warm, he's both forthright and downright 'saft'. He's a good friend.

I was first introduced to Jack as a fledgling assistant at Radio Clyde, called upon to help produce his phone-in programme. It was classic McLean. Listeners would harangue him on any subject and the UrbanV would harangue them right back. It was less a production exercise. More a case of holding him in check.

I listened from the control room, terrified, but nonetheless enthralled by Jack's wit and his humanity.

These days I can still hear the sound of his voice. It seems to float off the page when I read his Friday column in *The Herald*.

Jack and I have shared employers and now employment, as sports journalists. But while we've both sat in cold press boxes at the footy, Jack has moved on. These days he's not so much an 'out-and-out' fitba' scribe, more of a 'utility' man, filing reports on an incredible range of different sports. Some fascinating, some bizzare. Flounder tramping, I ask you?!

In truth, we've both undergone a kind of conversion when it comes to minority sport, (although that wretched mantle, in itself, does sport a disservice). We have both discovered the sociability, the fun, the enthusiasm and the new skills in new sports. Reporting on them is a challenge. They allow you to shake yourself out of the often formulaeic football preview/review mode.

They also make us reassess the nature of sport and take a stand. Jack's observations on the development of youth and women's sport are honest and important. Yes, he likes the company of the ladies! Yes, he makes the odd faux-pas! But we forgive him because Jack is, in truth, a bit of a feminist! In his inimitable style, he does a fair bit of campaigning for women's sport. He's always likely to take a heartfelt swipe at its lowly standing in the publicity pecking-order.

You'll become familiar with his opinions as you read this book. You'll be entertained, too, by his stories and by his wit. Doubtless you'll chuckle. His humour is infectious.

The Sporting Urban Voltaire is Jack McLean at his best.

Hazel Irvine
June, 1994

INTRODUCTION

WHEN I first joined the sports desk of *The Herald* I was aware of a certain animosity towards myself within the sports journalist fraternity; of course I was. Sports journalists make you horribly aware of animosity. The feeling was that yer Urban Voltaire was a mere writer, a dilettante, a fly-by-night, and in short, a bit of a spiv really. Also the rumour was that I knew sod all about sport, a rumour readily proved after my first sports report. It was a football game. I contrived, as is explained elsewhere in this book, to get wrong the names of the two players who were sent off, and the scoreline too. And in a vivacious burst of idiocy I got the name of one of the teams wrong as well. The sub-editors managed but laughed loud and long, especially long. I did footy for over a year.

But the time came when I expressed my disquiet over football. I did not like it. Football players aged 18 and destined to become fat, failed publicans were arrogant enough for Anton Diffring playing an SS Grupenfuehrer, and managers were serial killers. Most football journalists would pass for Brutus with a drink in him. The occasional exception to this sometimes brought tears to my eyes for their kindness. Arthur Montford proved to be an absolute gentleman and was extraordinarily nice to me: even buying me a drink at Love Street. Jim Whyte of Scottish Television told me things which he didn't have to and so did the then sports producer for Scottish TV, Dennis Mooney, an old chum from the days when we were students. Gerry McNee turned out to be helpful beyond belief despite his well known abrasiveness, an assistance I have often repaid sadly with churlishness. But I did not like football. I still don't. And so I slid out of pro footy.

My sports editor, Eddie Rodger, to whom I dedicate this book and stick in the rest of the lads on *The Herald* sports team, knew this and Eddie took me aside one day down in McEntee's pub. Eddie instead sent me off to something daft — I can't remember what it was, lacrosse or ping-pong or something — but I kicked off into a new dawn and it was great. I was a dreadful football reporter, and remain a dreadful reporter, but the so-called minority sports opened up not just avenues, but roads and streets and highways and countries which I suppose nobody, or not many, thought existed at all. I still do football — if it's girls or ladies or children or even sometimes junior, but it has to be a writing assignment: I can do that.

Naturally some of the sports I have covered have attracted a certain risibility when it comes to the response of my Scottish sporting colleagues. 'Where were you today?' I was once asked by Jim Traynor, chief football reporter and probably the top football writer in Britain today, the heir to John Rafferty of that Edinburgh newspaper many years back. I asked him where he had been. He'd been covering St Johnstone on a fiercely wet day in Perth. I told him I'd been in Edinburgh, covering the women's Scotland v Wales rugby international. The sun had split the skies, the game was great, Scotland had won, I spent a few hours in the Edinburgh Academicals clubhouse talking to The Great White Shark, a hero himself, and lots of splendid young girls. I got a lumber from another young lady, a meal in Raffaeli's and … the rest is none of your business. Traynor was green with envy. A day later he was still soaked to the skin. There you are then.

But almost instantly I took to the minority sports. For a start I got to meet so many cross-over sports people. It is amazing how many people involve themselves in different pastimes, and how pleasant they are to each other and even writers like myself. The late Norman Mortimer, who died tragically this year, Glasgow councillor, international fencer, PE teacher and on and on, involved himself in more sports than the entire Olympic Committee and was a wonderful source of information. He was also very good at shoving me a wee dose of the amber fluid too.

Sure, you get the odd zealots who are not really quite right in the head and in fact at one time *The Herald* seriously thought about cutting any copy about curling because of the dreadful criticisms of my fairly regular reports on this somewhat arcane game. I often got things wrong in this sport as in others because when you cover over 30 different sports in one year one sometimes gets things, well, wrong. I persuaded my editors that this would be dreadfully unfair to the overwhelming number of curling enthusiasts who put up with my errors and give me a welcome which would do credit to Charles Edward bloody Stewart in Moydart.

As a result I got involved with lots and lots of sports and the people in them. Some of the sports didn't seem, at first, to be sports. My editor wanted to know how come chess was a sport for instance. 'Sport for the mind, Eddie' I said. 'Aye; aw right,' he said. Flounder tramping at the Solway village of Palnackie, (it consists of catching fish with your feet and that's true), in the course of which I fell in love with a wee four-year-old girl who had more moxie than Harry the Horse or Little Isadore out of Damon Runyon. Quoits and clay-pigeon shooting I proved to be rather good at myself. Oh, there were many others and I have never enjoyed myself so much. Apart from writing it up on Sundays.

It is then that the real fun began. Swopping insults with the boys (they are all boys on *The Herald* sports desk), is the best fun of all. Not quite. The most fun of all were the sports, followed by the bonhomie, followed by the girls.

You will discover in this book my conversion to a sort of feminism. In the early days I became outraged by the absurd discrimination against women in almost every sport. My own current passion, bowling, has a long history of rather innocent, but nasty for all that, male chauvinism. Yet discrimination against females is endemic in sport, and worse than that, sometimes the females argue against sport for their own gender as well. I have been castigated often for my sexist attitudes and more often than not unjustly, I like to think. But in sport I done my best, as they say. I support women in sport because the women need support. And if anybody says I'm out of line when I report that such-and-such a girl is pretty, I never heard a pretty woman complain. Certainly, I never reported that a woman was ugly, partly because not one of them is as fat, old, and baldy as myself, and partly because it has nothing to do with sport, or ability.

And that might just be why I asked Hazel Irvine to do my foreword. She has had to take even more stick than a smart-arse like myself ever did, and has survived to be the most vibrant and refreshing and — the sports boys will not like this — one of the most knowledgable sports presenters of them all. And she, like me, found more fun in diversity than one can discover in the Upas tree of football. Just about my favourite piece in this collection is the one on children's games on page 144, for all sports start with children, and what their energy creates. What the hell, I know about that; I never grew up myself. Which is why I have had so much fun covering all this playtime over the years.

Jack McLean
Heraghty's Bar
Glasgow
June, 1994

SCHOOL'S OUT!

March 11, 1991

HERE I am in Irvine, with the smirr of rain on and off, and the perfect day for running about the countryside of this old and new town. As it happens, I was born here, but have not been back for 46 years, which is to say since I left Irvine Central Hospital as a swaddled infant.

There was no Magnum Sports Centre then, but there is now. Outside of the centre is the course for the biggest event which schools sport in Scotland possesses. This is the Scottish Schools Athletic Association Cross Country Championships, and Irvine has been the venue for the last nine years.

The 15-year-old Magnum Centre is big, but even it is a little stretched to accommodate the sheer number of competitors. There are 2000 young people here as entrants, of which 1500 will actually run. It is an awesome sight, 2000 children from wee to big, and all hyped up for the afternoon's events. The centre copes admirably; I don't know how.

The children are keen though, and this is one of the biggest events in the Scottish calendar — and from the results at this Scottish championship are drawn the 32 youngsters who will represent their country. In three weeks' time, the young internationalists will be at Boyle County in the Republic of Ireland running their hearts out for us.

The children are about in droves. You can tell the public and independent schools a mile off — they wear smart school uniforms. Glasgow's own Hutchie Grammar is well represented by a team of pleasant and modest girls. Karen Paton, from Newlands, also plays hockey and likes horse-riding. Her colleague, Alison Fowler, is also from Newlands. They both disarm me horribly when they tell me that they do not expect to win. St Aloysius (a school also from Glasgow) are expected to do well and certainly beat them. It is refreshing to discover sense and honesty in a school pupil at all, but, then, it is Hutchie, and one should not be too surprised.

As it happens, the public and independents do well at cross country and for an obvious reason: they have more space to themselves, and in the case of the boarding schools, a lot more time. There is not much chance of the average school in a Glasgow housing scheme being able to have pupils running around its local area.

There is, of course, plenty of opportunity for the independents. But this does not always work, however. The under-14 girls' cross country event was won, by several furlongs, by a wee waif of a girl called Pamellann Crawley, from Eastbank School in Shettleston, beating Scottish club champion Susan Scott easily.

Eastbank is not the most salubrious of schools — though its PE department is especially strong on athletics — and the wee lassie is regarded as a major prospect for the future.

The sheer effort involved in this stamina-demanding pastime could be seen in the exhaustion of the children at the end of the race. The courage, too, as I watched the second last girl come in limping as if it was myself after a football match at Airdrie. The very last girl to come in had most sensibly lost her number card from the front of her top, thereby ensuring that she and her school would not be humiliated by a mention in this blatt.

But there are stars in this sport and they emerge easily. St Aloysius was always going to do well in the team award, I was told, and they did, winning the gold for the over-17 boys. This was very considerably helped by the performance of Mark McBeth, who also won the individual gold.

He had been marked out by all the adults I met from the very first, as had very much the star, young Isabel Linaker, of Queen Anne School, daughter of the famous John and herself the British record-holder. Isabel, as was expected, ran away with the individual gold.

Incidentally, the team winner in Isabel's event was Hawick High School whose rector is, of course, none other than Scotland's own rugby legend, Jim Telfer. In athletics, it helps to have commitment from adults.

This is, indeed, a problem in school sports and was freely admitted to by lots of the teachers I met there who were in charge of their school teams. The ludicrous attitudes of many local authorities towards their teachers, PE or otherwise, by which most of the once committed dominies have been alienated against extra-curricular activities, has resulted in a considerable diminution of school sport of whatever variety, and it is reflected in the fact that clubs are now becoming more important than school athletics.

Dumfries assistant head teacher Scott Stirling was rueful on this point. 'Our major contribution to the pupils is now the six quid entry fee,' he said, 'and a lot of teachers discovered how pleasant a Saturday to themselves was after the strike.' Mr Stirling had driven the team down.

One of his ex-pupils is Hayley Haining, now at Glasgow Yooni and a prospect for the Olympic squad. Teachers like Stirling have contributed much over the years, but such splendid work looks hardly likely to continue for much longer.

The absurd behaviour of local education authorities towards sports' teachers lies in marked contrast to some other departments of the same councils. Irvine Development Corporation have spent a great deal over the years in sporting developments, and outside companies have too, (the Scottish Schools Athletic Association have been sponsored by Scottish Power to the tune of £25,000 over the last two years, and will be for £30,000 over the next two).

Education officials seem to get everything wrong and try hard to do so. They should have seen the health and enthusiasm of the 2000 children and young people at Irvine on Saturday. I felt a bit proud of Irvine, even at that.

A GREAT RACE RUN BY WOMEN FOR WOMEN

May 31, 1993

THE sun was splitting the skies on Saturday. Yesterday it put its hat on and it was a rotten trick. Was not yesterday when the first ever City of Glasgow women's 10km race took place.

Now I don't have a scooby what kilometres are (a colleague tells me right now that you divide by eight and multiply by five, but what you divide and multiply naebody seems to know) but it stretches from running them in 35 minutes as the winner, ex-Olympic athlete Lynne McIntyre did, to last runners who managed hours and were being picked up by Parks and Leisure Department cars all over the place, and didn't mind.

Said Susan Deighan, who is the event's co-ordinator for Glasgow P&R: 'It's a great day out anyway and the odd straggler is as welcome as the winner.'

It was a good day out for the runners and the spectators. I spoke to one onlooker in particular because she was awful pretty and I wanted to know why she wasn't running.

Anne Duncan, a geography student at Glasgow Yooni, told me she was too unfit herself but her chum was meant to be running and hadn't turned up.

When I was a student, pretty girls wouldn't be up in time for a 10 o'clock run in the rain if it was up to me, but students are different these days no doubt.

Also awake at this unholy hour were the City of Glasgow pipe band, with pipe major David Wotherspoon leading them off.

Despite the drizzle it was a grand display. All these ladies jouking about to the tune of *Highland Laddie* brought a lump to the throat.

There were two lassies in wheelchairs taking part five minutes after the horde began, which is unusual because, normally, disabled entrants start five minute before in a run.

This did not deter British junior lady champion and rated fourth in the UK, Karen Lewis, from doing the run in 38 minutes, which is some achievement despite, as fellow wheelchair entrant Evelyn Neave (who came in at 55 minutes) pointed out: 'We score a bit. We're a lot faster going down the braes.'

Cheating almost, I should have thought, but why not?

But there were a lot of people for this very first Glasgow 10km run for the weemenfolk. Out of 842 entrants, there were more than 700 who completed the course.

Some of them were very young — 18 was the youngest you could be — but there was also the indefatigable Betty Bunce, who did the course in 69 minutes — a mere six digits more than her age.

Betty, originally from East Anglia but long domiciled in Greenock, started running when she was 50 and is now something of a legend in athletic circles. She looks younger than anybody on *The Herald* Sports Desk, believe me.

Talking of newspaper folk, was there not Marie Whitelaw (who works for a blatt in Anderston Quay), who finished very late and took five minutes to get enough breath to speak.

'It was fabulous,' she gasped. 'Enjoyed it (gasp), do it again (gasp), did it for charity (gasp), the Heart Foundation ...'

I left her as she downed a free Diet Coke, thinking that if it had been me there would have been a serious need for the Heart Foundation at that.

But surprisingly, there were few victims. Two girls with minor foot injuries and two spectators with lovely wee hurts.

One was an ambulanceman who got run over by a bike. The other was a pregnant lady, who went into labour at a bus stop. A race against time youse would have called it if youse were working for a blatt at Anderston Quay.

A race against any kind of time it was for Hilda Murshedy (I think I've got that name right) who limped in heroically to fall into the arms of her husband.

Hilda is training for the half marathon and works for the Co-op. That's what she told me anyway. I am not sure if working for the Co-op or running the half-marathon has something in common. Probably.

Limping just after Hilda was a beautiful lady with pleated blonde hair who looked as if she should have been pirouetting at a mannequin parade. She was greeted by her dad and uncles. 'Away hame,' they cried, 'and dae yer ironing.' Such is women's sport.

The event was organised by Glasgow Parks boys and girls, especially the girls. The two officers for Women in Sport, both PE trained, Gillian Duncan and Angela Porter, joined up with marketing deputy boss Debbie Murray to tell me how important women's sport is, and I agree with them. What they said about yesterday's event was true. They hit their target for numbers and everything went absolutely smoothly. Said Angela: 'Perhaps we know, as women, what women need — creches and child-minding facilities. Promoting women's sport needs a bit of nous.'

The ladies said it without smugness, to which perhaps they have a right considering how well organised yesterday was.

The last comments come from Maria Cusack, a wee friend of mine from back in the days when she was at Lourdes School.

Now a systems analyst with Chivas Bros, she told me whisky was all right in moderation and I had no sense of it. The lassie knows me.

The other comment was from the runner-up, 26-year-old doctor Audrey Sym, who completed the course in 36 minutes and 20 seconds, just before 36-year-old Sandra Branney. There is something nice about being told off for smoking by a nice girl.

I will try to take her advice. That'll be right.

A SLOW GAME FOR THE FAST THINKER

November 23, 1992

HORRIBLY genteel but thick people call badminton 'badmington' the way they consume 'sangwiches'. Gentilities play badminton in church halls and the like: I should know for I was once one of them.

Admittedly this was the result of a determined effort to get off with Gillian MacIndewar in 1960 but the aroma of the church hall has ever been concomitant with this marvellous game. And it is a marvellous pastime. It is a slow and a fast game for those with brains. Generally badminton is slow on the shuttlecock but fast in the reaction.

But it can be a lot faster than you think at the highest level. When top player Chris Hunt was scientifically tested at last year's US Open he recorded shuttlecock speeds of 188mph. Yet speed is only one element. Watch a really good player and you will see restraint, smashes, deft little flicks, and the sort of spatial awareness which requires brains rather than limbs.

This last week saw the Scottish Open·Carlton Championships at the Kelvin Hall, Glasgow, and sadly the Scots did not do well. They were out of the competition quicker than Chris Hunt could batter a feathery object or two. Said a Scottish Badminton Union official when asked about the failure of the Scots: 'It's because we're crap,' a refreshing honesty on the part of any sports official.

Press Officer Elspeth Burnside said: 'None of the Scots won a match. Kevin Scott did get into the second round. Mind you,' she admitted, 'he got a bye in the first. And he's from Guildford.' It's grand when press officers tell you the truth.

The Scots are not very good at this sport which is surprising considering that we should be okey-dokey at inside games. Last Tuesday Caledonia lost 7-0 to Sweden in Arbroath. The Swedes are awfy good at badminton though: they are the European champions. All the Scandinavian countries are good at the game. This is quite simply because Scandinavians, like ourselves, have to play a lot of inside sports because of the climate: the difference is that Scandinavian politicians put more money into sport than we do.

The sport attracts a lot of girls. Anne Gibson, Scotland's champion and our only full-time player, had to pull out through injury, but Gillian Martin didn't show her ability too well. Given a bye in the first round, she lost out to England's Alison Humbly.

We should be doing better. Especially as badminton is so popular.

It is reckoned that over five million people play in Britain, with a goodly percentage of them Scots, which makes it the biggest participant sport after angling. There are 120 countries in the International Badminton Federation. I got all this from Finlay Tait of the Scottish Union.

'The facilities don't match with elsewhere,' he said ruefully, and they don't. Carlton, the racquet makers who sponsored the Scottish Open along with Glasgow District Council (another bouquet to Glasgow Sports and Leisure people), are naturally keen to promote the sport and tell me you can get your mitts on a badminton bat for between £10 and £100, which is reasonable at that.

Prince Edward, patron of the Scottish Badminton Union, was there yesterday and has turned up three times this year. For such a wonderful game and such an effort on the part of badmington (sic) players we could do with more Government meat in the funding sangwich (sic again). Sic anyway. At heart.

A WEE BIT OF HISTORY IN THE SQUARE

June 28, 1993

THEY raised the red flag in George Square in 1919. Why this was so heinous to the sensibilities of the decent people of the day one cannot quite understand but it resulted in a whole rake of chaps in respectable bourgeois suits and stiff collars getting the jail. Jimmy Maxton, Archie Kirkwood, and Willie Gallagher all got done. My dad remembered Maxton getting skelped with a police baton, a fate surely more appropriate to his great nephew. George Square wis great fur laughs.

Then again, George Square holds such marmoreal splendour that you kind of hold your breath with the solemnity of it all. There are 13 stookies in this heart of Glasgow. There is Sir Thomas Campbell and Robert Burns and — *(enough of this drivel McLean, this is a sports report, Ed.)*

Well there is a lot of history going on in George Square and a nice wee bit of it was made on Saturday when instead of wild Red Clydesiders cavorting about the statuary there were a horde of splendid youngsters dancing with a ball and putting it into a basket. For this was the Reebok Outdoor Basketball Challenge at which over 120 young people, from 10 to 18, were competing. They came from near and far. It will be further later on because the winners go on to the UK finals in Birmingham on the last day of July and the 16 to 18-year-old boys have the chance of winning a prestigious place in the first ever Euro-Blacktop finals in Milan. I got that off the press hand-out which saw fit to inform me that Milan was in Italy. I've been in Milan and I'm pretty sure it was in Italy and thank you for confirming it Mr Reebok.

But there was definitely something rather Latin about the spectacle in the Square. For a start, it was very exciting. This was three-on-three basketball, using only one basket and very fast indeed. Basketball is by nature fast and very robust: there is not meant to be physical contact but there is; a lot. There is not meant to be a real advantage in height among the younger players but there is. Certainly the girls I met from Aberdeen were tall enough to pass for the kind of hatstands I can't reach.

There were two teams from Aberdeen Beacon Sports Centre and Powers Basketball. Tom Clark, a PE teacher from Northfield Academy, and coach for the Aberdeen squad of girls who won the 13-15 girls' match, told me he had roughly 155 kids in train and, he said with justifiable resentment, no coverage from the *Press and Journal*. 'Youse huv goat to look tae the quality journalists,' I told him gleefully. The children were from Aboyne, Banchory, Keith, and elsewhere in the land of The Great Neep. Thirty-five teams played in the regional play-offs. Certainly the girls themselves loved the day out, even if they had started out at six in the morning. There was Fiona and Jemma and Clare, Arlene, and Dawn, all of them 13 or 14, and all getting medals.

That's not quite true because Reebok didn't quite manage to get everything right and forgot one of the girls' medals and a tee-shirt. They said they would rectify that in the future as I'm sure they will after this goes to print. Seriously, Reebok have sponsored well, as indeed, have the ubiquitous Glasgow Parks and Recreation Department. I am singing this lot's praises once again because they are due it.

Yet something worries me a little about this basketball development. All the Aberdeen girls said — and echoed exactly what the basketball girls said whom I interviewed a few weeks back in the abortive Glasgow Championships — that they preferred basketball to netball because it was, in the words of young Fiona from the Aberdeen team, 'less girlie'. I happen to prefer netball because it is faster and more precise and an ideal game for boys and girls, especially girls. But why should girls not want to be 'girlie'. If I was a girl I'd want to be girlie enough to make Marilyn bloody Monroe appear manly. Is there something in sport, or indeed in modern society, which makes girls want to be masculine?

I asked this question of the Parks and Recreation systems marketing manager (you get titles like that in local government whether you like it or not), Debbie Murray. Debbie turns up at all these enterprises like a lot of the parks people. Debbie couldn't answer the question either but admitted that there does seem to be a resistance among young women to sport, especially those associated with mainly female people.

Even Adam Horsburgh, vice-president of the Scottish Basketball Association, confessed that it is male stars in his sport who attract attention — Shaqueel O'Neil, who is 7ft 1in. and weighs 21 stone, is an enormous celebrity in the States, and Michael Jordan, who is sponsored by Nike, is another role model. Such stars do not exist in netball which is a shame really.

The Glasgow day, held in sunshine we are unused to, was part of a five-city tournament. As well as Birmingham there is Cardiff, London, and Belfast. Clearly this needs a wheen of commitment from sponsors and local authorities, but a lot more has to come from the the coaches, many of them teachers, and the young people themselves. After two months of competition the young folk were as keen as ever. Marr College, Troon, won the 10-12 competition. Inverness Royal won the 13-15 boys. Aberdeen won, as I wrote before, the 13-15 girls, and the Edinburgh Kings beat the Dalkeith Saints in the 16-18 final. I think I've got that right because it was a little hectic on the day.

A last glorious point. PR for Reebok is called Junior Walker. As an old bluesman I can tell you a chap of the same name once recorded a song called *Bread in a Basket*.

PLENTY OF SPORTING SPIRIT

May 6, 1991

BOWLING clubs have always struck me as mysterious, even sinister, places. Shrouded they usually are in foliage, trees, and mystery. Even in the depths of the urban landscape you find a screen of elms and oaks behind which lies a building of white stucco in a vague, Moorish style. Elderly gentlemen in dark blue blazers and white shirts sneak in from time to time, like Mafiosi trying to be respectable. Who knows what goes on inside these places.

Who knows, indeed. For many years the mystery of bowling clubs was penetrated only by the aged of this land. Bowling was a sport for the old fellows. You had to be 60 to even think of joining. For the last 20 years this has not been the case at all. What has actually happened is that lots of young chaps — worse, chapesses — have got involved in the sport. The result has been that the youngsters now dominate the sport in the UK. Tony Allcock, British and world champion, is yet in his early thirties, and you will find every bowling club has its fair share of father-and-son duos in which the sons invariably win.

Queen's Park Bowling Club has the both together. Queen's Park — which is next door to my own residence — has long been considered the top club in Scotland; the Hampden of Scottish bowling because, until last year, it was the venue for the Scottish finals. Queen's Park had that privilege for 98 years.

It is an old sport with as much of a Scottish connection as golf, for instance. Actually, the oldest club in the kingdom is Kilmarnock, which has been in existence for 250 years. (Next year Queen's Park celebrates its 125th anniversary, sharing this birthday with Queen's Park Football Club). As evidence of the sheer history of bowling in Scotland, you will not find a Scottish club without a portrait of Rabbie Burns. The bard was a keen participant in the game.

A very simple game it is too. You chuck a wee white ball up the greensward where the rinks — the lanes — are, and then try to roll the heavy and weighted orbs as near to the wee ball as possible. The wee white ball is called a Jack. It's bloody hard to cover bowling if you are actually called Jack, believe me. The word is never off the lips of the sportsmen.

Sportsmen it was, for women are not in evidence on most Saturdays. Bowling operates much the same policy as golf does and, while women pay considerably less than the men (Queen's Park demands a mere £80 from men and half that for women members) they cannot play while the blokes are on the greens.

QP also possesses a set of tennis courts where I watched the younger women, and delightful the scene was. There is a move to develop tennis for disabled players — they already have the facility for blind bowlers — but this is proving difficult due to financial problems and the municipal courts across in Queen's Park proper might establish such a set-up.

Finance is, surprisingly, a difficulty for this most august of bowling clubs. The indoor club across the Queen's Park recreation area takes a lot of potential members away, while the sheer reputation of this famous club has also had a tendency to lose potential members.

The fact is that there is no waiting list at Queen's, while a parvenu club like Croftfoot takes three to five years of your time up before you can roll the bools along its lawns. Surprisingly too, because Queen's is set in a scene of considerable loveliness and is famous — perhaps infamous is the right word — for its friendliness.

It will take me days to recover from the glorious sunshine I enjoyed there, but at least a week for the effects of the enthusiastic hospitality I encountered to wear off. Club vice-president Pat Masterson informed me that bowling was 'a sociable game'. Indeed it is. Sociable is a euphemism for a lot of large whiskies.

Sociable the players certainly are. Much given to smart sweaters and neat slacks, they troop in after a half hour out on the rink for a swift half and a half.

Dougie Rennie, an old whisky rep I have known for a good few years, is practically the archetypal bowler. Dressed as sharply as a Hollywood star on Oscar night, glad to talk to everybody, more patter than Les Dawson, and a taste for the product which he formerly sold to the likes of me, Douglas could sum up the Scottish bowler. Classless, well-spoken in a grand old-fashioned way, he has a risqué wit which is a little bit what bowling is about. Fun and witty and generally masculine is what bowling is, but courteous to the ladies too. It might be a time warp in some ways, but welcome it is to find it.

This is a cheap game at the end of the day. A really good set of firsthand bowls costs about a hundred spondulicks. You can play all day for nothing save your membership (which works out at about thirty bob a week).

The chaps this week were playing off for a wee wager of fifty pence, winner to take all and then spend it on a round for the lads. Winners this week were pairs White and Nicol, and I bet it cost them dear.

It might be a cheap game at that, but it cost me as well at the end of the day. I took a look around the lovely grounds. I witnessed the splendid gardens which greenkeeper Alan Bentley looks over. I listened to those who insisted that the club should be the home of Scottish bowling. I took a dram or two. Worse. I joined the club. So there.

SKIRTING THE LADIES

June 15, 1992

BERYLL Cook, the Lancashire lass who became a real artist, and showed the middle-classes what the lower orders were like, produced the finest painting ever of lady bowlers.

She had all these stout players in white skirts too tight for their bums and one of the weemenfolk poking her finger into just the right spot. An unerring eye. Throughout the whole of Britain, there are ladies with fat backsides skirted in white, chucking these spheres about.

Bowling men tended once to be elderly sorts of chaps with the sort of feinted arses which retired men somehow seem to inherit as of right, throwing bits of wood and resin about, and throwing even more weight in the clubhouse bar. Increasingly, the weemenfolk are taking over.

It was all weemenfolk at this weekend's bash in Northfield, Ayr, where the Seventh Women's World Bowls Championships took place. I was there the other year when it was the occasion of the Scottish championships. This year it was better.

World Bowls. There were 26 countries competing. Zimbabwe was there and Fiji, and Israel, and Jersey, and Ireland, and Hong Kong. But before I tell you about the last three countries, let's indulge in some national pride and congratulate the ladies who won the triples championship for Scotland.

However, our ain wee country got beat, as they say, by Hong Kong in the pairs, and put us into sixth place. Hong Kong were fifth. Their overall squad of five had three Scots in it, and the manageress, Helen Young, is from Glasgow.

Team member Rosemary McMahon — who delightfully describes herself as a 'home executive', that is, a housewife, — is mother to young Mark McMahon, a lad who has far to go in world bowling, and is across here courtesy of the Sports Council in Hong Kong. Rosemary is also wife to Bill McMahon, a school teacher in the exotic Orient and a dashed good player himself. All three are world class.

But they were not the only squad to have Caledonians in abundance. Virtually every one competing had Scottish ladies — you learn early on not to call them girls, for the girls are awfy commanding. Let's go for a second or two to Jersey.

Jersey has four teams and only one ladies' team, which is part of one of the four teams. I know; I couldn't understand that myself. Despite that, they managed a silver medal in the pairs, and you never saw more elaborate triumph in your life. They were that triumphant they bought me a drink in the beer marquee.

Manageress Pat Panter had strict instructions not to speak to the Press unless it was the responsible Press. Why she spoke to me, I cannot tell. 'We didn't expect a medal,' she said. 'We only have about 300 ladies playing on the island, but weren't we good today?'

They were, too. But not as good as Ireland. For the second world championships, but the first time in history, Ireland took the gold medal in the pairs. Margaret Johnston and Phil (Philomena) Nolan looked early days to be winners, and they were.

Tom Sutton, treasurer of the British Isles bowling associations and a Hibernian of strong accent and considerable generosity when it came to a wee libation, was well pleased, over the moon, cock-a-hoop, and happy as Larry.

'We done it' he said, in sports-speak. He also told me that there are only about 2000 lady bowlers in Ireland. 'But we are All-Ireland,' he told me, 'None of your sectarianism. North and South, there's nothing to beat a combined effort.'

Ladies is what the ladies call themselves, and why not? I will tell you why not. Because there aren't enough girls playing the game. In many another sport, it is hard enough to get the youngsters playing, but in bowls, it is quite clear that the girls are not going for it and that's a damned shame.

It turns out that the dress code, the uniforms, the blazers and the fact that you cannae take your hat off, and that skirts have to be worn at all times, are turning off the young females.

While young men have been shooting lightning through the sky in the last 10 years in this sport, young women have not even been joining the clubs. Considering that bowling is a sport at which men and women can compete on absolutely equal terms, this is an absurdity, and even the ladies acknowledge it. Something has got to be done.

Except I want the lassies in skirts. Short ones. I didn't say that: I only thought it and it went into print by sheer chance. Och, jings, help ma Boab, Beryll Cook would know what I mean.

IN GLASWEGIAN BLOOD

February 3, 1992

'YOU'RE a writer, not a fighter,' said Arthur Kerr, a legendary Glasgow boxer, to me many years back. Arthur was right: I couldnae fight sleep.

Yet boxing is in the blood of the Glaswegian. Some of us still try it of a Friday or Saturday night. If you are a Glaswegian you are second prize. Even the best Glaswegians — especially the best Glaswegians — are second prizes. I once skelped wee Tommy Gilligan outside a pub in Hamilton. I got a doing and Tommy damn near got suspended for life: only a lie on my part saved him.

But boxing used to be part of Glasgow, and it still is. Not a Southside man exists who cannot tell you of Benny Lynch: wee Billy Young, a man now in his seventies who looks my own age, or near it anyway, and who once sparred with Lynch, can tell you boxing till your ear is next door to a cauliflower one.

Friday's venue was the Holiday Inn, Glasgow. The fighters were wee. It is an argument for anti-boxing folk — I well remember Dr Edith Summerskill making it — that boxing attracts bullies. This is true, but the bullies are the fans, the sportswriters, especially the promoters. Boxers are almost always childishly decent and nice. It can be truly said that professional fighters are more likely to hurt themselves. On Friday night you could see that. It was a well-billed fight.

Nobody really expected Willie Beattie to win against the harder punching Gordon Blair. Least of all promoter Alex Morrison, himself a famous figure in the fight game. As it happens, both boxers are professionally represented by Big Eck. Who knows why this meant that both of them found themselves fighting quite so hard, but I can tell you that this Friday night bout was one of the most brutal encounters I have ever seen. Neither boxer is likely to fight again: if they have any bloody sense that is. I was there with a lovely little lady called Sarah.

When I spoke to referee Len Mullen after the fight he told me that he was thinking of calling the fight off after the second round. Only the heart-torn plea by Beattie — horribly cut above the eye but with more courage than Boy Cornwall VC — allowed him to go for a third round. As it happens Willie Beattie, a clever little boxer who, it is often suggested, fights with his face, won against an equally brave opponent in Gordon Blair. Blair is a good boxer and showed considerably more class in the two rounds than Beattie. What he showed in the third round was less determination. This was a brutal fight and there was blood and snot everywhere. Willie Beattie might well say he is ready to meet Gary Jacobs. I do not think he will. I hope both boxers never fight again.

Blood-spattered Len Mullen told me that it was one of the most awesome fights he had ever seen. Big Eck Morrison, the legend himself, who owns both fighters, doesn't want either of his stablemates to damage themselves again. Sarah, the little girl who was with me at Glasgow's Holiday Inn, doesn't want to see men hitting each other again for the rest of her life, and I don't blame her.

If you have never been to the boxing you will not know what they do to each other and you will never see so many well-off spivs. It is a part of proletarian life which allows big money and sovvie rings to stand side by side with big money and bourgeois snobbery. One thing is certain. The fighters always lose. Anyone who has put gloves on will tell you: losers are the ones without their shirts on. The expensive silk chemises on the backs of the spectators at a boxing bout are not likely to be sold.

Our promoter Alex tells me that he tries to look after his fighters, but it is an uphill struggle. 'Only daft folk fight,' he tells me. Alex fought himself, not wisely, as they say, but too well. Now a successful businessman he knows that the ring is the last place to expose yourself.

I spoke to many a boxing fan. Like me they all sported expensive suits and had big cars outside. Well, I only had the expensive suit. They had the big cars. Boxing is not for ordinary fans: they watch it on the telly. It costs a lot of dosh to see these little men knock lumps out of each other. The days of working-class participation are well over.

More than that: boxing is for males and the girls don't much like it. Tall and leggy girls parade around the ring and equally delectable girlfriends show themselves off with weel-off chaps. Boxing is money and style and perhaps the last bastion of sport without respectability. The boys at the top of the fight game don't look for respectability. Like bookies at racecourses they are smarter than punters. Smart enough not to put themselves up front on a hiding to nothing. Listen: I enjoyed myself no end. So did Sarah, if she but admitted it.

No laughing matter

June 17, 1991

THE laughter rose when I announced to the lads in Heraghty's Bar that I was joining the sports desk. When the sports desk heard the news there was a rush of resignations. Risibility and resentment followed me everywhere I went. Both looked over the fence, as ghostly cricketers do according to the poem, on my first assignment which was, in fact, a soccer match.

Association Football is next door to speech as the first thing a Scot learns, and I should know about football. My initial shot at the sport was gloriously disastrous. I am not a trained reporter. This was evident in the fact that my first report for the sports desk included the following mistakes: I got the chaps' names who were ordered off wrong. I got the size of the crowd wrong. I got the score wrong. In a magnificent burst of lunacy I got the name of one of the teams wrong. The sports desk wallahs were wonderful and corrected everything and then didn't let me forget my solecisms, not for a fortnight but forever.

I went from strength to strength. My best effort was falling from the press box at Airdrie's Broomfield Park. As it happens it was not really my fault for Broomfield would have been damn-near fatal to ex-President Gerald Ford. It was designed for falling down. All I suffered was torn ligaments which, eight months later, I still suffer from. A Mr Dixon Blackstock, reporter for another blatt, described the scene and said I was, and I quote, 'an eccentric Glasgow journalist'. I'm eccentric? At least I'm not called Dixon Blackstock.

I fell seven flights down the bench seats. An Airdrie official suggested that I had drink taken. My lawyer retorted that in all the years he has known me I have always had drink taken but he has never seen me fall down at that. Incidentally, Airdrieonians Football Club didn't permit my photographer —Angie Catlin, one of the very few female photographers in this business — to go to the toilet. Airdrie is not much of a town to include in the tourist trail but the footy club should most definitely be avoided.

But then, most football clubs should be avoided. Rangers then manager, Graeme Souness, made it be known that he would welcome Saddam Hussein quicker than myself, and Celtic's PR supremo, Mick Kelly, seems to have felt that I was the anti-Christ. Aberdeen manager Alex Smith was courtesy itself and I got a smashing profile of young Eoin Jess, one of the best prospects Scotland has seen in decades.

Alex told me to talk to everybody and anybody. He had an enormously important game the morrow but he thought nothing of dragging his players off to speak to myself. I think nothing of telling you that Smith is a gentleman and his players are lucky to have him. How about Alex Totten at St Johnstone who spends half of his time coaching kids, (mostly Asian), from Garthamlock? Alex works in Perth, lives in Dunipace, and coaches in Glasgow: a bed in Heaven to the man.

But by and large my sojourn in football has not been pleasant. Footy players imagine they are more important than mere hacks and certainly more than the fans. They treat everybody with contempt and they treat their sport in much the same manner. No matter that the majority of top footballers end their lives as fat, failed publicans, and unsuccessful ones end it with egos nearly as big as their overdrafts. Football is too much of a business to be a sport any more.

It was with relief that I turned myself to the so-called minority — what I prefer to call the 'specialist' — sports. I had a great time at the rugby where I viewed in torrential rain the efforts of the two lowest clubs in the lowest leagues. At the end of it the players came up to me and smeared me in the glaur they had bathed in, shook my hand, made their club captain take me off to the boozer, and bought me copious draughts of heavy beer. I wrote the report of the superb Garioch versus Birkmyre match with a hangover which would have done credit to Dylan Thomas in New York.

Other occasions when hospitality took over must be when I covered the tennis at the august Newlands club and wrote everything down the other way round. The tennis clubs involved enjoyed it immensely and wrote positively Georgian letters of complaint to the sports editor. Oddly enough, this was the sport about which I knew rather a lot, being the only one I have ever played with any kind of expertise.

The tennis chaps at Broomhill have forgiven me, however, and I am welcomed at that Glasgow west-end establishment, probably the only west-end institution to think of so doing.

But I have covered, over the last year, so many sports, some of them daft and some not. Surprised I was by such recondite activities as fencing and lacrosse. At the fencing, I encountered one of those public school fellows who makes one itch for the guillotine and the tumbril, he was that bloody condescending to me, and also a splendid girl called Rachel McFaddyen, a law student who made me want to become a father if your daughter turns out like her. Lacrosse was wonderful, given the fact that all the wee girls, (and some of them were really rather big wee girls), were so pretty, but also that lacrosse is one of the most exciting games I have ever seen — fast, athletic, intelligent, and graceful. It is a shame that state schools don't have a chance at it.

This came out so often at the specialist sports that I have become a touch evangelistic in the matter. The truth is that schools — the institutions from which sport must surely emanate if it is to flourish — are now doing little or nothing. The truly awful truth is that the independent schools — the schools to which only the better-off can afford to send their children — are doing so much better than the comprehensives, which appear not to be doing anything at all. When I covered the schools cross-country championships, (with a churlish reply from one of that organising body's members), it became instantly apparent that the state schools generally provide nothing at all by way of sports development.

The most depressing element of my last year on the sports desk was exactly that. I am sick of arguments concerning how much should be spent on the arts and whether or not we should shove fifty grand up for murals in the Lally Palais in Glasgow when, time after time, I have encountered healthy, confident kids being given the thumbs down for forty quid to take them to a tournament in Falkirk in whatever sport they have taken up. The stark fact is that sport is available to children with rich dads from the public schools — and so it should be at that — but not to children from poor and deprived areas and it is a damned disgrace.

I offered my reservations this year about sport itself. I'm not sure that the emphasis on fitness of the body is not sometimes at the expense of fitness of the mind. The sports centres, without which no self-respecting town council can be without, are often no more than mindless gymnasia with an intellectual pabulum akin to that provided by a Hitler Youth. I am concerned that working-class children are given opportunities for cheap sports such as those provided by martial arts organisations, but are unlikely to experience the so-called middle-class games like tennis or badminton or cricket or lacrosse or fencing. That bowling, as in green, is not preferred to bowling as, in inside, with hamburgers and Diet Coke instead of fresh air.

Another aspect of my year in sport which has surprised me and probably you is that women get a raw deal in sport. Golf and bowling might think this is all right, with their lower club fees for the weemenfolk, and doubtless some women do too. But the fact is that few girls continue in any sporting activity at all on leaving school, and we are killing females off early by such a discrimination.

I will bet you are surprised at the above coming from one of your leading male chauvinists. You shouldn't be. If there was one thing I learned over the last year it was learning. Eyes opened indeed.

NOW YOU SEE IT, NOW YOU DON'T

January 11, 1994

THE first reason why television loves sport is because you can see it.

The second is that TV sport is largely mindless. Bread and circuses, and at the end of the day, cheap. The sheer cost of televising football would take your breath away if it was not for the fact that the returns are huge. And that is why sport really is inexpensive.

Any company advertising during a major football match will expect to pay 20 times more for a spot than it would during a non-peak-time wee programme on a more arcane subject.

Satellite TV increasingly is geared towards live sport and especially football. It has to be. It is designed for customers who are paying extra for what other TV channels cannot provide. And yet the other channels could provide live coverage if it were not for the sporting organisations.

The Scottish Football Association is notorious for intransigence over a piece of European, if you like, legislation which would be outlawed in any other business in Europe.

This bit of law is called Article 14. Under this, the European Union of Football Associations could, and do, stop coverage of schools football if they want. They could ban transmission of the World Cup final on the strength of any football association in any country vetoing a TV signal.

The SFA can justify this on the basis that Real Madrid versus Eintracht were playing on the same day as Brechin and Alloa. In other industries this would be outlawed. Sport gets away with it.

Professional sport is scarcely a century old but, of all industries, it is hidebound to a degree unimaginable by multinational corporations in other spheres. Just why the media is quite so supine in the question of sport is difficult to understand.

One would have thought it might be a good idea, at some time, for the media to call a halt to the insatiable and unjust demands made by these sporting bodies. Put films on instead.

But the hunger for sport comes, of course, from the customers, and the people who, by and large run sport, know they have the seller's market.

Television companies know the clout these small, but powerful groups have. You will remember when Scottish were banned from the trackside at Ibrox because they ran a picture taken from a tabloid newspaper of the then Rangers manager, Graeme Souness, talking in the players' tunnel when he was barred from that area due to his misbehaviour on previous occasions.

The ban on Ibrox coverage was a clear interference with the freedom of the media, and no self-respecting TV executive would have put up with this censorship in any other area than sport. Scottish TV sport, at that time headed by the determined wee Denis Mooney, had the decency to react by telling the Glasgow club to stick themselves sideways.

Every other TV company should have stood shoulder to shoulder, but they did not. The developments in the last few years of satellite TV might be able to confront this problem. Certainly the appointment of Andy Melvin to Sky TV bodes well.

Melvin, once thought of as the natural successor to Russell Galbraith at Scottish, held strong views on telling sport about its responsibilities. Recently retired Ron Marshall attempted much the same but he is, well, recently retired. Whether the new chaps at Scottish can continue the campaign to fight for viewers, and that is sports fans' rights, we shall see, we shall see.

And yet this should be easy for the TV people. The producers, directors, and especially the front people on the cathode tube, are bright and sharp and strong enough characters.

The most successful former international sportsman who ever moved into broadcasting is the legendary Welsh fly-half, Cliff Morgan, who very nearly took the top job in the BBC, and could do so yet. Even further down, is there any sports commentator with more status — in his case rugby — than our own Bill McLaren?

Yet what can McLaren do with some of the faceless SRU?

Scottish Rugby has done well — consider the massive sums which have been spent in the last few years on the development of the game, and Murrayfield Stadium — but even he can but wait upon the lips of these unrepresentative fellows.

Consider too other remarkable characters who show the world of sport to the punters. I know and care little about horseracing but, crivvens, I know who McCrirrick is, and delight in him. Think of the sheer pleasure of listening to and watching some splendid front men and women in sport. Jonners, who died just last week, was one of a long line of sports journos who made you listen in to a report on a pastime you couldn't care less about. Golf leaves me cold, but Henry Longhurst had me spellbound. Murray Walker can even make motor sport sound — well, no he can't really, but he does try.

But why so little clout from these broadcasting heavyweights? Perhaps the answer lies in the nature of mass sport itself. You might just have noticed that I cover the minority sports.

The truth is that television coverage of specialist sport is woeful. And here's another one. Try being in women's sport. Or Sally McNair or Hazel Irvine covering any sport at all and getting ribbed by pea-brains who run it badly. It is up to the fans to demand more of us.

TIME TO PLAY BALL

February 28, 1994

THE distinguished American theatre critic James Agee was once told by playwright Tennessee Williams that he was a disgrace to the theatre itself. 'All you can do is close a show,' said Williams, 'but you could never open one.'

American playwrights have ever been castigating the critics for it is certainly true that they have suffered somewhat at the hands of these influential boys, and girls, from the blatts. British theatre critics once had a bit of clout themselves. Harold Hobson was certainly an important figure, as was the late Kenneth Tynan. Yet Britain has never quite possessed the critic journalist who could make or break a show, a book, a musical performance. Or a sport.

There have been, over the years, major figures in sports journalism. Until recently, however, many leading sports writers, especially those involved in football, have been somewhat supine in their attitude to the sports they cover. Newspapers have naturally been a touch extra analytical than those involved in broadcasting and television.

The recent spate of stories and articles concerning the state of play at Celtic Football Club has shown that footy writers are prepared to be less reverential than they were reputed to be. Indeed, our own James Traynor has been much vilified in the Celtic-orientated pubs and clubs in the West of Scotland, though, when I have remonstrated with the Paradise bhoys, they have eventually agreed that Traynor has been right.

But newspapers are different from the other areas of journalism. For a start newspapers can distance themselves, indeed they must, from whatever area in which they operate, whether it be politics, health, education, or sport, and especially football. Broadcasting cannot and there is a reason for that. For the truth is that radio and TV have a relationship damn near incestuous with whatever they cover. We in the blatts can stand aside. The other area of the media does not and they are under no illusions that at the end of the day they are there to provide, more than anything else, entertainment.

Thus it is that while our Mr Traynor is well respected by sports, football, and yes, Celtic supporters, Mr Gerry McNee is regarded as a turncoat, a pariah. One can quite easily suspect that McNee is perhaps a former Celtic fan himself, from the West of Scotland Irish community, and his highly controversial reports concerning this football club, so much, (ludicrously so if you think about it) a focus for Glasgow-Irish-Catholic aspirations, have hardly endeared him to that group. But he has been proved right. Few if any readers of *The Herald* know, or care, what — let us put it coarsely — religion Traynor is. For the telly is different from the newspapers.

Name any major sports presenter on television who can command the level of profile which, say, Raymond Glendinning had. Or Kenneth Wolstenholme. Those two used to have sports books out using their names as imprimaturs. Dicky Davies, Desmond Lynam, the more recent Jonathan Watson, are not seen in such exaltation at all. Instead we have sports 'personalities'. Some are very good at it. (Some took to it: Cliff Morgan in rugby, the late James Hunt in motorsport, Richie Benaud in cricket come to mind immediately as major stars in their respective sports who became superb commentators).

Today, however, we have, instead of journalists on the telly, sports persons. Perhaps the sheer dreadfulness of a number of sports journos who confused their role as presenters with that of sycophants has led to the present situation, but sports fans now note the major figures in television sports coverage are ex-sporting figures to boot.

Andy Gray and Gordon McQueen are regulars and seen as authoritative. Derek Johnstone is seen by many as a bit of a joke but not by anybody who knows about football, because he is very perceptive indeed and really does know what he is talking about. More: we have Ray Wilkins on Italian football. Trevor Brooking is sharp and articulate, too.

But am I alone in thinking that this is not necessarily good for any sport? Those who have spent their lives, from the age of 15 or 16, in what is after all just games, should be those who represent the critical faculty in their own field? Surely not. Of all the ex-sportsmen I can think of who had exactly that faculty, two were oft reviled by those in their sport. Both were football players. Danny Blanchflower and Eamonn Dunphy, both Irish, both internationalists, both (Danny even more than Eamonn) world-class players. But they were often criticised because they took no part in the cosy little world of telly-sports where bums are licked and hotel bills are paid. They were bright, clever, highly educated, and regarded sport as only a part of life, an enjoyable part, but only a bit of it.

Both were — and Dunphy remains — astringent, difficult, socialistic, challenging, and worrying for the Establishment. Neither of them was, or has been, employed significantly in television. They might not have been entertaining enough. Perhaps they might have said harsh things about the sport which they criticised.

Nobody in television seems to have said anything about the disgraceful hypocrisy of professionalism in the Olympics and in athletics, for instance. Or the fearful nature of increasing shamateurism in Rugby Union. Or the lack of coverage in minority sports. Or the lack of money for women's sport unless it is tennis, in which hypocrisy, social class, snobbery, and sheer bloody-minded false consciousness has made lots of spondulicks for the sport, but we still don't have enough kids out there playing that lovely game and the tennis clubs are strapped for cash. What we need are TV sportspersons who can close a show. As well as open it.

YOKER WRESTLES WITH CASH WORRY

November 16, 1992

THERE are times when minority sports go beyond the comprehension of your correspondent here. Celtic wrestling is on the edge. This weekend I am in Yoker Sports Centre witnessing the Celtic stuff; the traditional Scottish wrestling that they do at highland games when they are not wrestling with the committee, the local aristocracy, or the amber fluid.

Not much chance of the amber at Yoker. In fact, I couldn't squeeze a fag in. District council sports centres do not allow the nicotine, and in fact don't allow much at all, especially funding. This is not entirely fair.

District councillor for the area and an old chum to boot, Craig Roberton, was there on Saturday at the Traditional Wrestling Scotland-England Championship. Glasgow funded the event to the tune of £300.

What they are not funding is the sports centre itself, a rather splendid little place run by a former colleague of mine. Hilary runs it along with Andy, but there is very little money, the result being that the place — necessary, I should have thought, for a small district like Yoker in Glasgow and an area of deprivation — is normally closed on a Saturday and Sunday. This cannot be right, but that's what happens.

Some years back I discovered the saddest quote I have ever had to jot down in my notebook in another deprived area, an area of priority treatment, as they call it, Easterhouse. Said the young man there: 'There are only two sorts of young people here. Druggies or sporties.'

Yoker has not plumbed the depths yet, but it could. Quite easily. When young people are denied access to sport, among other societal phenomena, they will find something else to do, and the devil will be about to think it up.

There are more than 1000 members in Yoker Sports Centre, most of them unemployed, what else? The centre is helped by Urban Aid, but nobody knows how long they will continue their financing.

The scenario is that the Yoker community is likely to run out of money in two years' time. There are between 40 and 50 people working away here. Councillor Roberton has been active over the last few years, but even he cannot get guarantees from the council, let alone Urban Aid.

I have explained many times the benefit to young people and the local communities of sport, but money is tight. Perhaps the arts scene, with its massive funding in the visual arts in local government affairs, should be looked at in terms of priority.

Julian Spalding and the rest of the arts administrators are doubtless doing a grand job, but sport is more immediately effective in bringing weans and their parents into decency than a J D Fergusson ever would. Philistine I might be, but I am sure I am correct enough at that.

Traditional Scottish wrestling is Celtic wrestling. It is common to all the Celtic nations. Cornwall, for instance, is a highlighted part of the Celtic countries for the wrestling which is very different from that of Greco-Roman or free-style.

In Celtic wrestling, you have to overturn your opponent, and put him down first — simple as that. There are no wee tricky moves which you will find in the showbiz game, or in judo or karate, though a large number of judo exponents go in for this most recondite of sports.

Hugh Ferns, a 6ft 3in chap marvellously weighing in at 14½st, is a judo man who started this wrestling at the highland games. He beat his English opponent easily.

But it wasn't only the big lads who competed. There was Maxine, a wee, slight girl, aged seven, who did well. Or how about the two little girls, Leanne Whitehouse, aged nine, and her sister, Charlotte, two years older, who wrestled in front of myself and our photographer wearing kilts (the Scots wear kilts: I told you this was highland games stuff), and both did well.

Said wrestling supremo Willie Baxter: 'Wee Charlotte is probably the best athlete in the place. Just look at that grip of hers!' It is all very strange to me, wee lassies shoving each other about. I thought it was only me who did that.

But it is taken very seriously. Young Alastair MacEwan didn't win against his English opponent. At 14, you get dreadfully upset. His Scottish style didn't win against the so-called Cumberland — or was it Westmoreland? — method. Scot Stephen Ward, from Milton, however, beat his Cumbrian foe, Lee Elwood, despite the larger size of Elwood. Cumbria is big in this sport.

Wrestling in this form is big throughout the Celtic countries as I have said. Founded in 1810 by a certain James Scott, yet commemorated by a big stookie in the Cormac Islands, it started, it is said, as a result of trying to improve your sword arm.

Hector MacDonald, frae Springburn, is president of what is called The Scottish Wrestling Bond, and he told me that they broke away from the Scottish Amateur Wrestling Union. 'What they're doing isnae proper wrestling really,' he said. 'This has more skill.'

Myself, I cannot see it, but there you are. I am equally advised by Willie Baxter, sports facility manager. There are all sort of styles, he told me. Cumbrian, Irish, Cornish: there is even the Carachu Uibhist — the style of Uist. There are more wrestling styles among the Celts than there are religions, which is a lot of styles at that.

You even get it among the Catalans and especially the Bretons, where it is called La Lutte, if that's the proper spelling. Every year Brittany sees the Fest Noz, the Breton equivalent of highland games, and you will find plenty of Scottish, indeed British, competitors there.

There are times when comprehension breaks. I tried, I really tried, to find out if the Scots had beaten the English. It was impossible. The problem is that, as in many a sport which has civilised people, they don't much care who wins, and socialise after it.

I think Scotland beat England, or maybe our Anglo neighbours beat us. Or somebody beat somebody else. You couldn't tell. One thing is certain. Afterwards, everybody looked like a winner.

PS: I didn't want to admit it, but Scotland lost 5-3.

NO LONGER MERE PAWNS IN THE BRAIN GAME

May 25, 1992

MY EDITOR is an intellectual. Not my sports editor, who is as intellectual as Rab C Nesbitt and twice as bluff, but my editor. He believes that chess is sport. Sport for the mind he calls it, and I suppose it is. It must be sport really because, like almost every game I can think of, it is beyond me.

However, this did not stop me from taking myself off to the Clarkston Halls on the outskirts of Glasgow city to witness the goings-on during the West of Scotland Championships this weekend.

The last time I was in the Clarkston Halls was when I was 16 and it was Christmas night and we wiz all dancing to the music of Shane Fenton and the Chariots. What a difference during this bank holiday. Then there was mayhem and I had a bop hairstyle and an Italian four-button suit. Thirty years later on and the joint isn't jumping at all. It was quiet enough for yourself to hear brains ticking and what a lot of brains there were.

Steve Mannion, Jr, was there. Steve, whose dad is also an excellent player and an assistant chief constable, was playing and winning. Steve Jr, an internationalist who last won the West of Scotland Championship two years back, was the strongest candidate to win this year.

Scotland has a surprisingly strong record in chess. Two of our notables — Paul Motwani and Colin McNab, in their late 20s and both maths teachers from Dundee — are one win short of grandmaster status. Scotland, in fact, has done well in chess though we don't match the astonishing increase in capability which England has achieved. England didn't have a single grandmaster 20 years ago; now there are more than 20 of them south of the Border.

But even England cannot match Eastern Europe. When you consider that Gary Kasparov, now of the Russian Republic but originally representing Azerbaijan, has a rating of 2800, you can realise how far down the line British players are. Crivvens, the Hungarian Polyar sisters — Judith is the youngest grandmaster in the game at under-12 — could take any British player in half an hour.

Bobby Fischer, the oddest man perhaps in the world, let alone chess, and who has not played since 1972, would think you off the board before you put a pawn anywhere near it. British chess is adequate but barely so, and is not, as in Russia and Eastern Europe, a part of the national culture.

Once it was that the Jewish immigrants brought chess to this country and indeed the mainspring of Scottish chess came from the Jewish community. Time was when the Maccabi — the Jewish Institute — was Glasgow's biggest club. The biggest now probably is Giffnock and Clarkston.

A few years back the strongest was Castlemilk Chess Club but they, having won the Richardson Cup (the Scottish Cup of chess), went on to Europe, over-reached themselves, and, unfortunately, folded some years ago. My old school, Allan Glen's, had an especially strong club and ex-International Master Craig Pritchard was a star in the Scottish crown and was even a member of my old house, Barony. (We Barony boys were bright).

Scottish chess goes back a bit, about 150 years in fact. The weekend's trophy dates from 1877 and was first won by a Mr A Hunter. The stamped name doesn't actually say it was a mister but it was, for until recently women didn't enter, for they had their own competition.

In the past few years the ladies have disdained such a piece of sexism and now enter the open competition instead, and quite right, too, even if Comrade Kasparov is on record as saying that women chess players can never beat the best men. It appears that women are too polite and let satyrs like Kasparov sneak in a victory. Some male chess players mutter darkly that women aren't logical enough. Logical? I never met anything more logical in my life than a woman with a grievance in her.

Anyway, those chauvinists should have taken a wee glance at 13-year-old Sowmya Umush, who won the girls' championship at the weekend (she won it last year, too). A schoolgirl at Gryffe High School, she plays three times a week and beats everybody, including her dad — Dr Shivanna Umesh, who told me she started beating him at chess when she was seven. 'That's when I gave up,' he admitted. 'Now I'm just the transport manager.'

Sowmya is a shy wee lassie who — you just know by looking at her — is cleverer than you. She doesn't know what she wants to be when she grows up. Strewth, I hope she's doesn't want to be a journalist: I'll be out of a job in seconds. Sowmya belongs to the Houston YMCA Club in Paisley. I know the organiser there, Alex MacFarlane. Alex makes Graeme Souness look uncommitted.

There are 36 clubs in Glasgow alone and there is a strong lead in developing chess among younger people, especially among girls. Said this weekend's organiser Walter Munn, himself a player, (and ex-Hutchie boy like his co-organiser Bob Houston): 'We're pushing chess in the primary schools, but especially among girls, because there's an in-built prejudice against the game with girls, and their parents, too. What's more, we've found girls will stick at it.'

There you are, then. You thought I could get a sports piece out without writing about girls? Wrong.

SET PIECES ARE THE ORDER OF THE DAY

July 5, 1993

A QUARTER of a century ago, when I was young and daft enough to travel every day between Edinburgh and Glasgow, I took the train, then an hour and a half's worth of journey. Now that it is less than half that time, it is sensible. But The Glas-Edin and vice versa journey was much more exciting then.

The carriages were in Pullman style, with compartments and a corridor which led, inexorably, to the buffet car and the bar.

You made a lot of friends in the buffet car.

It was the first time I realised that the most august of the upper-middle classes drank like fish. And later, back in your compartment, you would have card games, usually brag or stud poker. You would also occasionally receive a visit from the card sharps who spent all day on the train — like Mississippi gamblers riding the boats. It was rare fun.

Less fun it is now on the 42-minute journey in which the only excitement is listening to boys talking of a visit to their pals in that institution for young offenders at Polmont, near Falkirk.

But Saturday suddenly recreated the magic of those heady days of my youth. For Saturday between, and back to, the two cities had a train with sport on it. InterCity Chess it was.

It was the sort of good idea which only PR men can think up.

A tale of two cities with all the trimmings; knights, kings and queens, bishops even.

I understand that the Irish want to change the rules of international chess. They want the bishops to be allowed to jump everyone.

But this chess was not the decorous, silent, and slow affair that chess normally is.

If chess is athletics for the mind, this was sprinting for the brain. The competitors — there were incidentally 15 players, for one of the number failed to turn up — had a mere five minutes to complete a match.

I nearly failed to turn up myself for the train was pulling out of Waverley just as I breathlessly got there. Senior conductor John Grey stopped the train. I've always wanted to pull the communication cord and this is the nearest I have got.

But once on the big, fast luxurious tube, I settled down to watch the chess. The train, which I am told can do 140mph, was nothing like as fast as the chess. With only five minutes to complete the match, there was an aff-its-heid excitement about watching two dead brainy people hitting the pieces and slapping the time clock.

A semi-final match betwixt two Scottish grand masters, Colin MacNab and Douglas Bryson, had me and everyone else hugging the edges of wur consciousnesses, let alone wur seats. MacNab won when Bryson's flag fell: simply not fast enough.

But Bryson can ponder on the fact that his foe went on to win against the other top Scottish player, also from Dundee Chess Club, Paul Motwani.

In third place was 16-year-old Jonathan Rowson, a pupil at Aberdeen Grammar, and awfy nice as well as bright. He actually drew with long time ace Peter Wright, a town planner who left his disgraceful profession to go full-time in chess-playing.

Peter earns, as all professional chess chaps do, a sort of a living travelling all over Europe as well as in Britain. And chess is for chaps by and large. Two women had been invited to this chess jamboree. Neither could manage. But why are women so thin on the ground in chess? There are the Polyar sisters from Hungary — Judith is now regarded as potentially a world winner and was the youngest ever grand master at under the age of 12 and was never sent to school, (as an ex-schoolteacher I commend this notion to parents). There is Sowmya Umush, a schoolgirl at Gryffe High School who keeps on winning against everybody. There is the women's champion in what is called Chinese Chess, Xie Jun. There is — ach, all I have to say is that the girls should get into this and be as superior at chess as they are at anything which involves thinking.

But the splendid thing about chess is that there really cannot be differentials in gender or age. Crivvens, Scotland's young Mark Russell, at 18, is Scottish boys' champion and has a world grading of more than 2000. Kasparov has 2800, and when Scottish Chess Association General Secretary Simon Kellet explained to me the statistical methods for establishing grades, I realised that I am thick beyond belief.

Grading is mair difficult than chess itself if you ask me.

But it was left to my old chum, Commander Steve Champion of the Transport Polis, himself a formidable player and whose son Steve Jr is a star in the world of the checkered board, to tell me what all this silly chess tournament on board a train was about.

Said Steve: 'InterCity is sponsoring this chess championship at the level of four grand, held in St Andrews next Saturday in that town's Madras College. It's our centenary year,' he said. And it is. For Scotland has a long tradition of chess and indeed George Outram sponsored it in this country for many years. Upsetting it is to me, though, that Glasgow is no longer the source of chess champs. For many years, my old school —Allan Glen's— was in the forefront, and Castlemilk Club got international status a few years back.

The Glasgow Maccabi Club — the Jewish community was once prominent in chess in this country as elsewhere — is still around but no longer a force in the game.

Ibrox Garage has folded as a club. The point is that chess has no class, gender, or geographical barriers. Sadly there is less chess being played by people, certainly by workies, girls, and Glaswegians.

But the game is genuinely exciting. And you never met more hospitality. It wasn't just the conductor who stopped the train. Commander Mannion damned near stopped my brain cells later on with two of the largest whiskies I ever saw.

As it happens, the five-minute chess hysteria is officially called 'Blitz' Chess. I could see why. Staggering off the train, I was blitzed myself. My companion that night refused to believe I had been covering chess. She castled me smartly and went home.

SCOTS END UP AS SHOOTING STARS

August 24, 1992

DO I not find myself in the sleepy little village of Kippen, (I couldn't resist the pun), on Saturday, and do I not find myself listening to the sound of the guns going off, for was I not at the Home Countries' Olympic Trap Shooting Championships? (Clay pigeon shooting to you).

Me and Phil, the photog, had travelled up this spectacularly scenic route to find wurselves in the heart of Stirlingshire. This rich country-side with its red ochre soil is the very place for such an expensive sport as shootin'. And it is expensive.

Like many a specialist sport the most expensive element is the travel. The boys — and they are mainly boys in this sport — came from Wales and England and Ireland and all the airts and pairts of our own country. More than that; a gun itself costs a few bob. A 12-bore shotgun costs between two and three thousand quid, though a gun can go much higher than that. The gun I myself fired, and more of that later, worked out at about six grand plus.

But then these guns are works of art. Rather lighter than you would expect, since a hand gun, for instance, can weigh very heavily. They are made of the best quality materials and the best quality workmanship. More often than not they are made in Italy, for that country is a major figure in the world gun championships.

Parazzi are the leaders in this class of gun. (The famous Purdey is for game shooting). The guns are what is called over and under, that is to say that the barrels are on top of one another unlike the traditional game guns in which the barrels are side by side.

There is considerable recoil in the guns: they are powerful beyond what one would think. Scotland has 1500 members in the Scottish clay target association. England has 30,000 members. Italy has 1,500,000 registered shooters. You have got a wee surprise at the end of this column concerning numbers.

First, I meet Iain MacGregor. He is organising Saturday's meet. Iain, who runs shooting parties for a business, is not just an enthusiast; he enthused me too.

Years of working as a driving instructor has taken him into instructing shoots. Today he runs loads of the increasingly popular corporate entertainment shoots, for there is nothing more exciting for tired business people than a day out at a range.

Clay target shooting, of course, doesn't kill anything more than a dod of clay, but it started off simply as practice for game and rough shooting. Today it is an Olympic sport, but for Iain it is also a business.

It is surprising how many people give the clays a bang or two. And though women have been in the past a little resistant to shooting, it is an ideal sport for the fairer sex, and more and more female parties are going in for it.

Target shooting has altogether 15 different disciplines, all with different names. The one thing it takes is concentration, and an eye for it.

Players like Scotland's Gary Peacock have more concentration than a snooker supremo because the shooting takes speed: no time to consider at all. Once most clay pigeon shooters were farmers. Today they come from all walks of life. Today, too, they have to shoot incredibly accurately.

Of the four home international teams of nine apiece, each competitor will have to shoot 200 times over two days. Gary Peacock, who shot at the New Zealand Commonwealth Games in 1990, had but recently won the Golden Clay in Germany, shooting 288 lumps of pottery out of 300, an awesome total. But all these people could shoot the ee'n oot of yer socket.

The pigeon shooting has done well for itself in business circles, but sadly it attracts — as Iain MacGregor admits — so few audiences that sponsorship is slight. The Scottish Sports Council donated two grand for the year but that just about pays for the sausage rolls.

Clay target shooting is for fans and adherents, and for the day out in business circles. I am hardly a businessman, but I intend to take it up.

Tony Lithgow, the clay association president, invited me to take what must be called a pot shot. The lads stood back. An Irish chap called David Evans, (there was a Welshman called Kevin there as well), called out encouragement. I raised Tony's six grand worth of gun to my shoulder. And I shot the beast. We artists have hand-and-eye co-ordination. Mind you I was coached by Joe Neville, the British Olympic coach. See the boys we get to meet? I will tell you this: I shall be boasting for months. I got a badge and everything.

Scotland has a mere 1500 members, though naturally there are a great many unregistered guns in the country. But England has 30,000 people sporting a piece.

It was a lovely day in the Stirlingshire dales. I shot a wee clay bird and didn't I do well? And best of all, Scotland won, for the first time. England came second as Scotland beat them by 16 points.

David Milton, sponsored by McEwans LA lager, whatever that is, beat Gary Peacock by 24 shots, if that's the word, out of 25, to Gary Peacock's 23. Me? I scored with every shot. The one I fired at that. It's the first time I've scored in years.

MORE THAN A SHOT IN THE PARK

October 26, 1992

'YOUR mission, Jack,' said my sports editor, 'is to boldly go where no man has gone before.' Thus it was that I embarked upon the very centre of split infinitives and minority sports.

Game shooting is probably both. Mind you, a lot of countrymen and women do the odd bit of banging away at birds, and hares, and the like, and in Italy, game shooting is an obsession, with stars of the sport akin to football players.

Shooting in Scotland is big business, and has been since the Highland clearances, when they put people off the land to make sheep the most important inhabitants, and then shoved off the sheep to make estates for English visitors to shoot pheasants instead of peasants. You might get a flavour of my democratic intellect by now.

I went to the first simulated game shooting meet in Scotland this week and I enjoyed it immensely. I did well, too, at Houston House last week. There is something horribly exhilarating about putting a shotgun to your shoulder and killing things.

But this was simulated game shooting; in short, it was clay pigeon shooting really except that it was in the wild. Houston Estate is 5000 acres of it, and about 20 minutes away from Glasgow, near Elderslie in fact, from where William Wallace came. The estate is loveliness itself. Twenty minutes from Glasgow and you are in the middle of what would pass for the Highlands.

Houston House, owned by Major Maitland, was especially splendid. The mansion is superb and the food grand, and the hospitality magnificent. The rooms are elegant beyond belief. But back to the democratic intellect.

I was invited to this first simulated game shoot because I cover the specialist sports. There is a difference between promoting minority sports and promoting promotions. This first simulated etcetera event in Scotland was a promotion for what is a commercial venture.

I do not blame Major Maitland, who is Renfrewshire's Lord Lieutenant, whatever that is, for wanting to provide an income for his estate, and I don't blame Bruce Gauntlett, a Wiltshire man who set up this day as a taster for corporate entertainment, or the companies who go in for such affairs, in trying their best to get the Press to give a jolly. But *The Herald* does not want to give private firms a jolly: it wants to tell the readers about sport.

Well, I will tell you this. The day out not far from darkest Glasgow will cost about two hundred quid, which is damned good value for a company executive. The reason why this is simulated game, and not the real birds, is because lady executives might not like the idea of shooting down nice wee feathery things and because the level of poaching, as well as out and out vandalism committed by local youths from Barrhead and the like, persuaded Major Maitland to stop breeding birds at all.

And another thing. Why were so many of the shooting chaps and chapettes such toffs? The names of half of the guests were as double barrelled as their guns. One wants to know why Major Maitland, and indeed the rest of the superannuated ex-service wallahs, are called by titles at all.

My father spent 20 years in the army, but nobody ever later called him Sergeant McLean. Major Maitland proved to be a very nice chap, who looked like something out of P G Wodehouse, but I'll be damned if I have to call anybody Major unless it is Denis Healey.

This is a sport for toffs and corporate entertainmant people will love it. All I have to say is that I cannot see the slightest reason why I am being charged huge bills by British Telecom, or some other monopoly, while they are giving a day out to a squad of Japanese entrepreneurs. There you have it: socialism at last in the sports pages.

But there were, indeed, lots of thoroughly nice people at the shoot. There were the Campbell couple who were doing the press and public-ity for the day and treated me royally. There was the magnificently clad Brian Pitchers, who wore a special shooting suit from Haggarts in Aberfoyle. He admitted to being less than a toff, but was a wonderful shot because he'd started off when he was a nipper on the very same estate. There was the doughty George McDermid who instructed me, and runs the Challenge Clay Company, and I never thought I would say something nice about an Argyll. There were lots of smashing people.

There were some that were not smashing at all. A Mr Martin Borthwick, who might be starting up a simulated game shoot at his own spot in Midlothian, was so absurdly rude to our photographer that wur snapper cut him out of the picture. I am putting Mr Borthwick right back into it. If you want to make a success of the corporate entertain-ment business, Martin Borthwick, try to be civil to people just doing their job.

But I did have a good day. My criticisms cannot override the fact that shooting is enormous fun and the countryside is breathtaking. If the taster day is anything to go by, then it will be a success. I boldly went and I would boldly go back — if they'll have me after this.

KIDS PAD UP

May 27, 1991

IF YOU should meet a Scot who enjoys cricket you will find, nine times out of 10, that he either attended public school or once lived in the Soft South. You will also discover that his appreciation of this most English game stemmed from the fact that the only place he could get a drink of a Saturday afternoon was the beer tent of the local cricket ground. Thus, it was for me when I worked in London in the mid-sixties.

Bit by bit I ventured out of the clubhouse to stare in ignorance at the boys in whites idling their time away with a bit of stick and a daft leather ball. I ended up playing the damned game, and a stirring figure I was in the white ducks and cricket cap of Richmond Select.

> *There's a breathless hush in the close tonight*
> *Ten to make and the match to win.*

I was a far cry from the flannelled fools of Sir Henry Newbolt's verses, but I was still a cricketer and a Scot at that. When I came back to our own, benighted land I kept the pleasure of the game.

Unfortunately, not many of my kinsmen ever get to see the splendours of cricket. Despised it is as an Anglo sport. In fact, it has got worse over recent years. When I was a kid we played a sort of cricket in the streets with a silly bat and a tennis ball and the stumps chalked up on a warehouse wall.

The proliferation of cars and the steady erosion of moral fibre among the nation's kids has left us bereft of childish sport, and especially those which are not soccer. Cricket was often played by boys and girls alike. (Incidentally, it is a virtually unknown fact that over-arm bowling was invented by public schoolgirls and once outlawed by the male cricketers.)

But the sport in Scotland is not quite as quiescent as most natives think. For a start, Scotland have been doing very well in the international scene, and more young people are at last being wooed by the cricket authorities. The recent development of Kwik Cricket, with its plastic stumps and bales and its softer ball, has allowed playground cricket to introduce the sport to more children than ever before.

Twenty Scottish clubs have joined this scheme to proselytise their game with every club pro taking on board four or five schools. There are currently 3000 plus children taking part in cricket and the Scottish

Cricket Union, with the considerable assistance of the Stanley Morrison Trust, has pledged £25,000 over the next five years to the development of the game.

It is, like many sports, not inexpensive. A good bat will be at least £100. Pads will cost thirty quid. Clydesdale Cricket Club, where I watched Drumpellier go down to the Titwood club at the weekend, has a subs fee of £70, though it is minimal for juniors and younger boys who are seriously sought after. Cricket has a scheme whereby wee lads of eleven, for instance, can play as mini-minors, and Scottish cricket takes its responsibilities toward the young very seriously indeed.

One of the most avid proponents of the game is Clydesdale's Sandy Strang, deputy heedie at Hutcheson's Grammar School, an institution but seconds away from the Titwood ground. Sandy, himself a fine cricketer (and a Cambridge Blue in football), has dragged so many Hutchie boys into cricket that he, Hutchie, and Clydesdale are thought now to have an unfair advantage over other clubs.

Unfair advantage or not, Clydesdale were good winners against Drumpellier — who have, of course, that magnificent cricketer Sajid Ali, a major prospect for Pakistan in the future — and the 50 runs scored by Clydesdale's professional, Stirling University's Bruce Russell, was a serious factor in their spectacular win on Saturday.

It was Bruce who caught Drumpellier's batsman out in the second-last over and the triumphal cheers were more akin to soccer than the Gentle Game. Sajid Ali disappointingly scored only 30 runs, much to the chagrin of his wife, Bushra. Baby Unzella didn't take a blind bit of notice.

One thing which is heartening about Scottish cricket is that the Asian community are made very welcome and have added much to the game. Clydesdale had Ricky Rutnagar and Muzaffar Mahmood in their first team at the weekend, and both enjoy their sport in this most opposite of climes to the sub-Continent.

Mind you, Ricky is an ex-Oxford man with an accent considerably posher than mine. He's a sight better cricketer than I ever was, too. It's no fair. That's what I said to Nancy in the clubhouse bar anyway. Nancy laughed, as well she might. She remembers seeing me play.

GREEN KNOCK IS CHAMPION

August 30, 1993

NOW Greenock is ever shrouded in monsoon, but while the rest of Scotland basked in the sunshine, Greenock also was wearing a sun-hat on Saturday.

Greenock Cricket Club has a lovely little ground, set amidst douce bourgeois tenements. Youse wid hardly know you were in the very crucible of the deprived western industrial belt.

The ground is, admitted club president, Graeme Sanders, very small, but groundsman Kenny Benson's ministrations makes this little patch of sward as decent a wicket as you will get. Kenny also does the clubhouse and pavilion. He's one of these chaps who can do electrics, plumbing, painting, and looking after journalists. This blatt could do with him.

Certainly the clubhouse is lovely, tasteful in its decor, in marked contrast to many a wealthier club, and this is not a wealthy club.

For a start, the club fees are a modest £60 per annum, and though there are between 350 and 400 members, the upkeep is high. There are tennis courts too, and a splendid squash court. In the winter the ground is used for hockey.

District umpire Alison McIntyre, (whose husband Donald I saw last year play at Riccarton), told me that, for once, in a male enclave like a cricket club, the hockey ladies get priority over the men and have first choice of the park. The men have to go to Largs. I commend this little club highly.

I congratulate them too, for they won the Western Union championship on Saturday, with 196 for six declared against their opponents Drumpellier from Coatbridge (don't tell me cricket is for toffs: a Coatbridge toff is anybody who puts water in his Buckfast and can read), and gained the better of a draw with 15 points, since Drumpellier managed only 179 for six wickets down, and were awarded only nine.

There are three main leagues in Scottish cricket — East, based in Edinburgh and the Lothians, the counties — that name speaks for itself — and of course Western Union.

Greenock is quite an old club in fact — founded in 1862 — and has suffered a little in past years from the simple fact that, by the nature of any sporting club, there are changes in membership.

A lot of the older members, once the backbone of the club, got so old that they, well, croaked it, and that is about as old as you want to get. Many members are now quite young.

This, said President Sanders, does present a little problem in that the young fellows are inclined to spend less time in the clubhouse, leaving early to get up to the serious business of chatting up girls elsewhere, and club revenue through the bars and functions is not as high as perhaps it could be.

Sanders points out that this will undeniably change over the next few years as the youngsters get older. When they get married indeed, I said, you might find the club will benefit from escapees from married bliss for an hour or two, for cricket clubs are nothing if not havens for male spouses.

But Greenock's success was something of a triumph in the Western Union — which has 10 teams altogether — as their full-time professional Darren Walker has been unable to play the last four weeks.

Atul Wasson, a well-know pro originally from India, had taken over and has done well. Perhaps not as well though as PE teacher Tom Black, who scored 108 last week and on Saturday made 76.

One of the most talented amateurs in Scotland, Tom, a Scottish international, has made a recovery from a bad car smash which put his career back considerably. Tom will be especially pleased at his club's win and his own form recently.

The deathly hush is over and I am enjoying a whisky and soda in the clubhouse along with sponsor Hugh McClure and a young lady who refuses to give me her name. I get it eventually. It is Emma. She is six and daughter of hockey ace Alison, already mentioned. The sound of leather on willow yet echoes in the mind. Play up, and play the game. That's what I told Emma anyway.

And suddenly I felt in harmony with the world.

PUT THROUGH THE HOOP

May 20, 1991

WHEN anybody thinks of croquet, they summon up images of tea-gowns and butlers standing by with silver trays of glasses of chilled Chablis. Sunny late-Edwardian summers and muffins for tea. Granchester would be the very spot.

At the weekend, however, it wasn't Rupert Brooke's old stamping ground at all: it was Glasgow Green, with heavy drizzle. When the boys and girls felt like a small repast, they nipped across the road to the boozer for a roll and sausage.

No wonder Lewis Carroll chose croquet as the game to exercise his surrealism. For all I ended up understanding about this most recondite of pastimes, the players might just as well have been using flamingoes instead of mallets. Only croquet players could grasp the rules of the game. Listen — the entire sports desks of all the British press gathered together in conclave could not make out what was happening on the greens.

Young Denis Mooney, in charge of sport at Scottish Television, told me the other day that he once filmed it and realised that a programme on the sport would have to go out in a ten-part series as a three-year course for the Open University. All I am going to do today is confuse you.

Mind you, nothing seems to confuse the actual players. They all know the rules, doubtless because almost all seemed to be academics — and mathematical ones at that. Rod Williams, a computer chap at Strathclyde Yooni, tried to explain what it was all about.

He was very patient, the way I remember my old teachers, and I could hardly comprehend a thing, the way my old teachers doubtless remember me. But I grasped a little of it. There are two players, each playing with two different coloured balls. The object is to get your ball through the six hoops on the field, and then change to the other ball, the one with the different colour. And then you can hit a peg, which is stuck right in the middle of the green. Is that clear so far?

Of course it is. But this is where it gets murky.

To get your ball placed in the position where it will go through the hoops, (they are one-sixteenth of an inch wider than the ball, so you have got to have the ball exactly in front of the hoop), you will have to think umpteen moves ahead, adopting the sort of tactics you will find in, say, billiards.

Furthermore, there is an interaction between you and your opponent. In this case, you employ strategies akin to that of an especially psychopathic snooker player on the drug, mescalin. Add the mental agility of a top chess player with murder on his mind, and you might just catch the flavour of the sport. Oh, I nearly forgot to tell you. Sometimes there are two games going on at the same time on the same green. That'll learn you.

The French claim that croquet was invented by them. They call it Mail ('mallet' to you) and it was the 11th-century precursor to many another sport. Golf it became in Scotland (it is only comparatively recently that golf became a game you played against the course and not an opponent, and the golf 'stymie' was ruled out). Louis XIV is said to have got so fed up playing croquet in the teeming rain that he had a courtier devise an indoor version which came out as billiards. Thus one can see why croquet is rather a courtly game. There is no place for temper tantrums here. McEnroe would not take to it at all.

This weekend saw a turn-out of 16 players, which is all Glasgow Green can really take. A lot of them were recent converts. Basil Townsend, secretary of Edinburgh, and a Hemingway look-alike, has been playing only four years, as has his wife Charlotte, secretary of the Bush Club, Edinburgh's other collection of croquet enthusiasts. Membership of Bush costs £40 per annum while membership of Ayr's Auchenruive Club is a mere four quid.

Croquet can be expensive — a full four playing set will cost up to £800 or so, but it also can be well within anybody's financial reach with a mallet costing about £40. Whether it is within the mental reach of most of us is another matter. Sometimes, as I understand it, there are different coloured balls to the normal four colours of blue and black, red and yellow. There are points lost for missing or something, and handicapping for poorer — or is it better — players. Sometimes they play different rules altogether.

The game cannot be said to attract more than a small number — there are perhaps about 300 regular players in Scotland — and most are attracted only because they know somebody who does play.

Elsewhere, croquet is a little different. France has several professionals who make a good living out of it, and the US has considerable sponsorship involvement. Yet the game is increasing, ever so slightly, in Scotland, and despite the arcane nature of what I saw over the weekend, I could see the attractions of it. Highly intellectual and convoluted as it is, there are physical as well as cerebral demands. It's just that I suspect I could not meet either.

CHARMING LUNACY AND BADNESS

September 28, 1992

I DON'T like croquet. I love it. I love it for it's sheer daftness. There I was of a Sunday, a year after my sojourn last season at Glasgow Green, watching white clad figures shimmy about, gently smacking the mallet against all these strangely coloured balls, and putting them through hoops.

Youse would have to go through hoops to understand this most arcane of games. There was part of the tournament on Saturday, and there will be part of it today. This is the Scottish Croquet Association's Chairman's Rosebowl event. It is not a rosebowl you should be getting for winning at the croquet — it is a week off just to get your brain back to normal.

I met Rod Williams again, chairman of the association. Rod is a computer boffin at Strathclyde Yooni. He explained the rules again to me, just as patiently as he had done last year.

There are two players, each playing with two different coloured balls. The object is to get your ball through the six hoops on the field, and then change to the other ball, the one with the different colour. And then you can hit a peg, which is stuck in the middle of the green. Is that clear so far?

The foregoing should be in quotes, for I am repeating some of the report I did last year. The reason for that is that I am none the wiser. All I know is that it looks a lot like snooker on grass, but with less money.

Certainly the croquet players are quite as single-minded as those of snooker, and just as polite and courteous. And as determined and as bright.

I met snooker wizard Mike Hallet at the weekend when we bumped into each other in Ralph Slater's splendid menswear emporium and he told me that snooker is about thinking ahead more than anything else. In short, about brains.

Well, croquet is the same. The origin is claimed by the French who called it Mail — mallet that is — and started off in the 11th-century. Naturally, this is disputed by the Irish, who named it Crokey. Croke Park, where I witnessed the splendours of the Gaelic Football Cup final last weekend, is named after the game apparently.

It became, say the Irish, golf. The Irish claim to have invented whiskey, the television, and America. I will commend only the discovery of whiskey there, and it was ourselves who made it drinkable at that.

Rod introduced me to a new and rising star in the Scottish Croquet game. Young Jeremy Dyer is a Lancashire man who now works in Glasgow with Scottish Amicable, doubtless doing terrible things to my investments, though he studied at St Andrews University. He was walloping red and yellow balls through the hoops, (which are but one sixteenth of an inch wider than the ball itself) with gusto.

His pretty companion, Nicola, read the Sunday papers. I have never met patient girls myself, but a true test of patience has got to be croquet. She is also a Yorkshire girl and rows, of course, for Clydesdale, in Cherry Wainwright's team.

You have met Cherry in my column before. Minority sports seem to attract patient and determined girls. I can't attract any sort at all myself but I can see why the lads are going in for specialist activities like sculling and skelping croquet balls.

Jeremy seemed to recognise that there is a certain eccentricity about the game and, indeed, the players.

Of the six who were playing on Sunday, there was not a one who did not eventually reveal a charming sense of lunacy. David Appleton, however, was gloriously dressed in an outfit closely resembling the bad one in *Mad Magazine's* Two Spies. For there is also badness at the heart of this game. The players take a terrible wickedness with them on to the green.

The Glasgow club has perhaps some 30 players, most of them academics — mathematicians are rather good at it due to the computation skills required.

There may be as many as 300 players in Scotland itself though few play all that regularly. The Glasgow club captain, Colin Rogers, told me that there have been strenuous attempts to get more recruits. Last year and this year he and his members have been organising introductory evenings each Wednesday at Kelvingrove Park in Glasgow, just beside the Art Galleries, from six in the evening till the park closes. Those interested can get him at 041-334-0689. It's very brave of him to issue that. But that's how keen the chaps are.

Chaps mainly as well. There is absolutely no reason, says Colin, why women should not take up the game. It requires no special physical prowess, only a decent hand and eye co-ordination and, I think anyway, a recommendation from the Great Grandmaster of the Mensa Lodge.

Certainly it is ideal for the relaxation. Says Colin: 'After you've relaxed with the croquet at Kelvingrove, you relax well and truly at The Brewery Tap across the road.'

I do not know this boozer, but I suspect it is just one of these ancient taverns I know under a previous name. Colin also holds the Dublin venue for croquet in great regard. I knew every single pub he recommended. For some reason, minority sports hold conviviality as part of the rules of the game. Apparently the Irish are keen on the game, and many a sojourn across the Irish Sea is enjoyed. To put the record straight, incidentally, I was not the only representative of the British Press, as I claimed, to cover the Gaelic footy cup final last week. The other was Scotland's ain Roddy Forsyth. It takes two Allan Glen's boys.

The Irish are doubtless keen on croquet because it attracts the sort of surrealistic oddness which croquet demands and the Irish frequently possess. Do not forget that the great Chronicler of Croquet, Charles Lutwidge Dodgson, was part Irish. Yesterday I could almost see him myself, stroking a red ball past a hoop with a flamingo in his hands in the dusk of the Glasgow Green.

A COLD SPORT WITH A WARM HEART

November 2, 1992

WHEN it is very late at night, and you are awakened by sports executives and told to record whatever you got up to that day, you have a tendency to say nothing.

'Nothing,' I said to my deputy sports wallah.

But that is not right. Minority sports need more than 'nothing'. I have told you before about the misnomer of minority. Curling is a minority entertainment, if you like, but how can anything be that when you discover, as indeed have done, that it involves thousands of people.

I have covered curling before. The sport has 20,000 people playing it competitively, and a lot more participants as well. Curling in Scotland is important. For a start, the sport has an international importance. And this small country is second only to Canada. Think about it. We have five million people here, and Canada has, I shudder to think, how many more. All the other cold countries have practically squillions. The CIS and Scandinavia have enough curlers to destroy us, but we are close to being the best. Scotland has international curlers who are tops.

We have the two Addison girls, (they are the daughters of my doctor as a matter of fact), and Kirsty was playing at the Dewars Rinks in Perth. Kirsty Addison is now Mrs Hay, and married to Mike Hay (sister Karen is in Austria studying), and the daughter-in-law of the legendary Chuck Hay, who is now in charge at Perth.

It is difficult for the younger curlers because this sport is expensive. An advertisement in the centre for shoes claimed that there would a reduction from £115 to £55.

You will have to be horribly fleet of foot to afford that.

The Dewars Rinks are magnificent. Young Alison has been working there for three hours and has three hours more to go. She is paid not very much but as a Perth girl, a local, she is glad of the money. The centre is glad of the help. Like everything else in minority sport, local communities are glad of any help they can get. It is an expensive business, the curling, but Scotland can manage.

The European championships will be held there next month. This is grand because the Scottish team do not have to pay for the European teams as they do if Scotland goes abroad.

At the European playdowns at the weekend, I met the usual chums of the sport. I also met an unusual lot. I don't know why so many young curling mums have decided to have weans, but there are an awful lot of little ones there. Alison is run off her feet trying to heat milk for the bairns. One of the bairns is none other than Hammy MacMillan. Anybody who knows anything about curling knows that there is always a Hammy MacMillan throwing a stone about.

Lorna MacMillan — herself once a rare curler — looks younger than my barmaid, but is now nurturing a wee Hammy. The Roaring Game is a very family sport!

But curling is a winter sport. It's damned cold out on the rink. And why not? Scotland is a cold country after all. But in the country, you have to think up things to do. Curling was obvious. It has a warm heart.

THE LADIES LOOK GOOD EVEN WITH CURLERS IN

December 14, 1992

PERTH is an awful bloody place: a bit like Dundee with brains and violence. But Perth also has the Dewars Centre, a sports centre which is second to none in its facilities. And the ice facilities were open to the curling fraternity this last week for the European Championships.

There were 19 countries competing, though only eight European countries managed women's teams — surprising, because many of the stars are in fact ladies, including Scotland's own Addison girls. Karen is in France just now doing her career no end of good, but Kirsty is Scottish champion and skip of the Scottish team; in curling the team is chosen by the captain, nae democracy about it.

It has to be understood that curling is a sport which has taken off but has not the level of sponsorship which many another, equally recondite, game can achieve. The European Championships were sponsored in fact by the Teacher's whisky chaps. Teacher's have sponsored curling since 1988 and they have put over 65 grand over the last three years into curling.

This sport has also seen a high level profile from Scottish Television, and rightly so, for it is a right wee Scottish game, combining the cauld, whisky, and sportmanship.

Well sportswomenship it should read, for undeniably the ladies have been taking the honours the last few years, due muchly to the presence of the two Addison girls. Kirsty Hay (née Addison: it would have been mair journalistic the other way round and I could have wrote née Hay) was there but also Hazel Erskine, there to help Kirsty's team to the final.

The Europa final in Perth is just about the world final and only the

US and Canada were missing to make it that, but the top curlers in the world were present. I bumped into Richard, the Austrian player. He played the stones as well as he spoke English which is, to say, better than me or you.

Curling is not big in the Tyrol, for there is only one curling rink in the entire country, but the chaps played out of their skins. Mind you, the Austrians were done down eventually by the Germans. I believe the reason for this was that the Germans were led by a skip who rejoiced in the name Andy Kapp.

Said Scotland's David Hay afterwards: 'We did badly. If we'd been on our game the Germans couldn't have lived with us.' He said this without rancour, bitterness, or envy.

Mr Hay, who is married to the delectable ex-Miss Addison, and the both of them about 20, is already a seasoned player. Mother-in-law Dr Isobel, whom you might remember me telling you has the thankless task of being my GP, said she thought the boys done good.

And so they done as well. Scottish curling is world class. As I wrote earlier, the men did well indeed, even if they didn't quite manage the heights. The ladies managed the final itself and, considering that Canada and the United States have levels of sponsorship beyond the wildest of dreams, Scotland has nothing to complain of.

What we can mention is the enormous difficulty of getting yourself about in the various competitions. As I said last week, it takes parents with money and commitment to allow the young ones the chance of really taking off in sport, and curling is no exception.

The five girls of the Scottish team — that's four with a sub — all have the benefit of parents and the dubious opportunities given with being students. Once again I have to say that this smashing game would be impossible were the people concerned unemployed from Easterhouse.

As I said to my chum, broadcaster Iain Anderson, who does the *Week in Sport* for the Beeb every week, I would spend all the Arts poppy for Strathclyde in issuing a grant for weans to play sport: it would be money better spent.

Curling is well attended though, and there were sizeable crowds there. Some changes — much for the better — have been made. In an especially drastic change, the rule now is that you can take a stone which is in front of the house out in your first two shots. This is a little like ending the off-side rule in footy, and the soccer boys could take a leaf out of the curling book.

It has meant a much sharper game. The players themselves are in favour. Said Hazel Erskine: 'It's a more attacking sport now; you don't feel so defensive as we did.'

The Scots girls weren't, as it happens, attacking enough, for they lost 9-3 in the final. I spoke to the losers afterwards. They were enjoying themselves no end, like Partick Thistle fans who have only lost 10-0.

The triumphant Swedes didn't look nearly as mirthful. Pretty though, I'll tell you that. Aren't they all, except the boys. I never really noticed them.

NOT ICE AND EASY IN CURLING

November 29, 1993

CURLING has always been bad for me. Somehow, I seem to get everything wrong in my little essays on the sport.

The major problem is that curlers all seem to have the same name. The Addison sisters — the two young women who have dominated Scottish curling for so long — have caused me much grief. Their mum is my GP, and long in a practice which was once headed by a Doctor Hay.

One of the sisters married, of course, Mike Hay, another top curler. So Kirsty Addison is now Kirsty Hay. There is also David Hay, another ace curler, and John Hay.

Youse'll love this. The chap in charge of looking after the press is a curler called Gordon Addison. He is no relation to the Addison girls. Have I cleared all that up?

Gordon turns out to be a pleasant young chap who works as a lawyer. He is also pleasant enough to buy me a wee hauf, because curling is not just about chucking stones down the ice, it is very much about socialising. A cauld day would be the caulder without the drams.

Gordon was also very frank about his sport. 'We do need sponsorship' he said, 'and since the television coverage has gone down, we need it even more.'

More about the telly later. There has been some sponsorship for what is an expensive sport. A pair of stones will cost roughly seven hundred spondulicks, though most players hire them.

This makes the rinks expensive too, and the cost of keeping the ice itself is damn-near ruinous. It is therefore very costly. We are talking of £5 per hour for each player.

Though this is not impossible for a lot of curlers, just think about the added cost of travel — most curlers are rural people and far away from the rinks — and you are dispossessing most of the unemployed, a lot of children and teenagers, those on low incomes, and heaps of folk who have never tried it. It is a great shame, said Gordon, and I agree with him because if you have ever been at a curling rink, you will want to try it yourself. It's a bit like bowling crossed with the dodgems at the shows. It is the way I play it.

But Mr Addison was more candid, and admitted what many people in the specialist sports shy away from.

'This is a sport which, sadly, is mainly for the middle classes' he told me. To illustrate he pointed to the winners board in the smashing little bar of the Murrayfield Curling Club. He showed me the names of the schools which fuelled the Army Cup. All the schools were fee-paying, with George Watson's prominent.

I have written many a time on this unfortunate circumstance. The truth is that the private schools give sporting opportunities, and in more sports, and minority ones at that, than the state schools do and frankly it is a disgrace.

The education authorities, right up to the Scottish Office itself talk great gobs of unctuous nonsense about sport for all and the importance of fitness and health, but they do very little to promote sport in any form.

Admittedly some local authorities try the best they can, and indeed Edinburgh Council helped to sponsor the three days of this nineteenth Edinburgh National Mixed Curling Championships, though they were outmatched in sponsorship by the nearby Braid Hills Hotel which put up the visitors gratis, but organisations such as Direct Line and ScottishPower will be targeted in the future because sport is underfunded.

The Curling Championships had major stars there at the weekend, including Norwegian ace, Eigil Ramsfjell, DiDi Kolb of West Germany, and Tommi Stern of Denmark, and this was once a premier event. All this for only £1000 winner's prize.

The change in the rules — the new three-guard zone in which the first three lead stones cannot be put out of play — has meant a more attacking and spectator-interest game.

Despite that, curling is not doing as well as once it did. BBC Scotland still covers it, but Scottish Television, once in the vanguard of curling coverage when Russell Galbraith was sports editor, does not touch it.

Quite simply, Scottish decided to extend its football scene and the extra resources and programme time required meant that 'some sports had to be reduced'.

There you are. The footy mania is a damned Upas tree. And certainly, curling has lost much due to the lack of the telly. Scotland has done well in the sport over the last decade, though is accorded scant respect unlike other countries which engage in the ice sports.

In Canada, for instance, sponsorship, especially by companies like frozen chip firm McCain, can lead to prizes of $70,000 which is not, well, Hay.

I knew I'd end on a Hay note at that.

AN ICE BUNCH OF PEOPLE

February 21, 1994

LAST time I wrote about this marvellous ice game I admitted in advance that curling has always been bad for me. 'I get the names wrong,' I explained, 'and nae wonder.'

There are so many sisters and brothers and intermarrying at a level which would have driven the Salic Law daft that no reporter can ever be accused of accuracy.

But thank you all the same to the non-curler called W M Kidd who wrote a vituperative letter to the Blatt last November at the Edinburgh Mixed Curling Championships, and thank you, too, to the correspondent to the Summitnews, the informative newsletter of the magnificent Summit Ice Centre in Glasgow. This writer complained heartily that I got some things wrong, especially the cost of curling. I was not, in fact wrong, but he was. Throughout his diatribe he managed to spell my title as 'MacLean'. I am not a Mac. I have ever been, and at all times, a right wee 'C' and no Macs about it. But why cavil when one finds oneself in the splendour of the Summit Centre?

Peggy Smith of the Summit Centre, resplendent in tartan outfit and the sort of buttons which Alan Breck sported, dragged me unwillingly into the bar and introduced me to the worthies, mostly older than the players themselves, (officials, mums, dads, hubbies) and told me with pride — and the entourage a bit swelling with it too — that this was the first time that the west of Scotland had put on a Scottish Championship. This was the Scottish Ladies.

Next week sees the Scottish Men. Out of these 14 teams will come a champion side to go to the World Championships in Oberstdorf, a mere two hours south of Munich, at the German National Centre where the very Torvill and Dean duo did their training all these years back before they took the ice world by storm.

The two Scottish teams — male and female — will be there from April 9 to 17 and are expected to do well. This would be a touch surprising to Scots sports bodies outside of curling. For Scots curling, especially ladies, is of world stature.

Now think of this: Canada has more than 1500 venues in which to exercise this sport, which originated in Scotland of course, and Scotland has 30, few of which can come up to standards of size which would permit international competition. Yet Scotland has done consistently well, and more.

Despite the fact that there are 48 curling lanes in Calgary and that 384 people can play at the one time; that the Granite Club in Toronto has curling going on on five floors and despite the slightness of venues in Scotland, this country has world-class winners.

And there are other constraints in this country too. I spoke to Richard Harding, an old acquaintance from past meetings, and him the manager of the Lagoon Centre in Paisley. He told me, and I believe it, that as a pupil at Glasgow Academy he was forbidden to curl because the only place he could was at the late Crossmyloof. His headie forbade the boys because it was where neds went.

And then he told me more. 'We need more support from the schools. We have plenty of coaches to teach them, but we need the schools'.

This was echoed by Peggy of the Summit. 'Saturday morning children's sessions — from whatever age, from wee to big — cost £1.25 per two hour session, and the top players, including internationals, do their instructor bit all for nothing.'

Much of what the Summit does is funded by the extent of their magnificent social club, one which would do credit to any club in any sport in the country.

Curling started off in the rural areas, among farming folk, and was popular among such communities. If anybody wants to argue that the world climate hasn't really changed since the War, let them look at curling.

The mild winters of the last 30 years have meant that the seven inches of ice required — for safety purposes if nothing else — has turned Scottish curling into an indoor game. (In Canada the climate is so severe that it has to be an indoor game). Don't forget that curling has the advantage of being more than a sport: it is a game as well. One in which you can grow old, and gracefully.

This weekend saw upsets of course — I was disappointed myself to find my doctor's daughter, Kirstie Hay, losing in the semi-final to Rhona Martin, a housewife from Greenock who has built a formidable team herself, though Hay may well go on to greater things with the two Louden girls with whom she teamed for the first time this year.

I was betting money too, always a daft thing to do. Still Sheila, the president of the Royal Caledonian, made up for it. She bought me a large one. Oh, and Mr Kidd, who criticised me last year, and skip

Christine Cannon won again. That's five years I've been losing wagers on the wummin.

But I am not as big a loser as a greetin' face like this Kidd person at that.

WHERE BRAINS FOIL BRAWN WITH FINESSE

March 4, 1991

YOU went up the road from the old Kingsway Cinema with your trench coat buttoned at the neck and the rest of it gangin' free — you were D'Artagnan. Fat boys would be Porthos. The quick illusion of a garden cane to a rapier worthy of a musketeer allowed romance to enter the average 10-year-old's life in moments.

At once I was Errol Flynn (himself an Olympic champion swordsman). Romance and fencing go together, and it was with the spirit of the swashbuckler that I found myself covering the Scottish Under-20 Fencing Championships at the weekend at the well-set-up Blantyre Sports Centre. You have to swash a buckle a bit in Blantyre as I remember: it must be the last town on earth where Teddy Boys cause trouble of a Saturday night. Fencing in Blantyre is not unusual. Doing it for sport rather than for real is what is out of the ordinary.

Blantyre Sports Centre is indeed splendid and has been going for eight years: it is not doing as well as could be expected. Blantyre folk have an awful tendency to regard sport as basically hitting each other with screwtops outside the chip shop, but the centre tries hard and former PE teacher and now centre supervisor Gerry Kane is happy enough about the increase in users of the place. There are a lot of PE-trained people about, including an old colleague of mine from back in my teaching days, Norman Mortimer, a one-time member of the Scottish sabre squad.

Sabre is different from foil and épée and each takes on board differing demands — except two. You have to be fit and you have to be bright. Fencing has been described (by David Mends of the Scottish Amateur Fencing Union among others) as 'chess in three dimensions'.

My old chum Norman says that Glaswegians — who number themselves well in fencing circles — call it 'fighting with finesse'. Watching the sport, you cannot help but be taken aback with the finesse. If the sport of fencing started off with duelling, and it did, it took with it a basic courtesy which has become endemic. There was a time when sabre allowed scarring in Heidelberg, but Schlager fencing has long been outlawed, even in Prussia. Today's fencers win not by blood but by skill.

Skill it is; strength will not work in this sport, as a result of which there is genuinely no problem about girls playing with boys: let me rephrase that. Fencing is to do with aptitude and ability and not at all to do with the kind of physical demands which exists in most other sports, though stamina is a necessary portion. A somewhat recondite sport, fencing does not attract many adherents and, in fact, there are a mere 1000 practitioners in the country. This competition, for instance, managed to attract six contenders for sabre on Saturday and it is reckoned that there were no more than 250 under-20s competing in the entire two days at Blantyre. One of them, however, was young Rachel McFaddyen, from Dumfries, now a law student at Edinburgh Yooni.

Rachel is a fine, decent girl with a pleasantly laid-back attitude who spoke as freely to myself as I have ever heard from a sports person. She is also a pentathlete and told me that fencing was her worst discipline. You could have fooled me when I saw her in action. She would have speared our man Errol in seconds. Epée is what she was doing. (In foil you can only hit target on the trunk, in sabre you can touch anywhere above the waist, in épée you can score a point if you were to touch your opponent's big toe or somewhere even more risible, and it is all done by electronics. Hits are recorded by means of an electric judge.)

This is a sport which ladies and men can compete in equally because strength is no measure. It is not even confined to age groups, though the weekend's jamboree was indeed for the youngsters. David Ness, from George Heriot's School in Edinburgh, is only 17 but is already a prospect. He took the gold in the sabre, fencing against his fellow Heriot pupil, Justin Crozier, and told me afterwards that he started off simply because he saw Stewart Grainger in a movie and wanted to be like him. I wanted to be like Stewart Grainger myself, but not at the fencing: I wanted to get off with girls really.

But fencing is a little bit more than romance; it has a splendid reality about it. It levels everybody, male, female, upper-class and what one used to call lower-class. It is only a shame that, like many another minority sport, fencing is rarely an option in the ordinary State school. Everybody I spoke to said it was a sort of chess with bodies involved. It is more: it is ballet with brains. Blantyre should be so lucky.

FLOUNDER MEMBERS IN A MUDLARK

August 2, 1993

D'YE know, I have never done fishin'. This weekend, I embarked upon a report on the sport which, it is alleged, has more active participants than any other. Not, as you would think, angling, or fly fishing, or even trawling for herring.

Back to the very primeval form of it was what I was looking for.

Flounder tramping. To be exact the Grande Internationale World Championships Flounder Tramping. At Palnackie. Got you confused there, eh? Youse don't know what flounder tramping is and you don't have a Scoobie where, or what, Palnackie is.

I will tell you what the press release told me. 'The village of Palnackie on the Solway Firth for the 1993 Black Bottle Flounder Tramping Championship is the only plaice (?) to be on Saturday, July the 31st.'

Well it was the plaice I was that day. More of Palnackie later.

But first to the event. 'Flounder-tramping,' said sort of treasurer and secretary of the Palnackie Flounder-thingmy committee, Harry Ellis, originally a chap from Partick but now a civil engineer residing in the little hamlet of Palnackie, 'is a straightforward sport.'

I should jolly well say it is.

It is about as straightforward as you can achieve. The aim of it all is to wade into, in the case of Saturday, the muddy estuary of the River Urr and try to stand on a 'flattie,' a flounder. To be successful, the competitor then reaches down, picks the fish up, and has it weighed.

The winner of the chief title is the lucky competitor who has got the heaviest fish. Last year it was a chap from nearby Kippford, John Robertson, with a flounder of two-and-a-half pounds.

The year before it was a lady who won. This is such a daft sport that children could win it. Even I could have won it if I'd taken part. But I didn't, believe me.

More power to young Paul Hackett, our photographer. Struggling along the hills and not-quite beaten tracks of this spectacular part of the country, he and me managed to get right down to a rocky promontory overlooking the mudflats of the Solway Firth.

Says Paul: 'Are you sure you can make it down this 40ft rocky tor down to the mud?' Says I: 'Aye.'

Immediately I fell over a splendid piece of granite and into a thorn bush. Picking thorns out of me and being attended to by local observers, it occurred to me that it was not an entirely good idea to send a middle-aged writer with arthritis on a mission which would pass for the Guns of Navarone. I let young Paul wallow in the flounders' fields himself whilst I was ministered to by competitor Carl Holland and his wife, Sally.

Now I will tell you where Palnackie is. You'd never find it yourself unless you knew about it. Even on a rather bleak day the area is startlingly beautiful. Across the water is Kippford. There is a terrible rivalry between all three villages, each a mile or so apart, but I shall be back here for it is an astoundingly scenic area. Dalbeattie is near and Dumfries within a 15-minute journey. But this area is away from such bustling towns.

A lift from Dave Fittes and his family all the way back up the track to the centre of Palnackie, the Glen Isle Inn, revealed that he too was English. There were a lot of English actually living in this hardly-spotted part of the country, but they are not the retirees who so disfigure Scottish remoteness: they are all young and working here and loving it and well accepted by the locals, who feel they have added much.

And there I was at the Glen Isle, where publican Cammy Herdsman presides along with his wife, Cecilia. I never met more welcoming hosts in my life, and saved me they did, with a large one of Black Bottle. The whisky company had sponsored this bizarre event to the tune of £260 plus whisky. Representative John Rutherford told the crowd at the prizegiving that they will be sponsoring the event next year, too.

Sadly there were only just more than 100 competitors this year, the weather over the last month being bad enough to deter the extra hundred Palnackie had received in 1992. But winner of the biggest flounder, Chris Clark from Dumfries, got £150 and a three-litre bottle of the Aberdonian nectar and is allowed to keep the big silver rosebowl trophy for the year. This a sport in which the second prize is won by the competitor with the wee-est fish. 'Frae big tae wee,' said a young lad salaciously. 'If yer oot there in the cauld fur hauf an 'oor, ye get fae big tae wee nae bother.' I do not know what he meant by that: I am only reporting. Anyway, Neil Crossan was a wee boy you couldn't see above the table and had to be stood up on it. The heaviest catch won the third prize for Stuart Kiltie, the children's one was taken by Neil Whennel, and the women's prize by awfy shy Tanya Glendinning aged eight. She got a silver cup and 30 quid. Nae whisky though.

Later the dancing went on into the small hours. You never saw such talent in the bar. I fell in love though with a very small girl called Katie MacQueen, a wee lovely lassie with flaxen hair and glasses and a wild determination. Her smashing mother said she made a lovely niece but a terror for a daughter. I can't wait till she grows up.

Incidentally, they throw the fish back. Just as well. God knows their fate if Katie got her hands on them.

NOUGHT CAUGHT BUT A COLD

January 17, 1994

WUR favourite quote seems to be ill-based factually. When W C Fields rejected the offer of a glass of water in a New York bar because, he said, fish fornicated in it, and he didn't say fornicated at that, he was not well informed. Do not come back as a fish. The poor things don't fornicate at all. Atlantic salmon do it maybe twice in their lives and croak it afterwards. Pacific chaps do it once and then meet their makers. The lady fish live longer. This sounds a lot like humans, really. But I'm still not coming back as a fish.

After my weekend in Kenmore, Perthshire, I am willing to state that I'm not coming back as an angler, either. Let Bernard Corrigan supply the McLean household with its haddock in the future. I know that angling and fishing is the biggest participatory sport in the UK but it is also the coldest. And cold it was on the banks of the River Tay and the edge of the loch at the weekend.

But there were lots of loonies in Kenmore for the start of the salmon season on Saturday, the famous January 15. The most famous start of all is in Kenmore, a small and beautiful village near Pitlochry and one of the nicest places in the world to get cold in. The venue is the Kenmore Hotel, Scotland's oldest inn, dating from 1572 and complete with a poem pencilled on the wall by Rabbie Burns no less and preserved for ever by successive hotel owners. (They wouldn't let me add to the verses.)

The new owners are very nice people indeed and took up the great tradition of the salmon angling start of the season with a will, with one of the partners, the rather dishy Miss Suzanne Glasper, originally from Durham, opening the proceedings by throwing a quaich of whisky over the first boat out. When I was told about this by PR chap Bill Nolan (him late of Tennents, a company for whom I once laboured as a drayman), I got him wrong over the phone. I thought he said 'A crate of whisky' and nearly had a heart attack.

But there was well over a crate dispensed to the 200-plus anglers who turned up for this important ceremony. The piper was out in the square early on Saturday morning and then the wee march down to the river (and me in it as well, clad in Nolan's deerstalker fishing hat and looking grand). The Boar's Head bar was doing brisk business giving whisky away. Cheery is not the word for it.

But there was a less amiable note to the morning. A demonstration in the Kenmore Square by locals from Perth complaining that the river, as other rivers in Scotland, were not open to the public. I spoke to demonstrator Brian Keith, a careers officer. He claimed that the private river-fishing system was losing opportunities for jobs, especially for young people. It is true that Canada, Greenland, Ireland, and many other countries have a level of public control far removed from what are, Keith says, 'private fiefdoms' on Scotland's rivers.

I spoke, too, to some anglers from Stirling who had come up for the opening to fish, they said, rainbow trout, and had been threatened with police action.

I have considerable sympathy with anybody who insists that people don't own rivers, or land if it comes to that in the case of walkers, and those who feel entitled to their own country. So did most of the anglers that day, and what could have been a tense confrontation was defused by the simple decency of the angling people. (True it is though that part of the argument lies in the now very considerable problem of the 'White Settlers'. Certainly there were a lot of smart Southern accents bouncing about.)

But there are problems elsewhere in the angling industry, and industry it is. The Tay Salmon Foundation has been raising money in recent years to buy out the netting on the lower stretches of the river in an attempt to increase the numbers of salmon. Commercial salmon fishing makes money, but the tourist industry, allied to salmon angling, will make much more money for the country and the communities. Canada, the USA, Greenland, Iceland, and Norway have all responded favourably to the call to ban salmon netting, but the UK government have been very tardy in this matter.

Admiral John Mackenzie of the Atlantic Salmon Trust told me that the netting off Northumberland — what is called the North-East Drift — is scarcely viable but is interfering dreadfully with the numbers of salmon in Scotland. 'Scotch salmon is the most famous in the world and we have a massive potential in jobs and leisure being destroyed by small-minded greed and the inertia of government.'

And now you're asking what I did. I fished. Caught nothing. Mr Nolan caught a rod on the other side of the river, making him the biggest catch of the day really. The biggest catch was a 22lb salmon, a big silver beauty, caught by Philip Redford on Newtyle beat, near Dunkeld. I tried to catch a girl that night at the dancing. She got away.

THE GREATEST PLAYER I EVER SAW ...

February 2, 1990

IT is rare, though not entirely uncommon, that legends of this city meet. Thus it was that your Urban Voltaire encountered the greatest football player this country has produced, if you don't count Maxie Murray. Maxie Murray might just have been pipped at the post by Frank Haffey if it wasn't for the fact the Haffey was a goalkeeper and therefore entitled to idiocy.

Other greats in the field of football lunacy are as follows: Willie Telfer, who scored more own goals than Ron Brown MP, a bloke called Valentine who allowed Celtic to make the magic margin of 7-1 in an Old Firm game, and the redoubtable Albert Murphy of Clyde FC who used to cross himself before fouling an opponent. Cross himself? Albert couldn't get absolution from St Peter himself for some of the fouls he committed. Stars to a man. But not a star like Jim Baxter.

Slim Jim they called him when he went to Glasgow Rangers. Glasgow Rangers never entirely knew what they had, except a headache. Glasgow Rangers still suffered from the great days of Bill Struth when even wayward characters like Torry Gillick could be made to toe the line. When Slim Jim came across from Raith Rovers, Rangers were run by gentlemen who had never encountered a Jim Baxter in their lives. A shock it was.

For a start Slim Jim was an ex-miner. That was all right back in the days when huge numbers of footballers came from the pits — people like Jock Stein and 'Tiger' Shaw, grim and determined men with the sense of humour of a Wee Free meenister — that was all right then. Knew where you were with such chaps. Baxter came from the mining community, no bother. The bother was that he came from the kind of background where men were their own ones; and Baxter was worse than that: Baxter was bolshier than Arthur Scargill. Baxter was a one-off: a legend from the very start.

I will tell you how good a player Jim was. He was so good that my dad, and even older men, fraught with frustration at the modern game and filled with the Homeric legends of yesteryear, said of the greatest player Scotland ever saw, that Jim Baxter was the greatest player that Scotland ever saw. That was not just praise indeed. The old men were greetin' at the notion of admitting that anything was as good as the old days. They were having heart attacks at the sight of anything better. And Jim was better. Jasus, Jim was better, I can tell you.

He was so much better that one of the greatest halfbacks of all time — Paddy Crerand — has never been able to take his place in the football Hall of Fame because he was overshadowed by a genius. Baxter was better. Better than that: his greatest pal was Paddy Crerand. The two of them used to trawl the city at night, showing off, and hitting what nitespots Glasgow had at the time.

The old and fondly remembered Sans Souci had Baxter's white Jag permanently placed outside the door. A notorious bridge club (which wasn't really a bridge club) was another location for the Baxter Jag. Baxter was thin, vibrant, larger than life, and the very image of a rebel. Football's own James Dean.

Slim Jim always treated football as a game. He toyed with it, as he toyed with a ball. Baxter couldn't be bothered with seriousness, even in football. He still can't, as it happens. In football, Jim played as if nobody else was on the park. In truth, most of the time they weren't, and especially if he had the ball. There were those who said he couldn't tackle. Why should he, my dad asked; when he had the leather at his feet nobody could take it off him anyway. Critics said he was slow. Slow? Baxter wasn't just slow: he took a wee musing to himself and couldn't be bothered with anybody else's opinion. Work rate? Work is for honest tradesmen. Geniuses just breathe on an idea and make substance out of it.

Jim Baxter is no longer the slim Jim of the past. He is a big man who has put on a bit of weight, but not as much as the new legend has it. The new legend, from mouth to mouth in the pubs, is that Jim is about 50 stone and is living in penury, like some kind of latter-day Benny Lynch. The truth is that Baxter is like many a middle-aged athlete — and he will hate me for that — a lot bigger than once he was. He earns a living, though not as much as he would have done if he had exercised his art in another arena, like opera and the like, and he is still about.

I should know. I have been sharing a spot of the amber fluid with Mr Baxter for years now, but sooner or later you have to pay for the pleasure of it. The other day, over another amber-fluid tasting, the legendary James Baxter had a wee request.

A request from a legend has got to be considered. After all it was the very legend who stuck a ball up his jook during an England-Scotland game, and you can't get mair cheek than that. It turned out to be cheekier. Baxter wanted my new camel-coloured fedora. Brand new it was. What can you do. I gave him it. I took — take — my hat off to him. There you are. He's got my hat. I like to think I've paid him back a little. But not enough.

THE TIME OF THE SORCERERS (PART I)

September 5, 1990

THERE I was in the middle of Taylor Street in Townhead, shod with a football boot on my left foot and a carpet slipper on the right, endlessly skelping an old soft bladder against the tenement gable end. I looked a right idjit, and much was the wonder of the female lieges at one so strangely attired.

The football boot, and its absent partner, was — were — a recent purchase. I had bought them with the money I had got for my 11th birthday. 'Continentals' they were called, slight little things like shoes really, with two thin wee yellow stripes (aptly enough, considering my subsequent footballing career) down the sides.

Continental boots were all the go then, for the magic of the Magyars and other European sides was fresh and smarting in British footballing minds. Hitherto I had forced my feet into a pair of brown boots which would have done service with Alex James of the baggy pants and which were stiff enough to be worn by a Nottinghamshire collier.

In Taylor Street that day I only had the one new boot on, though. It was all the fault of George Young.

Big Geordie Young, big Corky, was then the most celebrated foot-baller in Scotland. Not the best in fact and nothing like it, but the hero of the game all the same. The captain of Scotland and Rangers, and then his country's most capped player ever. George Young was a Titan and a sportsman of the highest order. And I had read his book. *Football Made Easy* was its absurd title. Absurd, because no matter how you try — and I tried, believe me, I tried — football can never be made easy.

Big Corky's book was full of splendid diagrams showing feet and wee dotted lines in curves, like dancing manuals, about the various ways to get round your opponent. Oh, there was advice on every page, and I followed, unsuccessfully, every piece of it.

The slipper on my right foot was to make it painful to hit the ball with that extremity, and easier with the left, booted, one. It was George's advice on how to strengthen your left foot. 'A one-footed player,' said George loftily, 'is a liability to himself and his team-mates.' As it hap-pens my liability with the left foot was next door to a disability, for I could hardly use the thing for standing on.

I was determined, though, and my left did get better. It was not all that I attempted, though. There were the endless hours stotting a wee rubber ball against Mrs MacAllister's close wall, up and down, up and down. This was to get perfect control with my head. (The only head affected, at the end of the day, was that of Mrs MacAllister's, for she was slowly going off it, what with all that interminable bump-bump-bump coming through into her parlour.)

A player called Albert Quixall, who I think appeared for Sheffield Wednesday, could run the entire length of the pitch with a ball on his head, not dropping it once. I wanted inexplicably to emulate this feat. I wanted to emulate all the players. I practised the volley for hours against the playground shed, jumping in the air so that I could look like the photograph in Charles Buchan's *Football Monthly* of Puskas doing exactly that. The word 'endless' comes to mind at every activity.

Endless playground games, endless kicking the ball about before tea of a winter with the frost sparkling on the ground or the rain eddying in the gutters and the streetlights making brilliant reflections, like an Orangeman's sash, in the puddles of the cracked pavements.

After your tea, football round the lamppost till it got dark enough for you to be called in by your mum. Before I went to sleep I kissed the face of every footballer in the photograph of the Rangers team which I had pinned up on the wall. My father thought this normal, and my mum thought all wee boys were demented anyway. Sorry, I have just admitted that I was a Rangers fan; there you are then.

Of course it was normal then for every little boy to carry such an obsession with what is called the Beautiful Game. Back in the mid-50s every boy was obsessed by sport. We played every game you could think of. We played a sort of cricket, with a makeshift bat, a rubber ball, and three lines drawn on a warehouse wall. We played rounders and went swimming, and lots of lads went to the boxing up in the ABA rooms.

There were then no diversions such as television or those ridiculous home computers whereby the weans play with their fingers. Only older boys had bicycles, and none of your BMX bikes about it. Games were the thing, and although there was indeed cowboys and indians to play and kick the can and all those amusements of Molly Weir-type legend, the games indulged in were mainly sporting games.

And of them all football was the noblest. You played it summer or winter, rain, hail, or snow. You drove your mum daft with the clothes-washing as a result. As a result, too, even the most meagre talent could sort of kick a ball about a bit. It was only a sissie who couldn't.

Even the most meagre talent, I said, could sort of kick a ball about. No wonder, considering the amount of time we spent with nothing more than a ball. It is only in recent generations that young boys (and girls too) waste their leisure time inside a house, or waste even more of it posing in fashionable clothes. Back in my day a childhood was very little different from that enjoyed by the children of 30 and more years before me. And for generations football was the game quite simply because it took so little in terms of equipment.

Oddly enough — or not really — Jock Stein and Bill Shankly, both men of mining stock from Lanarkshire villages, almost paraphrased each other in separate sentences. 'We played football with a ball made out of rags,' the Big Man once said, 'because there wasn't anything else.' Shankly was even more sanguine. 'I'd have played with my mammy's heid if I had to,' he once remarked.

For in the bleak mining villages of Lanarkshire and the dank slums of Gorbals, and anywhere else where the children of the huddled masses yearned to be free, football was played — with anything. At my school, where a ball was prohibited in the playground, we played with a puck of wood filched from the technical department. It is amazing what skills can be developed with just a cube of teak.

The greats of the inter-war years all came from backgrounds of deprivation. By the immediate post-war years you were seeing British players who had been drawn from that background — Jackie Milburn of Newcastle, Stanley Matthews of Blackpool, Tom Finney of Preston North End — just a few of the English legends I remember seeing.

The Scots, too, were grim-faced wee men, sturdy within the slightness of their physiques, made small by the diet and deprivation of the Depression years. What strikes one now, when one catches a glimpse of old photographs of past football teams, is the sheer age of one's heroes. Take a squint at the Old Firm captains of the early 50s. Jock Stein of Celtic is burly and thick-set with hair visibly greying, his face lined and worn, curious mottling on his arms. (Stein, an ex-miner, had the strange marks which every miner bears on his skin — little blue marks where slivers of coal had become embedded.)

His opposite number at Rangers, Jock 'Tiger' Shaw, was so squarely robust he looked faintly unreal, like the way you imagine an American footballer under his shirt. His hair was almost white, and his face so grim and craggy he would have passed for a Soviet general at Stalingrad.

The rest of the teams looked similarly aged. Of course in the aftermath of the war many of the players were old men: the war years had suspended football and few young players came through during that time, outwith the army sides at any rate. But one thing is certain, and old newsreels display it time after time: the old players had skills that have now largely disappeared.

Even the newer players who took over from the Steins and Shaws and Willie Waddells showed the same agility with the ball. Gordon Smith, of the legendary Hibernian Famous Five, who played into his 40s, had the same elegance of style which I am told Alan Morton also possessed.

And there were youngsters coming up. Into that Hibs side came a 16-year-old bombshell, Joe Baker. What would amaze the young fan now is not just that Joe Baker was, at 16, one of the highest scorers in what was the First Division in season 1956-7 (renamed from Division A in 1955), but his opposite number at arch-rivals Hearts, Alex Young, a mere 18, was running him a close second. Both played for their respective countries when they were under 21. (Baker played for England, actually, and gained eight caps.) Today you would be hard pressed to imagine youngsters of that age playing in the Premier Division (though Dundee United has recently played the 16-year-old Christian Dailly, also, as it happens, at centre forward).

The point is, however, that the level of skills continued to be passed from the old to the young for a long time. Admittedly there was a certain falling-off during the 1950s as some of the older greats left the game, but there were new players coming up. Perhaps not quite so hungry as their predecessors had been during the Depression years, but much of the bemoaning of the British football fans of the 1950s and early 1960s was the result of the overshadowing of British teams by European and South American clubs that had emerged after the war.

But it was hardly surprising that the foreigners should have surprised British football. Britain is, after all, a small island, and Scotland a tiny nation set within it. British fans expected world dominance as their right, and a very silly expectation it was too.

Even then world-class players kept on being thrown up. When the legendary Jim Baxter was chosen to play for the World against England our Scottish hearts burst with pride. Even Baxter's heart did, and James was never a man for an ersatz patriotism.

Baxter wonders at the game now. He tells the tale of himself and another Ibrox magician, Ian McMillan, the inside-right they called the wee Prime Minister, at a game recently. 'Wee Ian disnae swear, but he came close a while back there,' he told me. Both men had been at one of those modern-type matches in which everybody is doing under the four-minute mile and nobody beats a man with the ball. Baxter posed the question to his companion. Would they themselves get a game in today's frenetic world of football, he wondered? McMillan doesn't swear. 'Well, Jim, we feechin' wouldn't,' replied the majestic little man.

Baxter doesn't entirely believe this and neither, surely, does Ian McMillan, a player of wonderful silkiness in his day. And neither do I. But I can understand their apprehension.

Baxter was an entirely different sort of player in his day, and he would be a different sort of player now, and so would McMillan. I doubt, though, if either of them would be permitted to show anything like the kind of insouciant skills with which they tantalised oppositions back in their glory days. Baxter was perhaps the last great genius of the game in Scotland, though there were players abounding back in his time who would take the breath away today and whom we often ridiculously took for granted. (Baxter had a special skill, hardly encountered today. He could *see* everything, and he still can. Today's football is played at the pace it is partly because there are so few players with that ability.)

Baxter himself knows the part his background played in his development. 'I come from a wee mining village called Hill O'Beath,' he said. 'There was 1200 of a population.' He recalls that he captained Scotland himself a few times. 'So did Willie Cunningham, against Hungary in 1954. He came from three doors up.' The number of professionals who hailed from that small, tight community seems ludicrous now, but the same phenomenon was echoed in Lanarkshire and Ayrshire and everywhere you found small places and lots of kids.

Baxter is, as many another veteran I have spoken to during the course of this article and before it too, less than happy about the attitudes of the clubs today. 'Celtic have been more prolific,' he said,' than my former club, Rangers, in bringing on new lads, but none of them seems to have any idea of how to build a player from scratch. They just buy what they want. And they no longer know what they want either.'

Jim Baxter had something else to say, and it was a strange statement, too, coming from perhaps the most sophisticated performer the Scottish game has ever seen. 'There's no rawness allowed now,' he said. He explained it. There is no room for young raw talent, he meant, and damn-all for fun in the business. The young lads are hardly being allowed to emerge.

Baxter was 20 when he signed for Rangers and started on his trail to the Hall of Fame. A colleague of his when he went to Nottingham was Joe Baker, who has already figured in this celebration.

Joe was 16 when he first started scoring for Hibernian FC. He was a raw youngster, but fast. Dear God, he was fast. He scored 159 goals in four years with Hibs before he went off, one of the first, to Europe and the big money with Torino. Says Joe: 'I was too young to know if what I was doing was right when I played for Hibs, but it seemed to work.'

Baker's idols were strikers, the lack of which today he bemoans. Idols such as Lawrie Reilly of Hibs — 'Last-minute Reilly' — and Willie Bauld of Heart of Midlothian, Buckley of Aberdeen. Baker hails from Wishaw. There were hundreds of fine players within, well, striking distance. Ian St John came from two miles up the road.

Baker remembers the great days of his youth, but doesn't live on his memories. When he finally hung up his boots he went into a plethora of businesses — pubs, selling cars, ice-cream vans, but all that time football remained his life. 'Mind you,' he said, 'I've been lucky in my wife and children. Fifty percent of footballers are on their second wives. My wife has stuck by me for 27 years. It makes a difference. When my playing days were over it took me four years to adjust.' Baker has a daughter of 27, and a son of 21, and he is clearly very proud of them.

Here is an articulate and well-spoken man who talks well and passionately of the game which has surrounded his life. He wants to set up a school for strikers. He now works with Albion Rovers and loves it, and retains his zest for the game he loves. He and Baxter share such an enthusiasm, and I was to find that with all the one-time greats. That and a remarkable dignity seems to mark all of them out.

All the old players of the past whom I talked to worried about the lack of basic skills of the modern game; all of them were full of praise for young players who showed promise. All of them were scathing over modern demands — and modern methods. 'For heaven's sake,' said Baxter, 'what's all this nonsense about fitness? A young, healthy man should be fit enough. It's a ball in front of him he needs to make a footballer. I hated training,' he says, 'but if you put a ball at my feet I'd be there all day.'

Iain Munro, the new manager of Dunfermline Athletic, and a mere stripling in comparison to Baxter and Baker, argues the same course. 'Football is now reflecting other aspects of society and it is like life today — far too fast.' He points out that football is now often seen as being for mere athletes, and that the old magic is disregarded by too many people in the business.

'People don't seem to have time for each other and it shows up even in something like football. Not losing becomes more important than winning. Kids are being exhorted' — this came out with every single ex-footballer I spoke to — 'to play for trophies instead of for the love of it.' Munro also points out that the commercial pressures of the game, as well as the sustained idiocy of many so-called football fans, has created 'abuse towards players that is absolutely scandalous'.

He is right there. I can remember that old Rangers team I once supported. They seemed to have the same team list every week for a decade. Ritchie, Shearer, Caldow, Davis, Paterson, Baxter, Scott, McMillan, Millar, Brand, and — Wee Davy Wilson. I can remember Davy Wilson playing his heart out, and I don't remember him having a bad game. He must have done, but back then you stood by a player. You knew he was doing his best.

Let us go back a little. I knew the Rangers team before Niven, Shearer, Caldow. The first game I was taken to starred Torry Gillick. The way my dad had promoted Gillick I had imagined a hero right off the silver screen, like Errol Flynn in a blue jersey. Torry turned out to be a heavy wee man with silver hair. Waddell and Thornton looked older than my teachers. Celtic had newer players.

Brian Wilson, MP and lifelong Celtic fan (he is the club's historian), remembers getting fed in his high chair to a litany of old Celtic teams, and he remembers the idols of his day. 'Evans, Stein, and Peacock,' he recites (Brian didn't know that that halfback line was known as 'the three brothers' due to the fact that they were all, rather surprisingly, Freemasons) — 'Charlie Tully, Bobby Collins, Willie Fernie.'

As the parliamentary consultant to the Professional Footballers' Association, Wilson is very conscious indeed of the problems facing Scottish football. 'There is so much competition in football nowadays, and at every level of the game, from kids to crocks,' he says. Socialist as ever, Wilson also draws attention to the appalling transfer system. 'No other profession would allow such bondage of contract,' he says. But scratch Brian Wilson and you will find another football fan, ready to talk blissfully of the footballing sorcerers of the past, all of whom suffered under contractual systems which made medieval serfdom look democratic.

Football today is very different from the game as I was introduced to it a mere five or six years after the war. Back then the players were paramount and every football fan can chant a mantra of the great names. Today there are a mere handful of players you would go out of your way to see and none of them can compare with players of even quite modest teams. Willie McNaught of Raith Rovers, or Jimmy Mason of Third Lanark, and later that formidable forward line of Hilley, Harley, Gray, Goodfellow, and McInnes. The Hibs Famous Five. Bauld and Wardhaugh at Hearts, the Ancell Babes at Motherwell. Graham Leggat with Aberdeen, Johnny Coyle and Tommy Ring with Clyde.

Celtic had a seemingly never-ending stream of great players and wonderful characters. Rangers was my team as a boy, and I can assure you that I was never permitted a breath of sectarianism by my father and am appalled at the absurd continuance of that poisonous concept into the nineties, though I am hopeful for the future on that score.

Those of you reading this who wonder at the hold football has on Scottish life might not understand this, but there are many strands to the tenacity of the wonderful game, a tenacity which every football fan reflects as he stands on the glorious but bleak wastes of Hampden. One is that football is indeed a substitute, not for religion as is often stated, but for politics. Football takes the place of politics for the dispossessed of this land, those who know that they have no stake in the politics of the country; for whom a vote is meaningless. Football, and discussing it endlessly in pubs of a night, is the means by which the sort of dialogue which politics would serve as at a dinner party in the New Town, is at least adumbrated by the working classes.

And something else, too. It has to do with me, and those like me, who once put that slipper on our right foot and a boot on the other. Who tried to play that game, to excel in it; to make art. And who couldn't, but yet caught the artistry of others and marvelled at it in our souls.

THE TIME OF THE SORCERERS (PART II)

September 6, 1990

THE artistry in football is given to but a few: I don't know why. As a boy, like most of those who were the smallest in the class, I had a certain facility with a ball myself. A wee ball, though — a tanner ba'; I was a tanner ba' player. In the playground me and a little fellow called Robert Craig were kings of the asphalt.

It was when I was 14 and played my first game on a grass pitch, with a full-sized football and 11-a-side, that I had to face up to a tragedy of a truth. I could do tricks with a ball, but I couldn't play to save myself. Football is only partly to do with ball skills: even an adequate player needs a bit more than circus tricks. But he needs to know the basic skills first, all the same.

Those who know little of football often take elementary ball skills for granted. Few women and girls are aware of the sheer difficulty in merely controlling that sphere on a bumpy pitch. For the benefit of those ladies — who make up the majority of females, of course — who know nothing of the game, I will tell you the most fundamental of moves in football. It is not kicking the ball, because every toddler does that. It is trapping the ball.

Trapping the ball, killing the ball, getting the ball under control, is the starting point of the game itself. That all of us brought up in the Beautiful Game know that, that it is axiomatic to a footballer, can be seen in the fact that it is almost never mentioned by a fan, for he expects every player to do just that.

There are different types of players, of course. Jim Baxter hardly worked a ball, Jimmy Johnstone couldn't keep it off his feet. Both made themselves masters over that wayward rolling globe. They killed, ensnared, made a prisoner of, and ultimately ordered it about. But they started first by making sure that the ball did not control them, that they were the boss over it. That is the beginning of footballing genius: without that, no player, no matter how athletic, can hope to become an artist.

It is becoming clear, however, that athleticism, heavily underlined by the constant commercial pressures of the modern game, has become more important than art, and how much it shows can be seen by a certain sense of despair among even the leading lights and authorities of football as it is played today. Frankly, too many players, at world level too, are insufficiently grounded in the most elemental of skills.

Iain Munro, ex-Ranger and now manager of Dunfermline, is an

especially articulate critic of what is happening today. He is particularly vehement of the demands made by 'over-the-top idiots' at schoolboy level, and is sometimes incensed at the behaviour of fond papas on touchlines. 'There are wee boys of 10 and 11 doing tours of Germany, for heaven's sake,' he says, 'and all playing for trophies instead of the fun of it.'

Munro ascribes many of the problems of schoolboy football in recent years to the tragic effects of the last teachers' strike when the dominies, not unreasonably, decided to withdraw from their traditional role as coaches and managers. (Even yet PE teachers, once the backbone of the schoolboy game, are being forced to do extra hours in the school at the whim of directors of education, and any extra-curricular sporting activity is not taken into consideration: no wonder the teachers have decided to give up on the outside activity front.)

Munro believes that, for football to survive — and he is sanguine about that — there has got to be more community involvement, and that many of the century-old traditions of football have got to be circumvented. He himself has been experimenting with coaching a team from Garnetbank School in Glasgow's Garnethill.

'Out of 14 kids only one was indigenously Scottish — the rest were Asian, without any cultural traditions in football. What we wanted to do, more than anything else, was to get kids to enjoy playing. Not trophies or medals or cups; enjoyment. We were starting from scratch, and it's been great.'

Dunfermline has also organised coaching courses at local secondary and primary schools. 'We're teaching dribbling and keepie-uppie. And we're not doing it to capture youngsters at an early age. We're doing this for the sake of football itself.'

Munro manages what is, after all, a small Scottish club, albeit with a distinguished enough past. Alex Ferguson manages perhaps the best-known club in Britain, Manchester United, and he echoes Iain Munro's conclusions. Says Ferguson: 'I remember telling Scotland coach Andy Roxburgh 15 years ago that the best thing he could do for football in Scotland would be to get rid of schoolboy football. I mean the organised game. There is too much organised football at schoolboy level, and not enough boys are playing for pleasure. Some of these kids are as feart of losing as if they were professionals, and they'll never make great players with an attitude bred in them like that.'

Ferguson is scathing about the screaming parents on touchlines and, too, about the so-called 'managers' of schoolboy teams. 'I know a lot of these volunteers who run kids' teams have got a commitment to soccer, but too often the same people are playing some kind of role as kid-on professional managers, telling the kids to go out and win at all costs, to "close down" an opponent, to get intae them,' he says, 'but it's not good for the game, and a disgraceful way to teach children.' He ascribes the problems of over-competitiveness at that level to the early days when boys' clubs like Drumchapel Amateurs got the cream of the players, and later when the Rangers and Celtic boys' clubs began to use such organisations as nurseries.

'Fifteen-year-olds shouldn't be playing competitive football,' says Ferguson. 'Schools football is enough, and not too much training either, apart from one — enjoying yourself.' In advance of his views Ferguson — a highly competitive manager and player himself — points out that the decline in skills and indeed fun in the last World Cup was startling. 'People run faster, but at high speed you need even finer skills and quicker thinking, and it just didn't show in the World Cup. And it doesn't show in the domestic game, whether in Scotland or England.'

But yet another argument that Alex Ferguson came out with, and which has been uttered by everybody I spoke to on the subject, was the behaviour of players on the park — and fans on the terracing. Ferguson bemoaned the behaviour of many players today. 'Anyone who played football in the 50s and early 60s will tell you of the camaraderie on and off the pitch among players and of the sheer enjoyment of playing this marvellous game.'

He is not alone in this attack, and he is joined by most in the professional game when he reveals his distaste for the attitudes of many fans. It has been an increasing feature of football supporters over the past 20 years that they just want their team to win, and at any cost.

Football fanatic Donald Findlay QC is perhaps an unlikely supporter. One somehow does not expect lawyers and other professional people to be football fans. The ingrained working-class nature of the game and the bourgeois espousal of other sports, as against the People's Game, has seen to that. But Findlay is a fan; worse, a Rangers one. Yet he, too, is unhappy at the parlous state of his chosen sport. He maintains that football is the greatest watching game in the world. 'I've watched rugby,' he says, 'but it's only in internationals that you get something approaching the excitement of soccer. It's in soccer that you see the blend of athleticism, skill, thinking, grace.'

Findlay, however, is disturbed at the 'big money' which is the prompting of today's game; at the obsession with winning and making sure that entry to Europe is assured. Findlay is also concerned, as everybody in Scottish football is, that Scottish teams, headed by Rangers, are not bringing new young players into the game. He ponders on the fact that there is hardly a Scots-born player in the Ibrox side.

Before manager and director Graeme Souness came to Rangers the Scots were parochial and fatalistic; they accepted that every new Scots talent to emerge would be snapped up by English and continental clubs because that was where the big money for the players was. Scots simply accepted this fact, and accepted, too, the second best, and the third-rate role that their clubs allowed themselves. Souness changed all that and bought big-name players from everywhere. Perhaps Souness's vision is a little warlike, and by no means pretty; he demands victory rather than style or charm. But it is undeniable that Souness rejected the century of Scottish football parochialism, and that fact alone has prompted a wider sense of purpose among Scottish clubs, as well as dealing a body blow to the one-time arrogance of the big English teams who simply thought of Scotland as a nursery for players and came with blunted chequebooks and blunter manners at the end of every season. Souness has been a trail-blazer here, and his courage in tackling a moribund situation has been considerable.

Yet staunch Rangers fan Donald Findlay has his doubts, too, shared by many in the game itself. 'Where are the young players going to come from if we rely on outsiders and don't rear our own stars?' he asks. And he has another question to ask. Though he himself can well afford the ticket prices, he is anxious that many fans will not be able to see matches on a regular basis. 'Clubs have got to strike a balance between meeting the needs of ordinary fans and obtaining money from big business. How can an unemployed chap stump up £7.50 a game, and maybe a couple of pints after the match? How can a father on the dole take his kids to a match and afford it?'

Rangers and Celtic now vie with each other as to how much business money they can pull in. (Rangers are streets ahead of their rivals in this, however, and the Ibrox club is a vast earner out of the corporate business leisure set-ups which large companies now go in for.) Naturally there is considerable resentment from other clubs over the way that both Glasgow teams have exerted such power over Scottish football for over 80 years. Much of the resentment is earned too.

When I set about this exegesis I was surprised to discover how many people in the game were not only willing to talk to me, but to take time out of busy schedules to do so. My experience of the attitudes of both Old Firm clubs had not prepared me for openness or indeed the sort of friendliness which I encountered from some of the biggest names in British football. For Rangers and Celtic, for all their vast support, and for all their overweening triumphalism, are not always pleasant organisations to do business with.

But Celtic had appointed as a new director none other than Dr Michael Kelly, the public relations supremo. Celtic need all the friends they can get at the moment. Last season was perhaps their least successful in 40 years, and the start to this season has been equally disastrous. Yet Celtic proved hard to contact.

When I wrote a profile on their returned prodigal son, Charlie Nicholas, the other week, I had to compose it in circumstances in which

Celtic manager Billy McNeill refused to speak to me, Nicholas was forbidden to meet me, and Michael Kelly put the telephone down on me on several occasions. Preparation for this series had to go ahead without Mr McNeill or Dr Kelly permitting a word. The sheer arrogance of the Old Firm — the fact that I can speak to a Cabinet Minister more readily than I can to an Old Firm club manager is scandalous — is quite stupendous as well as absurd.

The Old Firm have been the Upas trees of Scottish football for most of this century; their fans hail from the Hebrides to Berwick and beyond, to the detriment of local football. Both clubs believe themselves to be impervious to the demands of fans (witness Celtic director Jack McGinn's curious defence of his team's appalling performance last year that it was actually the fans' fault) and behave towards the media with a combination of condescension and paranoia.

In marked contrast, Aberdeen manager Alex Smith arranged to meet me in his Glasgow hotel on Friday night, just hours away from his team's meeting with Glasgow Celtic. I spoke for nearly two hours with this busiest of club managers and he could not have been friendlier — or more honest.

Another scion of a mining community, Smith is an ex-player who went into management. Unlike most of them, he has been successful too (he was particularly successful the next day — Aberdeen cuffed Celtic 3-0 on the Glasgow club's home ground), and that following two of the most capable managers you can think of, his predecessor Alex Ferguson, whom we have met above at Manchester United, and the one-time Hibernian legend, Eddie Turnbull. It is not false modesty which leads Smith to tell me that it was Turnbull who built the platform for the remarkable challenge to the Old Firm hegemony which Aberdeen have made for many years now.

It is decency which prompted him to insist that I 'put that in about Eddie Turnbull'. And — like so many other people in the high-pressure business of football — there is a strange streak of romanticism in Smith. Naturally, he wants Aberdeen to win everything, but not at any price. For a start, players have got to be looked after and not treated as chattels or numbers on club accounts ledgers. Young Eoin Jess is a case in point.

I first noticed Jess about three years ago, standing out from other young would-be stars. He is 19 now and is just beginning to measure up to that early promise.

Eoin is a raw-boned young man with a large frame which he will need to start filling out soon. On the pitch he has an easy elegance and a certain slowness which will surely sharpen up within the next season or so. Hopefully not too much, for the Scottish game needs, above all, players who can calm the pace down.

'I want to get good enough for a regular team place,' he says, which is understandable in a young man at his stage, but he is genuinely a modest young fellow. He lives in digs and, in common with the Aberdeen club policy, has to meet the demands of college courses.

He has recently bought a car, and it is grand to see a young man get so much pleasure out of working hard. His mates up north come from his own background, and he doesn't drink or mess about in nightclubs. Were he a wee Glasgow lad he'd be a lot more gallus, but I will tell you this: he is going to be, if things go as they should, a star. Aberdeen know this and are conscious of their responsibility for him and their other young prospects.

Not all clubs meet their responsibilities towards youngsters, though. Tony Higgins, secretary of the Professional Footballers Association, points out that things are getting better in terms of education for players regardless of age. 'We encourage, through the Professional Football Education Trust, as many players as possible to consider their future outwith and after their playing career,' he says. 'Not just the youngsters. But obviously young players are very vulnerable.'

A club can sign a boy of 13 on an S form and can sign over 30 such boys in one seaon. It's reckoned that about one in 10 boys might have a chance of earning some sort of a living from the full-time game. It is only natural, says Higgins, that schoolboys' attention is undivided on making it in football and, he remarks, 'it is a very outstanding sort of boy whose scholastic career doesn't suffer from early club recognition in the sport'.

There have been clubs who have abused the S form system. (Some clubs do much worse and offer inducements to parents of boys of 11 and 12 of holidays abroad etc. This is illegal but it does occur.) However, increasingly, a club's bad — or good — reputation goes before it, and there are more clubs now serious in their responsibilities towards young prospects.

Here Higgins cites a number of teams, in particular Aberdeen and Dundee United. (Interestingly, United's concern seems to be paying off. They now have the youngest first team squad in Britain.) Football is big business and the clubs are beginning to realise that they have the same sort of duties to staff that other business concerns have to shoulder. The Youth Training Scheme for young footballers, run by former Celtic player Mike Jackson, now has more than 80 boys on its books.

The S form system may well benefit the big clubs; it does not do so for many smaller clubs who don't have such glamour attached to them. But the smaller clubs are necessary to the health of the game, and there are traditions that should not be allowed to fall into desuetude.

One of the quaintest traditions in world football is enjoyed by Scotland's oldest club, the fabled Queen's Park, home of Scottish football.

Queen's Park is amateur, the only such club in senior football in Britain. Not kiddie-on amateur with a handful of fivers tucked into a boot in the dressing room. Queen's was once a breeding ground for many a big club, but less so now. Some youngsters no longer want to play for nothing other than fun and glory, and there are those who find the traditions of the club — the compulsory wearing of the jersey outside the shorts and other splendid lunacies, irksome. And, says club stalwart and fine player in his day, David Letham, it reflects on behaviour on the terracing too.

'We now get louts at the games,' he tells me, and this from a club which used to attract fans who showed their approval by thumping their rolled umbrellas on the floor of the stand, and who wore bowler hats as their version of club colours.

At least there are still supporters going to see Queen's Park. A major problem with football for many a year now has been the number of formerly keen fans who no longer attend matches. Another legal eagle who once frequented the grounds of Scotland and beyond is kenspeckle Glasgow solicitor Joe Beltrami. 'I went to two matches last season,' he admits. Until five years ago he could be seen at every Celtic game and travelled everywhere abroad with the club. 'What's depressing about the game today,' he says ruefully, 'is that I don't miss it now.'

He ascribes this disillusion to the amount of physical contact in the sport and the frenzied approach by many players. And the lack of wingers today. And something else too. 'Even just a few years ago every single pitch at Glasgow Green was used. Today the pitches are empty.'

Perhaps this is the greatest problem which football faces: fewer youngsters are playing it and for less of the time. Most boys don't really play the game; they dress up instead in expensive strips and pose on the field. Their dads seem happy enough at this. The skills which I learned as a boy with a tanner ball are indeed disappearing as every child now practises — and less often too — with full-sized footballs and assumes the same absurd rites that are now endemic to the professional game, from professional fouls to copulating with fellow players on scoring a goal. Even the psychological impact of thinking of a team with five backs rather than, as in the days of my youth, five forwards, has to be taken into consideration when one looks at the undoubted demise of football in the past 20 years. For, despite the near-superhuman efforts of many of the people in the game to whom I have talked in the preparation of this article, the fact remains that Scotland's international performance in the recent World Cup was so woeful that every football fan knows that something has got to be done. Not a few of us are beginning to wonder if it is not too late. Surely not, though.

There must still be boys out there with the dreams I once had, and still making sunbeams in the dark.

GIRL FOOTBALL PLAYERS DON'T CRY

September 9, 1991

WHEN the English FA decided that it was OK to permit wee bits of girls — up to the age of 12 (as is currently the position of the SFA) — to play soccer they were just a little presumptuous. It is up to girls to decide to play football and not a collection of boring old jossers in blazers.

The girls will play anything at all if they want to, as any dad with daughters knows. And if they wish to cavort about like the big girls who call themselves professional football players that is up to them.

As it happens, women football players generally don't cavort about like their male counterparts.

Oddly enough, they don't kiss each other after having scored, and they don't writhe on the field upon occasioning such shocking injuries as a sock garter snapping. They get up.

In yesterday's Clydesdale girls' game against the fair ones of Glenrothes, I even heard an injured player tell the referee that she required no assistance. Had it been a male professional he would have needed Joseph Lister for the anaesthetic.

Truth to tell, the women are nice and sporting and try awful hard, but they are not very good at football. Their ball skills are a little basic, though the teams I saw showed some splendid individual touches with their feet. Ball control was sufficient and sometimes rather good.

Clydebank's Debbie Hegarty, who plays for the Scottish women's under-21 squad, could hold her own against many a professional in a one-to-one encounter.

But the girls lack aggression for one thing, and their kicking is poor. Simply put, it is grand fun, but girls are never going to match the lads.

Of course they're not. For a start, the men are going to make sure they don't. Funding in women's sport is utterly shameful and women's footy follows the same pattern. It costs the girls £7.50 just to join the Scottish Women's Football Association and they pay for their travel and facilities.

Administrator Maureen McGonigle is scarcely paid for looking after women's football (she does this two days a week and three days for women's wrestling). The women have to work against levels of male chauvinism now largely unknown in an office for heaven's sake. They are grateful for any help they get, which is not much. Andy Roxburgh is a strong supporter (probably due to his past career as a PE teacher) and the Scottish national women's coach is male, David Wiseman.

The Football Trust (a group sponsored by the Pools Association) has given £15,000 this year, plus a grant of £3500, to assist the women's game which is going from strength to strength.

There are nearly 500 registered women footballers in Scotland with 24 teams in three divisions. Scotland does well. Our Under-21 team beat England 4-2 last year and we are going on to join UEFA — the next ventures include fixtures against England and Iceland, in which we should do well.

As one would expect there is a male input into women's soccer. At the Clydebank-Glenrothes game, one discovered that Glenrothes girls are coached by science teacher Eddie Doig, a qualified SFA coach.

Also on the sidelines was Lindsay Horne, a junior referee from Fife whose wife, Susan, was playing in goal despite bearing a wee one just 10 weeks ago. It remains true, however, that women are not exactly wanted in Scotland's national sport.

Younger girls are taking it up now. Youngest on the field was Glenrothes High School's Cairyn Byers, aged 14. She started playing because she likes football, and supports Aberdeen. Her brother doesn't play at all, the jessie. I said that, not her.

Clydebank won, as it happens. For much of the game they had been winning at 3-1 but two minutes from the end came tragedy. An appalling pass-back by Debbie Haggerty of Clydebank saw the Glenrothes striker move in quickly.

Clydebank keeper, student nurse Ann Stevenson, brought her opponent down in what was a blatant professional foul, but one of the gentlest I have seen. There was no alternative, given the new ruling. Referee Willie Anderson had to send the young lady off.

There is something daft about a game in which nobody in a Rangers and Celtic side (pay attention, Mr Huistra) gets red-carded, and big blokes of referees red-card wee bits of girls — and angels to boot.

I tried to speak to Miss Stevenson as she left the field but she was in tears. It's no fair; that's what I say. Played a damn good game too, if you ask me.

The little blonde, Bridie (that's my first bit of sexism in this report) missed the penalty strike which ended the match at 3-2 for the Clydesiders.

Lets have another wee burst of sexism. I had expected a whole set of big wimmin looking like Bobby Shearer with lipstick. Instead I met smashing girls aged from 14 to what is none of your business.

They were that nice they would have made Ian McMillan sound foul-mouthed. They were committed enough for Dave MacKay to appear lackadaisical. They were a bloody sight prettier than either, especially Dave MacKay. Now that's sexist, but so is my last sentence. They wouldn't let me interview them in their bath.

PUTTING THE FUN BACK

March 23, 1992

WHILE my colleague James Traynor was being entertained (ha!) at Ibrox on Saturday and the baying fans were exercising their respective sectarian ideologies, I was watching football at its very best. For I was at the Scotstoun Playing Fields to witness a cornucopia of footballing delights with the Tudor Crisps Cup semi-final stage for the primary school weans. And I enjoyed it.

It was one of those days when the sun shines for 10 minutes and is followed by the sort of torrential rain you can only get in that Key Largo movie. We have all been listening for what seems like a century to irrefutable arguments about a winter lay-off, but nothing could exemplify the argument better than the taut faces of mums in the Scotstoun pavilion watching their weans playing in monsoon conditions.

Notwithstanding the weather, the actual football was a glory to the game. Seven-a-side it was, with small pitches. This is the way ahead for children's football, and that goes for secondary school children as well.

The Scottish Schools Football Association is aware of that as well. Said the assistant general secretary of that organisation, Alex McMenemy: 'Kids need to play on pitches they can cover — not those great stretches of red blaes which we used to run up and down on.' He said a lot more, and so did the programme notes.

Included in them was the injunction to put fun first. 'Fun and skills should be higher priorities than winning. Adults should remember that, when dealing with young people, tomorrow is more important than today.' I may say that the overwhelming majority of fond mamas and papas observed that very well.

There were eight teams competing, with four of them going through to the final stage itself, which this year will be held at hallowed Ibrox itself on Friday, May 1, prior to the Scotland-England schoolboy international. The two final teams from the four will play during the half-time interval. It should be a grand occasion for the wee ones.

No matter what, every player will receive a plaque and medallions. The sponsors, who are also giving full strips and tracksuits to each of the four teams, kitting out the Scottish Schoolboys' squad, and donating £5000 to Scottish schools, are to be much commended.

I should be commended myself for clambering up eight flights of bench seats — and me wi' a bad leg tae — to interview young Miss Julie Fleeting of St Winning's Primary (I didn't know Tom Winning had been raised to such a lofty position).

I had just witnessed Miss Fleeting's team beat St John's Primary School 4-0. It was a splendid game with every player trying to beat their man as well as using the space. We were looking at the sort of football which, sadly, one rarely finds at the more mature levels of the game.

Some of the goals could have been entered for the Goal of the Year farrago on the telly, believe me. I don't know who manages St Winning's, but he/she should apply for Andy Roxburgh's job.

One of the difficulties for your reporter was that it was impossible to identify any of the players (*Youse couldnae identify Diego Maradona with a red light on his heid and an arrow pointing to him: Ed.*), but I could identify wee Julie. She was the only one sporting what I believe is called a French plait, for out of the 64 players she was the only girl.

The Elders of the SFA have but recently decreed, liberals as they are, that girls can now play in the same teams as boys, and awfy good of them it is, too. Did it occur to the chaps that being the only girl might just be a touch lonely? Nobody to greet with in the dressing room if you lose and nobody to celebrate with if you win. I went along to see this plaintive child. What I saw was different from my preconception, believe me.

What I saw was a devastating player. From start to finish she was undeniably the man of the — I beg your pardon — the player of the tournament. She controlled the back and the midfield. Her passing was immaculate, her control superb. She was spraying passes like Kenny Dalglish had been merged with 'Slim' Jim Baxter.

Her accord with another fine St Winning player, wee Chris Strain — who showed splendid ball control and an ability to rove around — was uncanny. Far from being a wee waif she is a very confident young lady indeed. A bit shy, actually, when I talked to her, along with her mum, her auntie, and her granny.

It was a difficult interview in some ways: a dog kept barking at me and attempting to detach a silk sock from my ankle. I'll guarantee that Traynor didn't meet such challenges at Ibrox. Julie told me that she can only get one other girl to play footy where she comes from. I wondered why her dad wasn't there as well. I should have known. Her dad is Jim Fleeting, the Kilmarnock manager.

Going through to the final itself will be St Winning's along with their runners-up, Holy Family Primary, and Castlepark and runners-up Crombie Primary. All these teams showed class. Me? I'm betting on St Winning, just as long as young Julie keeps free of injury.

FOND MEMORIES OF THIRDS' WORLD

April 27, 1992

THE Third Lanark Volunteer Rifles were obviously regimental in origin, but about the least soldierly football club in Britain, Europe, the World.

The club also was the most loved, and there was a reason for that. Glasgow had five on-going clubs — the city was not called football daft for nothing — and Partick Thistle and Clyde should have been the Old Firm quite simply because they existed in areas in which the largest numbers of people lived in a thriving city.

It was not to be: the importation of Ulster sectarianism put paid to that. Thus decent working-class chaps sent their wee boys to the home of Third Lanark, Cathkin Park.

The South Side of Glasgow had three other teams to support. There were the boys in blue; another club was Queen's Park, for the toffs; and Clyde was for entire idjits with a fondness for lost causes.

Third Lanark — the Hi-Hi — were for the kind of football supporter who didn't support the game at all. Thirds' chaps went to football as a duty and a stirring demand for democracy and decency. Winning was left up to those folk who thought it was important.

The major reason for the existence of Thirds was the belief that, in the South Side of Britain, let alone Glasgow, there could be a football team that was free of sectarianism, or even nationalism if it came to that.

Hilley, Harley, Gray, Goodfellow, and McInnes: I remember them all. The glory days of the Third Lanark team. I wasn't the only one to remember the glory days at the weekend. Glasgow's Dixon Halls, a municipal venue but 10 minutes away from the former ground of this famous old club, held a wee memorabilia exhibition of Third Lanark at the weekend. There were the old newspaper cuttings, the old programmes, and, too, the old photos. Hilley, Harley, Gray, Goodfellow, and McInnes, of course, were prominently displayed, and why not?

They were the boys at the end of the day when Thirds disappeared, still supported to the hilt by the kind of fans and their dads who disapproved of religious bigotry. The entire team was broken up when the club fell apart by the appalling machinations of businessmen, led by Bill Hiddelston, late director of the Parish. You cannot believe the distress Mr Hiddelston caused when Thirds went. It was like Robert Maxwell, only worse. Like the People's Palace had been razed to the ground. Thirds were a part of us.

At the weekend I had to off to the Dixon Halls to see this exhibition; to revel and wallow in the nostalgia of it all. Third Lanark beating Celtic in the Glasgow Cup Final, and us with the wee-est goalkeeper — Jocky Robertson — in the world. More than him, too, for Thirds had some genuinely world-class players. How about Jimmy Carabine, tough, and silky and Scottish to the core? Or Matt Balunas? Or Andy Anderson, whose son was at the exhibition? But of them all, I remember most Jimmy Mason.

There were copious photies of Jimmy, and quite right too. The old Horse Shoe Bar, back in the days when Jimmy Marshall of blessed memory used to run it, had a framed photograph of the Third Lanark team with Mason in it. That was just after the war when every team in Scotland could boast top players. And Thirds could boast, horribly, of Jimmy Mason.

My favourite was of the little man in an international jersey — and he had few caps — standing like the sort of wee man who didn't just look like your dad, but like your dad's dad; the sort of wee fellow who would win medals in the Great War — being presented to the Duke of Edinburgh. For some reason he seemed, in the photie, to have the Duke of Edinburgh being presented to him.

He was flanked by the Deedle himself, Willie Waddell, and by Billy Houliston. Mason stands wee and with stature, with a knife edge to his side shed, grim-faced but smiling. Scottish to the hilt, side by side by the big earners with the big clubs.

He even had shaved himself well that morning. A little man but his own.

I spoke to a lot of other Thirds fans. My old chum and former Hi-Hi ball boy Tam Crocket — well I knew he'd be there. He told me affectionate stories of the old team back in the early 60s, and was especially sentimental over the decency of Korky, big George Young, who used to pay the players out of his own pocket and gave the ball boys money for fish suppers. 'A lovely man,' said Tam.

His eyes misted over when I asked about this club of his. 'I go to see Dumbarton now,' he said, and there was a sudden note of bitterness. 'They put us out — the last team to play against us. We got beat 5-1.' He brightened at the memory.

'Drew Busby scored for us. Christ, I couldnae tell ye the names of the Dumbarton boys, but Thirds had Hilley, Harley, Goodfellow, and ...' His voice trailed off in memory of Joe McInnes.

The organiser of this splendid show, Bob Laird, put it all on for nothing. He didn't charge a penny. Thousands went through it, and I have a wee suggestion that every Hi-Hi fan should shove a quid or two towards his expenses, care of *The Herald*, and I mean it.

IN A LEAGUE OF THEIR OWN

November 30, 1992

WHAT a capable, charming, clever, decent, polite, pretty, and splen-did lassie is young Hazel Irvine, she of BBC Television and the commen-tator at yesterday's four nations' women's indoor football champion-ships, held in Glasgow's Kelvin Hall.

Hazel was the commentator throughout the tournament in which England, Scotland, Wales, and Ireland competed. She is a petite blonde with a dazzling smile who looks and sounds like the daughter you wish you had. And she is absolutely committed to sport.

Television actually covered the day, a bit. She commentated on every game, all 15 of them. She was eloquent on women's football.

'I don't much like the phrase "ladies football". It should be wom-en's football or sport for that matter,' she said, though admitting that old buffers like myself call such folks ladies anyway.

'But women's football is something to come. When I was at school,' she reminisced, 'I got to play every game except football. It was a damned shame because I'd have loved it.'

Changed days it is now. There are now three women's leagues in Scotland, 10 in the first, and eight each in the second and third divi-sions. The under-16 youth league is based in Aberdeen and in the West of Scotland.

Kelvin Hall on Saturday had a come-and-try session for girls in which 260 took part — and it was so over-subscribed many left disappointed. The hundreds of girls who could not get a game have had their names taken and will be contacted by the organisers, among which we can mention firstly the Scottish Women's Football Association. I have to mention here, too, the ubiquitous presence of Glasgow Parks and Lei-sure Department. They stuck thirty grand into the weekend, and it is money well spent.

They do so much to promote sport. Bernard Connolly, supremo of the above, was there: there is hardly a specialist sports event I cover in which I do not find the hand of Bernard and his staff. Sometimes the staff are there incognito.

Iain MacDonald from the department was there on his day off, partly to watch the football and partly because his wife, Karen, is interested in playing. And his wife was not alone in her interest.

There were more than 900 spectators at the championships, most of them young girls who once were forbidden by male idjits from play-ing at all. Clydebank had three young lasses there. Donna and Sasha, both aged 14 and pupils at Gryffe High School, have been playing for some years. 'It's easier to get to play football in Scotland,' said both the girls, who originated from England, and their pal Tracy agreed. 'It's a lot easier now, my mum says.'

The women's game is naturally, at eleven-a-side level, a little less powerful, and much less aggressive — you will not find the dreadful fouling endemic to the man's game — and not quite as fast. This allows for more skill to be enacted and certainly a more rational use of the pitch.

In five-a-side women's footy, it is different. If anything, it is faster than the male game. There is, in my view, a reason for this. Girls play netball, a wonderful game in which you have seconds to release the ball and cannot move more than a step. Netball sharpens the reactions, and I commend this as a training game for professional clubs.

Talking of professional clubs, England has a national league set-up, unlike Scotland, and that is an advantage to their girls.

There are the Millwall Lionesses, Doncaster have their Belles, Arsenal, in particular, promote a women's team, and there are many other big English league teams. Scotland has only Kilmarnock running a women's team. Could this be because of Jim Fleeting, until recently the manager there, whose wee girl, Julie, is the star of current primary football?

But what a lot of good players Scotland have at the moment. Italy — which has a substantial women's football development — possesses top Scottish stars in Karen Peirie from Aberdeen, and Eileen Casey, who plays for Verona. Ayrshire's Rose Reilly once scored 45 goals in one season in Italy and at 38 looks set to continue for ever.

And Scotland had more to boast about this weekend. We won the championships, Scotland A team beating Scotland B in the final by 7-2.

Yet most considered the real final to have been the semi in which Scotland beat, overwhelmingly, a much-fancied English side by 9-2. It somehow makes up for the famous debacle when Frank Haffey picked nine bladders from the back of the net.

Our goalie, Gillian Lyall, had a marvellous game and the two goals scored against us was a measure of her ability. Player of the tournament had to be Pauline Hammill who scored eight goals, with wur ain Sharon McAllister a close runner-up. I know the men's game doesn't permit the girls. Celtic should be eating their hearts out.

ONE OF THE BOYS IN BLUE

December 28, 1992

ISOBEL woke up quickly, in seconds. She checked her room. There was the sun streaming through the window. She liked that. It meant it wasn't raining. Rain always was bad for football. Your mum and dad didn't let you out when it was very wet. Mum said your clothes would get ruined. It didn't seem fair when the boys could go out and get absolutely filthy and nobody said anything about that.

Underneath the glass of her dressing table were the photographs. Isobel stirred again and hugged herself for it was cold. Her arms, outside the blankets and sheets, were goose-pimpled, but her heart was warm when she thought of the photographs.

Her eyes opened she looked around. There was Mr Teddy and Mr Rabbit, pink and fluffy the last one. There were other toys about. Silly names really and childish but then she'd always had them. She didn't know why she'd called them that or even, really, if she had called them that. Perhaps Mummy or Daddy had suggested the names. She liked the cuddly toys, to be honest, but, being older, pretended to be indifferent to them. Girls got fluffy toys but boys didn't on Christmas Day.

The photographs had to be attended to now. She took the blankets and sheets off the bed and pulled herself out of it. Standing in her night-clothes she felt bigger than she knew she would when she was dressed. Today she felt excited but still like a girl whose Christmas Day this was. Tomorrow she'd get to play out in the street but not today.

She knew what was going to happen. Grandma was going to kiss her and say she was so pretty and so would Daddy and all the aunties and uncles and the people who came in. The other children who visited briefly would have to say that too. Mummy had put her hair into ringlets. Her new dress had been put into the wardrobe. 'Aren't you lucky,' Auntie Janet had said two nights before, 'just being the only one. You are a little princess,' she would say this morning. It would make you sick, thought Isobel. Her dress was velvet, the colour of the wine they would have at dinner. The collar had lace around it, cream like cheese, frilly like frâiche. Isobel gave a sudden shudder and went to the dressing table.

There were the photographs under the glass. There was Sammy Baird. She loved Sammy Baird most of all. He had blond hair which went in waves back the way. He had hair the colour and ripple of the field outside Grandma's. Sammy Baird had a big long body and oddly short legs but he still looked elegant in his blue jersey and long white shorts. Ian McColl was balding but distinguished. Once, when Uncle Tom had taken her to the Grosvenor Hotel on a Saturday lunchtime she had sat, exalted, at the table with Ian McColl. She'd asked him if George Niven was better than Billy Ritchie, and Ian McColl had said, in his distinguished way: 'We are using Mr Ritchie just now for the present. Would you like to meet Mr Symon?' She met Mr Symon who was very grave and very grey and courteous. But she liked Sammy Baird best.

Moving to the dressing table she kissed Sammy full on the lips as she did every morning. She was frightened of quite a lot of the others because they looked so fierce but liked Ian McMillan (he looked like Daddy), but kissed every single one of them, even the young ones like Alex Scott. Her daddy had taken her to see Torry Gillick's last game for Rangers. The way Daddy had talked about it she'd expected Errol Flynn. But Torry Gillick looked very old and squat, white-haired and burly, the way you imagined a grandpa. Isobel kissed every photograph and gave Sammy Baird a last and extra one. 'Belle!' came the cry from downstairs, 'Breakfast!'

Washed, dressed, and adjusted by her mother, Isobel went down to breakfast. It was all as she imagined. A special day, Christmas, and the grown-ups loved it. Everybody waited for her to open her presents but there was only one she really wanted, only one she had really asked for, only one which her mother had worried about, only one her father had, she suspected, been pleased about. She opened all the other presents, leaving the biggest one for the last.

When you are 10 you are not self-conscious, but a lot more aware of others than grown-ups believe. Isobel took her time. The big present. She slowly unwrapped the box. There it was, the reindeer-laden paper peeling off. The box revealed. A blue jersey, white shorts, and dark stockings with the dart of pillar box red at the top. A Rangers strip. Another box was there. She knew what that was. Football boots. Little boots with two stark white stripes down the sides, like the Hungarians wore. Continental boots. Like the Hungarians wore. Boots like slippers.

Standing in her velvet frock Isobel stroked the boots and thought of a real romance on the Ibrox pitch. Playing against Willie Fernie, pulling inside then out, past Bobby Collins, inexplicably playing at left back. Maybe Bertie Peacock was injured and everybody had to move but Isobel knew she had, above all, to beat Bobby Collins: he was about the same height and looked like a girl anyway, or maybe Audie Murphy. On to her left foot, slipped over to the right side. A winning goal now. Time still for a hat trick. The crowd roared. 'THERE'S ONLY ONE BELLE!' they cheered, 'ONLY ONE BELLA-BELLA!'

Isobel stood there with her prizes, her trophies. Her velvet dress lay stiffly upon her. Her eyes took in the boxed gifts. Today she would not be allowed to lay aside the dress for it was Christmas but tomorrow she might be allowed out in her boots and the Rangers strip.

Christmas morning. Isobel wasn't Belle any more. It was a later time, a lot later. The year 1956 and Sammy Baird a long time ago. Upstairs she could hear her grand-daughter stirring. Amanda-Jane would be up and about now. Funny how children nowadays don't wake up first thing the way we used to do. Grandchildren are even more different than your own are really. Perhaps not. Her own daughter, Amanda-Jane's mother: she'd been football mad too. She looked down at the presents around the big Christmas tree. The boxes, the big presents, all these years later. Strange that it was a green and white jersey, the shorts with a No.9 on them (Amanda-Jane loved Charlie Nicholas), not the splendid blue she had fallen in love with those years ago. Isobel thought back to when she was a girl in love with Sammy and Ian McMillan. When Willie Woodburn was suspended for ever, she had wept.

Amanda-Jane had a new velvet dress with a cream lace collar ready for her but later she would put on the football jersey too. She'd play in the street the way Isobel hadn't been allowed to all those years ago at Christmas. Ten she was, thought Isobel. Playing for the the school she was, the only girl in the team, though there were others coming up. 'Julie Fleeting last year: I saw her in the Primary Schools tournament and she was great. Good to see the girls coming through now. A journalist turned up as well and wrote about her. Eventually the wee Fleeting girl could even make the women's international scene. Italy has professional girl players. I had dreams about that too,' she thought.

Dreams. Once there was Bobby Collins in front of her. First inside and then pulling back. The ball into the blue. End of the game, was there not George Young and Ian McColl and Mr Symon patting you on the back. Gruff praises. Big Malky said in the press next day that Scotland could no longer afford to ignore your challenge for the centre job. A sudden bitterness took hold of Isobel when she remembered that dream of hers so long ago. Today is different though. The SFA allow the lassies to play. Another bitterness came up. 'They don't really mean it,' thought Isobel.

A noisy day, really, Christmas, children about and adults. A lot of football discussions later. Isobel liked it and joined in, as much as she could and was allowed to until the men breenged in and took over.

Amanda-Jane would be up shortly and the sun was streaming in through the windows on this Christmas Day. Green and white hoops and Charlie Nicholas. Ally McCoist in blue. Not much really changes, Isobel said to herself. Boots like slippers. Velvet dresses. Isobel shouted up the stairs: 'Breakfast!' she cried.

CALTON ATHLETIC ARE STILL ALIVE AND KICKING

January 25, 1993

DROOKIT. If I was drenched to the shirt it was as nothing to the boys on the football park and the boys and girls who spectated at the Calton Athletic Recovery Group versus Govan Central in Barrowfield's Crown Point Sports Centre on Saturday.

The game of course should never have been played, but referee Danny Boyle knew that the lads were desperate to trudge through the glaur. Mr Boyle is heedie at Ayr's Queen Margaret Academy and a well-kent face. This was, he revealed, his first game as a referee, having passed his final exams just in December.

If the weather was vile, the football wasn't, especially from Calton. Professionals cannae appear in the rain while a team of recovered drug addicts can play an entire game out there without greeting. For Calton Athletic Recovery Group are exactly that — ex drug abusers.

Calton have become famous. They were the inspiration behind the BBC drama *Alive and Kicking* which starred Lenny Henry and Robbie Coltrane (both of whom have gone on to be members of the Calton advisory committee). Their success in helping drug abusers has been startling. Since February 1991 when records were first kept 208 addicts have made a sustained recovery from dependency. Since finding premises that figure has increased to 240.

The success of the group is unrivalled yet funding is still an enormous problem. David Bryce, founder and ex-addict himself, tries to explain some of the problems. The Calton policy of total abstention from drug abuse is not echoed by many of the social agencies which involve themselves in the problem, certainly in this city, where there are at least 12,000 users, and more deaths through heroin abuse percentage-wise than anywhere else in the UK.

'The official policies of clean needles and heroin substitutes are only encouraging drug abuse,' says Bryce. 'What consolation is it to grieving parents to know that their son or daughter died with a clean needle in their groin? What we do at Calton,' says Davie, 'is a simple programme for complicated people.'

But funding has been hard. This is a seven days, five nights a week project. The Calton needs £50,000 a year to continue and expand. The Glasgow Health Board is a source of funding but there has been a serious threat to Calton over the years.

Yet some quite surprising bodies have been very supportive of this largely working-class, street-level group, though drug dependency cuts across all the social classes, especially among young people. Some of the E drug users look down upon the injecting addicts. The heroin users reply: 'See you soon pal — you'll end up using what we did just to come down.'

But Glasgow Trades House, that august and largely conservative body, recently donated £1000, and Merchant House five grand. Rotary Clubs have invited the Calton group to talk to their members, as have the Samaritans and many schools and colleges.

The workers at Greig's bakery gave a thousand pounds too. Talking of Greig, John Greig of Rangers donated the profit from signed footballs at auctions. Paul McStay gave a running machine and a treasured Scotland strip. Charlie Nicholas and Tommy Burns both give welcome support.

Calton Athletic are not merely ex-drug addicts, however. They are also top of the Glasgow Welfare League (they won 9-1 yesterday against Govan), and took the Scottish Welfare Cup last year. They are a formidable outfit, managed by John Jarvis, winner of the UK Postman of the Year recently, and captained by Davie Main who has been with Calton for three years and once played for Scottish Under-16 Schoolboys.

For success, read the astonishing failure of many of us to recognise the pressure which led these young people into drug use in the first place. Davie Bryce — who admits to having gone through years of wasting his and other people's lives — once fought for a boxing title.

He could have been a contender. So could Marie Fitzpatrick, who once represented Glasgow at badminton and who held down a good job as a qualified hairdresser until the drugs scene caught her.

Marie is a clear-eyed, shiny-haired, well-spoken young woman of 23 looking a lot younger. Into aerobics and fitness programmes, she looks more like a teenager. 'You should have seen me nine weeks ago,' she told me. 'I was a wreck.' It is hard to believe. By coincidence, referee Danny Boyle is her uncle.

Another coincidence. I met 20-year-old Jackie Heron. She is slight and blonde, neatly-dressed and looks like a daughter you wish you had.

She is, like Marie, very pretty. She was very pretty when I last met her, too. You see, I taught her, a pleasant, rather quiet girl. She has been nine months drug-free and last year came in third in the 10km run at Bonnybridge. These are young people who should have met their potential. They are beginning to now, and more power to them. Part of the secret is the sheer determination in the Calton group, and the support shown by wives and husbands and sweethearts and parents.

Outside the ground, I spy a police car. They didn't know it was Calton Athletic; they had just come to watch the game. 'Is that Calton in the blue?' asks one of the officers. 'Bloody good team. Look, there's another goal scored.'

OLD FIRM GAME WITH A DIFFERENCE

March 22, 1993

AS you may have read in the past, I loathe an Old Firm day; the streets awash with bigotry and teenage mutants, their faces blurred with stupidity and sectarianism. I also loathe the fact that my normal ports of call are out of bounds to me because they are filled with chanting zealots who would do well in Teheran during Ramadan.

The truth is that the Old Firm game is probably the last real focus for the sectarian divide in the West of Scotland. If it was up to me the game would be played behind closed doors in an empty stadium, and both teams would lose. There is more logic to that, in a strange way, than there is in the celebration of ancient atavisms which have no place anywhere and should not be there in the first place.

But yesterday I strolled along to an Old Firm game which was a revelation. On Saturday, Celtic and Rangers played out their curious conflict at Parkhead. Yesterday they played out another, also at Parkhead, but this time it was not at Celtic Park but at Helenvale Park, a little ground operated by Glasgow District Council with a nice little stand and a wide wee terracing. It is used for all sorts of sports.

Unfortunately, it is also covered with Astroturf, and not a very good version of it. It showed up in the Rangers versus Celtic game which I witnessed. The surface is unsuitable for controlled football and, in my view, downright dangerous.

Actually this was not entirely my view: I got the statement from everybody else, including Bobby Lennox, the Celtic reserve team coach. For what we were seeing yestreen was one of the games in the under-18 Glasgow Cup, now known as the Glasgow's Alive Cup (after the slogan adopted by Glasgow District Council and sponsored by them to the tune of £12,000).

Sponsorship also comes from the STUC, Glasgow Football Association, and the GDA. The Glasgow Cup is actually the old one, the most aesthetically lovely of all Scottish football trophies, a riot of ornate silversmithing.

On a sunny, if somewhat windy, day we were to witness two attacking teams of young Rangers and Celtic hopefuls. The result, a 2-2 draw, was justified, with Charlie Miller and McGinty scoring for Rangers, and the Celtic scorers being Smith and Donnelly.

The goals were all the result of defensive blunders but this was doubtless largely due to the condition of the pitch. Astroturf has long been a source of some controversy but frankly this particular artificial surface is inappropriate to ball skills. The ball skids off the ground at too fast a speed for defenders to do their job and hardly adds to attackers' control, either. It bounces higher than a stot-up would on a trampoline.

These are very fit and extraordinarily enthusiastic young teenagers, desperate to prove their worth to the managers of the first teams. They are inclined to run too much and to bunch a little.

Some of the youngsters have indeed played in first-team games for their clubs. Lee Robertson has already shown considerable potential for Rangers' first team, and Smith and Cochrane, 18 and 17 years of age respectively, have graced the Parkhead pitch in first-team games.

This has got to be a good thing for players and clubs. I well remember when 17-year-old Joe Baker of Hibs and Alex Young of Hearts, a year older, contrived to be the highest scorers in the Scottish League. It is a shame that Scottish football has been unprepared to put teenagers on the park in recent years.

These boys come from all over Scotland and are real prospects, which is why people like Benny Rooney and Bobby Lennox were out watching the youngsters yesterday. Rangers' Billy Kirkwood and Ian Ferguson were urging the kids on and their manager, Walter Smith, also was present. There was a crowd of nearly a thousand. Children were everywhere — the littler ones running about daft behind the stand and having a great time not watching the footy.

What was truly splendid about it all was the lack of the venomous hatred one sees at the big boys' games among the supporters. There was 10-year-old Daren Fernie, from Barlanark, in his Celtic colours, flanked by cousins, nine-year-old Brian Ferguson, from Shettleston, and Kareen Hurley, aged 11, and both bedecked in the red, white, and blue. They were polite and well-spoken youngsters. All confessed that their dads did not allow them to go the Old Firm games as, said young Daren: 'They are a bit, well, rough.' Sensible dads.

Another sensible dad was construction worker Ian Stewart, who had brought along his wee boy, also Ian, for his first Rangers-Celtic game. 'I wouldn't take him to the big game. In fact,' he pointed out, 'he's not much bothered about this one, either.'

You know the concentration span little ones have, but he was clearly enjoying the day out. And, like a lot of the spectators at Helenvale, Mr Stewart clearly enjoyed supporting his club — in his case Rangers — but had no time for sectarianism. 'Truth is,' he said, 'Celtic deserved their victory on Saturday. They could have scored four.' It is genuinely refreshing to meet a football fan who does not have darkness in his heart.

The boys and girls and mums and dads were a tribute to sport, cheering good play from all the young colts out there (with the exception of one foul-mouthed halfwit who was eventually silenced by other spectators).

It is possible, under the competition's rules, that both teams, who remain unbeaten after three games, could be in the final at Ibrox on Sunday, April 25. It would be a grand occasion. Doubtless we would see the same parents there, and also the legendary Junior Omand of The Spiders, whom I met once again yesterday, deep in conversation with Rangers director Jack Gillespie.

I'll bet the two wee Dundonian lassies, Laura, sister of Celtic's Ally Paterson, and her pal Susan will be there as well. I always get girls in the column at that.

STILL STREETS AHEAD

July 19, 1993

LIKE all very small boys, I wis a wiz at the tanner ba'. When I grew up, I wis a wisnae. Wisnae any good that is.

Sweet Lord, I could write a salivating book about it. About teasing a tennis ball round a celestial lamp-post in Townhead and fondly imagining I was getting round Billy Wright and skelping the leather orb into the blue behind Gil Merrick, the only footballer who sported a Clark Gable moustache outside of Celtic's Billy McPhail, who scored two of the goals in the great sivvin-wan celebration of the ethnic-minority consciousness. He was a hairdresser. Back in the 50s, hairdressers scored a lot off the pitch at that.

Like all very small boys, I ran circles round the bigger boys in the playground, and even in the street, round the lamp-post, like a wee moth I fluttered fully. Wee boys always did. Then came a time when I didn't. It was when it was a full-sized ball, a full-sized pitch, and full-sized opponents.

Then I looked like the sort of mouth-organ player who done well up till the time he encountered Fraser Speirs, (moothie players will recognise this implication in seconds).

In short, I was a splendid wee tanner ba' street playground show — youse up there watch this wan — see me, mammy, ah'm dancin' — ma tea's oot, and da's gonny kill me ah'm that late.

If youse listen to the likes of me, you will be hearing drivel about how long we stroked that tanner ball and how dark it wis in the lamp-light.

Molly Weir would have wrote it if she had the sense and came from Glasgow anyway. But there is nothing like atavism and sentimentality, and even big companies like Reebok know it.

Reebok is a big sporting company and have organised lots of things sporting to sell their products. To be honest, I haven't a scooby what their products are except for sloppy-joes with their name on them and expensive sandshoes. But Reebok has embarked on a nationwide and sponsored tournament concerning footy.

Street footy. Put yer jaickets doon to make the goalposts, play till dark, get a skelp on the lug frae yer da, and a fine frae the magistrate fur enjoyin' yersel' in the street.

Jings. Reebok would huv ye thinking it wis 1954 and the sweetie rationing had just stopped.

Crownpoint it was in Glasgow yesterday where the Reebok Fives were held. The sponsors wanted, they said, to recreate the street football of yesteryear. There were a lot of children about, playing the way I remember myself — no very well, really, but loving it. Out of the 60 teams taking part, there were five girls' teams. I watched the girls' final — 9-11 age group.

Eileen of girls' winners Rapa Pumas from Dennistoun and Whitehill Secondary, herself aged 13 and quite big in comparison to the others, scored two splendid goals obtaining the finals' prize, but truth to tell, it was the two wee lasses from the losing team, Wynford Primary, I noticed most.

One was wee Donna James, aged nine, and the bravest player on the park. The other was Deborah Garment and the man, if you like, of the tournament.

Seriously, this wee girl showed the sort of class I once saw in Charlie Nicholas, Paul McStay, and indeed young Eoin Jess when they were schoolboys. Deborah was everywhere, chivvying away, defending like George Young in his heyday, passing like Paddy Crerand, and charging down the wing as if The Deedle was still alive.

Manager Doreen Park , a teacher at Wynford Primary, told me that she got started in football partly because sports commentator Jock Brown was the best man at her wedding.

A 'Nae Luck Award' there, I should have thought.

She also seriously embarrassed young Elizabeth when, as Primary teachers do because they know such things, she pointed out that Elizabeth joined the mixed boys' and girls' football team because she fancied someone called David. I wish I was 11 again.

Frankly, there is something terribly wrong about football when these girls are not permitted, and they are not, according to Scottish Football Association rules, to play alongside boys. But let us not carp. The refs were official.

Charlie Sermani, refereeing the finals, told me it was a delight because nobody told him he was blind, deaf, or daft, and the only people who swore at him were the linesmen.

There was a three quid entry fee, and none of it went to Glasgow District Council who provided the venue free, the decent folk. The money went to Barnardo's Child Care. Everyone who took part got a certificate and there were medals, and trophies, and Reebok T shirts, and everybody got a laugh when I couldn't quite get over the fence, an attempt I made unwisely, and for which I deserve a medal myself.

Reebok have 50 regional finals on the go, and the winners of the older age group, who were Sacred Heart — and nobody seemed to understand that there are three squillion Sacred Hearts and I never found out where they were from — well, the winners go on to the regional final in Renfrew on August 1.

From there they go to the national final, in Bolton, the lucky lads — or so I'm told. The luckiest lads and lassies will lose at Renfrew, if they have any sense.

SEVEN'S NO HEAVEN FOR THE WOMEN

November 15, 1993

LAST year, the Scotland women footy players were more than triumphant, winning first and second places in the Four Nations' Indoor Championships, Scotland A beating the national B side in the final. This year Scotland did well at the Kelvin Hall venue too. The B team were in third place with Scotland's A side losing to Norway, the European Champions, in the final.

Scotland's teams do well and get better every day. However it has to be said that the victory of the Scandinavians was a touch outright. For the second time in three weeks, I have witnessed a legendary score. Shinty saw seven-wan a fortnight ago, and so did women's football yesterday. And the Scots were the recipients of this magic figure.

In all honesty it was a score which reflected the class of the Norwegian girls, but Scotland had lost the presence, because of a broken leg, of talented goalkeeper Gillian Lyle, who had played so well at last year's tournament, and reserve keeper Lyndsay Wilson of Hutchison Vale was also out with a broken finger.

Late replacement Carole Anne Wilson turned up just this morning and is perhaps a little young and slight, though I should say that her performance was brave enough. It was just that she had not knitted into the defence enough.

It's a shame really that women's football is not given the advantages of regular training with each other. There were other fitness problems too, with players forced to call off, though Lynda Brown of Clyde Ladies met a late fitness report.

The final itself was not quite the debacle for the Scottish girls as the scoreline suggests. There were the injury problems, but there was also the simple fact that the Norwegians were very much bigger than their opponents.

The Scots were certainly fast — women's five-a-side is surprisingly speedy as well as physical — but the Norwegians had a pace resulting from their stature and their longer legs. The Norwegians had skill, too, and perhaps an edge on preparation, and certainly the Scots did look tired in the second half.

Yet the most skilful player on the pitch was undoubtedly the little number five, diminutive Pauline Hamill, from Cumbernauld. Last year's finals saw her score eight wonderful goals. This year she wasn't permitted to go as daft but she teased and tormented the opposition with the little frills, pirouettes, shifts and feints which would have done credit to Jimmy Mason for heaven's sake.

Yet the Norwegians were too strong. Hege Gunnerod scored a marvellous goal from just over the halfway line, but she could never have done that if it wasn't that she is nearly six feet and her legs have a longer stride. And, after all, Norway have a long-standing reputation and this is just the second year that Scotland have set up this tournament. Wales, Northern Ireland, and Eire joined in.

All the teams showed promise. Northern Ireland manager Trevor Erskine has much to be proud of in his team, especially the youngest player of the contest, blonde bombshell (I had to use a wee bit tabloid stuff here), Ceara McCulloch from Ballymena, who is only 15 and will be back at school this morning. She had a grand game.

Later I meet Scotland B player Pauline Martin, who berates me for some imagined slight in my report last year. She cannot remember what it was, and neither can I but says, and quite rightly: 'Some of the men think we don't really play, but we can you know.' She trains with the men of Renfrew Juniors and Scotland's team coach suspects that the lads expect the women to train twice as hard.

And before you start on the sexist nonsense, women do chest the ball down, and head the ball: I don't want to hear another silly word from boys. What is more they take a zest, sportship, and pride to their game which is often horribly lacking in the lads. And the large crowd is there to enjoy it all.

There was Barry, Paul, Martin, and the only girl, Leanne, all Primary Seven from St Benedicts in Easterhouse, along with their teacher, Miss Bertolacci. They enjoyed themselves enormously. Nice children, well-spoken, and hoarse with cheering on their national team.

The boys freely admitted that Leanne, a defender, is a smashing player. I didn't want to tell any of them that Leanne will not be playing with them when they all go off to secondary. A bit like telling children there's no a Santy Claus.

There was Jean and Robert McIlreavy from Linthouse, taking their two children to see the matches as it was the birthday of their eldest boy, Robert. A good day out. A good day out too for the 315 children who took part in the pre-event Soccer Skills Coaching Clinic on Saturday. The thousand odd spectators saw it that way too.

The lassies are a bit different from the lads though. Everybody got kissed at the end of the tourney. Everybody clapped each other and everybody went away happy. Maureen McMonigle, executive Administrator of The Scottish Women's Football Association was among the last to leave, along with Sheila Begbie of Teamsport Scotland.

Both were happy with the weekend, as well they might be. There was a healthy sponsorship for the event, though more is needed. A bit from the Press too, I was informed. There are lots of girls out there who would like to find out more about how to join the thousand women already playing footy in Scotland. Try Maureen at the SFA in Park Gardens. I wish I could join myself.

GAELIC GAME STILL UP AND RUNNING

April 13, 1992

IT may well summon up to you a notion of little men like myself if you were to call anything Gaelic, but Gaelic football is designed for my own people and even possesses a grammar which is nothing if not classical.

So is Gaelic Football. For a start, it is a precursor to soccer which is so called because it is officially titled association football. Rugby football is called that because William Webb Ellis actually picked up the ball and ran with it, the blaggard, while he was at Rugby School.

The cheeky sods thought then, and doubtless still do so now, that he had invented a new game along the same lines, as the idjits believed Neville Chamberlain had invented snooker in Poona. I will tell you this: Gaelic football started it all off.

Soccer, rugby, Australian rules — they all started from Gaelic football. In this game, which I witnessed in the open spaces of Espieside Park in Coatbridge — it is also, for some reason, called Drumpellier Park, and it is Lanarkshire after all — I encountered the Gaels at their best and worst.

Gaelic football permits you to pick up the ball and run with it, but as is the way with all games which men invent, there is a limit to it. It leads one to the conclusion that men are not entirely right in the head and enjoy inventing stupid limits to everything; like morality for instance, a notion inexplicable to females.

Well, we were in Coatbridge, and the drizzle was there, and there were all these chaps running about throwing, punching and kicking the ball — that's what they do in Gaelic football.

It comes from Ireland. The two teams playing, naturally, have Irish origins. The Sands-MacSweeney team from Coatbridge are named after two of the most famous hunger strikers. The Glasgow team playing against them are named the Mulroy Gaels.

It is a very Irish occasion, and why shouldn't it be?

The brothers and sisters from the other isle have been here for a while, after all. How about supporter Donna Gallagher, a nurse from Donegal town who told me that she is along the lines of getting to know a certain Alex from the Emerald Isle. Or Sean Duffy from Armagh, and here for 25 years, or Seamus Sweeney, the referee who used to play himself and came from Fannad. Or the two splendid Scottish lads from St Aloysius College, Liam and Noel, themselves the sons of a major influence in the development of Gaelic football, lawyer Frank Nugent.

He played yesterday, but his team lost. It was not by very much, for in Gaelic footy you get goals for under the post and points for over it, and although both teams contrived to kick well, the Mulroy Gaels eventually got a three-point advantage over their Lanarkshire opponents.

It is a very fast-moving game in which you can run and play just as long as you bounce the ball off your foot every four steps. It is an aerial game and fast: the players in Ireland are regarded as they should be — athletes and sportsmen.

Oddly enough, the game has done well across here, with nine teams as well as children being taught. There are even girls' teams being started up. It will not be a professional sport, however, despite the speed, skill, and argument surrounding anything Irish people do as a hobby. Gaelic football will remain a minority sport. It is important enough in the large cities in England, especially in London where there are more than 20 clubs, but naturally less so elsewhere.

Gaelic football is fast, direct and the perfect ball game for young people who are enthusiastic, if not terribly skilful. I hold it as better than rugby, for instance.

Out in the park, there was a splendid wee dug who, I am told, makes a regular appearance. This is a game which could be played by everybody. It is not, indeed, a game for faint hearts. Women play it in London, and it must be frightening to see it. It is a little part of Ireland in this nation, and a little part of the free Celtic spirit, and grand it is to see the Celtic spirit without the slightest breath of sectarianism at that. Even Wee Frees could play. But no me. I'm too auld for that.

Gaelic football possesses about seven referees in Scotland, and not many in Ireland either if it comes to that, but like most games, it has an awful lot of rules, and an awful lot of people determined to see them respected.

An awful lot of tradition too.

There are teams from Dundee, and Saltcoats, and Edinburgh. A bit like Irish dancing, Gaelic football is an importation from the land which gave us Count John McCormick, Joseph Locke, and a sense of humour.

During a weekend when it also gave us tragedy, it is salutary to see our cousins giving us pleasure in the green fields.

I liked the dug too.

JOY UNCONFINED FOR 'CULCHIES'

September 21, 1992

DUBLIN'S Croke Park saw history in the making yesterday as Donegal fought their way to a famous victory over a one-time triumphalist Dublin team in the All-Ireland Gaelic Football Cup final. I know this because I was looking over the shoulder of Anita from the *Donegal People's Press* and that's what she was scribbling. Anita is not what one could describe as a neutral and she was not alone in her support for the 'Culchies' against the Dubs.

Dublin were, of course, expected to win. Indeed Donegal were considered very lucky to be in Croke Park at all — their first time in the final. A shocking display by the north-west team in the semi-final was matched, disastrously, by an even worse performance by Mayo, and there was plucky little Donegal in the final against the near-professional Dubliners. This is a wee bit like Queen of the South playing Rangers.

But the Donegal side had its day and there were 31 counties urging the bucolic peasantry of the Gaeltacht against the city slickers of Joycean Dublin. I could get quite used to this sort of prose.

Dublin on Saturday night was awash with country folk. The green and yellow of Donegal was everywhere, much of it worn by Glaswegian-Irish. Sure, were there not about 18 publicans of my acquaintance about wining and dining in the best places and saying novenas for the success of the north men.

Nobody really held out much hope for Donegal but all agreed it was grand to get there. Dublin itself was a touch ambivalent. The Dublin team haven't won the Sam Maguire Cup in nine years and their last appearance in the final was seven years back. But your Dub is a decent man and the truth is that the taxi drivers, and the barmen and shop assistants in this most loquacious of cities were quietly telling me that they wouldn't really mind if Donegal were to take the ultimate prize in what, in Ireland, is the ultimate sport.

Gaelic football is a quite astonishing game. For a start it is incredibly fast. The rules of all football games started here; the idea of rules stems from Gaelic football. You can run, kick, throw, bounce; you need speed, fitness, spatial sense, courage, and last but not least, sportsmanship. All these were in evidence in Dublin on Sunday. Add a bright, sunny day, and a crowd exuberant enough to go on the stage. Donegallies are nothing if not theatrical and you have what scribes like myself call 'a glittering occasion'.

Donegal started well. I have a suspicion that when the splendid Irish tenor sang, to the accompaniment of a red, white, and blue-clad brass band, the Irish national anthem, the country boys were given the sort of jolly which the Welsh describe as Hywll. From the moving sound of thousands of throats Donegal took off and from the start looked both threatening and confident.

Even when Dublin's Charlie Redmond kicked the first point, Donegal did not let go. A second Dublin point meant nothing for the city boys were never allowed to settle.

In hindsight the settling of the game was decided in 21 minutes by Declan Bonner, a cousin of Celtic's own Paddy, when Donegal went into the lead 6-5. From then the Culchies were on top. The last minute of the first half saw Jim McHugh hoist a wonderful kick on the turn to put Donegal three points ahead. Dublin had been snuffed out, not through the rummel 'em up play which had been expected of them, but through sheer skill and elan.

The second half kicked off well for Donegal again, but Dublin are a skilful and determined side and for a good 20 minutes Donegal were defending desperately. Dublin had the peerless Vinnie Murphy foraging, but somehow his efforts seemed ineffectual in the end. Keith Barr was solid and inventive but still the Donegal defence was impenetrable.

It is difficult to explain to soccer fans exactly what is wrong with their own game. If they had been at Croke Park they would have discovered it. Gaelic football is open but tight — and athletic, balletic, and rough. Skill and courage are indivisible. When someone scores, a polite handshake and a demure bow is the way of it.

The game continued end to end. On a clear day in Gaelic football you can play for ever and that's what it all looked like. Good things come to an end though. The end, really, was man of the match, Declan Bonner, scoring a snatched point out of nowhere. It was, as we sports wallahs say, a spectacular end to a wonderful occasion. Donegal, never expected to win, and just bloody glad to be there in their first ever final, had won 18-14. No goals were scored for it was a well matched game, but superb football was played. Anita wept and hugged me, decent girl. The Culchies ran on to the pitch. The Garda were beaming. The Dubs took it well and applauded.

Donegal captain Anthony Molloy made a spirited speech as he accepted the cup. He made it in Irish, which, I'm afraid your correspondent could not quite grasp. As I write this the celebrations can be heard from my window.

A GRAND DAY FOR THE IRISH

February 8, 1993

I ALWAYS encounter a girl at my sporting events. Yesterday it was young Angela Baker, aged 10, playing for the Glasgow Select against a Tyrone team in the under-11s match at St Aloysius' Park in Millerston, on the edge of Glasgow. She was playing Gaelic Football at that.

Just when male-oriented sports are going to wise up to the idea that it is not very good to have only one girl in a team, I do not know, but, to be honest, I have a wee suspicion that Gaelic footy is not for lassies anyway.

It is most certainly not for the faint-hearted. But then who said girls were such? Certainly even the Mayo boss, the legendary Jack O'Shea, admitted that the Gaelic game is tough and rough. In a grand comment he declared: 'Common decency demands you stop short of deliberately damaging an opponent. After all,' he said, letting us know that Gaelic is essentially still fun, 'we all have to go to work the next morning.'

Clincart Construction Ltd were sponsoring 13-year-old children, who played at half-time, and the Edinburgh building boys, Keane Development, sponsored the other team. Both companies were also sponsoring the strips for the grown-up Donegal and Mayo teams who played a splendid charity match in front of a sizeable crowd.

Most of you should know by now that Donegal won a famous victory last season when they beat Dublin in the All-Ireland Cup final at Croke Park, Dublin. Donegal is still not back to normal and celebrating will be continued there after the result of the Glasgow game against Mayo.

The result was overwhelming for the Donegal side with one goal and 15 points (a goal scores three points and occurs when the ball is put underneath the posts: mere single points are scored over the posts) as against the Mayo team's 13 points. It was a clean, if energetic — and there's a wee Irish euphemism — game, and Donegal had the edge throughout. Half-time saw the Mayo boys losing but early in the second half they came to within a point of the champions.

But Donegal's magnificent goal, scored splendidly by Tony Boyle after a move started off by big, burly Barry Cunningham, put Donegal not only in front but in the driving seat. There were enough Boyle relations in the crowd to have passed for a nation itself and Tony was toasted like a Taoiseach later last night at the celebratory dinner which your correspondent himself attended.

The Donegal man of the match was surely Manus Boyle who scored seven points (Manus had also been top scorer in the All-Ireland Cup final), with James McHugh showing up well. Mayo's Jakleth Jennings scored five points and altogether there were good displays by individuals. How do I know this? The fans told me, for heaven's sake. Our photographer told me this too because he is an Australian and Gaelic Football has a certain affinity with Aussie rules. Such an affinity in fact that an antipodean fellow, unbelievably called Richard Gough, a student presently at Glasgow Yooni, is playing for the Glasgow Gaelic Football team at Pearse Park. And Pearse Park is what this is all about.

It was in order to produce funds for the Scottish Gaelic Games at that venue that this charity match was set up. To get adequate playing surfaces at least 70 grand will be needed and yesterday's event will have generated at least £10,000 for the purpose. Sponsorship was high, not just from the two building firms but from elsewhere among the Scottish Irish — indeed the Irish-Irish — community. Allied Irish Bank put in a right few bob, as well as being represented by the lovely presence of Suzanne from Motherwell who did much to put me right, including a wee libation. I know her boss, Niall, an old chum. He was telling me a lot, but frankly I found myself listening to Suzanne a touch more, for some reason.

But this was a celebratory day out for the Irish community. Not just the football either. A bit more. Johnny Boyden and Kevin McLafferty were there, cheering on the lager, sorry, the teams. Big Devlin was there too. The reason why I am mentioning the above is twofold. One: they asked me to. Two: it makes sense. But the other day I wrote of the Donegal connection. The boys above represent the sheer healthiness of remembering your roots in generations past but knowing who you are now. There is no Balkanisation of culture among these people: they are perfectly happy to be Scottish and Irish at the one time. Think about the notion of being Scots-English: the brain cells cannot comprehend such a paradox.

DERRY ARE THIS YEAR'S GAEL FORCE

September 20, 1993

IRELAND exists just to confuse you and themselves. It was the Gaelic football final. The Sam McGuire Cup is the prize.

It was fought for yesterday at Croke Park by two teams who sported exactly the same colours. Cork and Derry wear red and white. The teams decided against neutral colours in the final. They, and the supporters, were dancing about like Mivvi ice lollies. Two hours before the game in the Gresham, I spoke to a chap who rejoiced in the name of James Connolly.

He's bedecked in the red and white — his children have their faces painted in the colours. It took a half hour to discover what team his family supported. Cork it was in fact. 'Sure,' said James, 'the game's the thing.'

Well, there was a disappointment waiting for him but only after an immensely exciting game in which Derry won in the last minute, by a scoreline of one goal, 17 points, to Cork's two goals eight points, a total of 14 points.

Thirty seconds before the final whistle, Cork could well have drawn against this unfancied Ulster team. This is now the third northern team to have taken the ultimate trophy in Gaelic footie in three years. The three Ds it is now called — Derry this year, its first ever all-Ireland trophy win. Last year it was Donegal. 1991 saw County Down pouring the celebratory Guinness into the famous silver vessel.

And this year had Derry. It was a popular victory throughout Ireland. As Derry manager, Eamonn Coleman said after the match: 'We have three and four generations of young people who have never known what it is to have a job, let alone win anything. This is for the youngsters of Derry.'

The Irish are an emotional people anyway and this simple and decent speech brought a tear or two itself. But the elation of winning brought out the very best of all Ireland. Even the Dubliners were for little Derry, who were not expected to win. Every major Irish blatt plunked for the experienced Cork side. There were nine all-Irish players in the south-western team and not a one in the Ulster team.

In fact, Derry super-sub Dermont McNicoll played in 1983 for the All Ireland minors, and there were a number of ex-All Ireland minors in the Derry team. Incidentally, Cork's visit was not entirely in vain for their minors — under 18s that is — beat Meath in yesterday's juniors final. But nothing makes up for the disappointment of not winning the Sam McGuire.

Not that Gaelic football people cannot cope with a defeat. The feeling in the Dublin bars and hotels after the match was that this had been a classic match and the best team won on the day. Even Irene Hoolihan, a Cork girl, agreed to that despite the fact that Cork were greatly discomfited by the loss of Tony Davis, who inexplicably was dismissed early from the field and left Cork with only 14 men.

There had been a previous disturbance but certainly Davis had nothing to do with that, and no-one on either side could understand why Davis was sent off. The loss of this particular chappie produced a duller second half than should have been the case, with Cork moving into a defensive position, but everything hotted up in the last 10 minutes.

And when the final whistle blew, the hordes rose as one and embraced each other, fan to fan. Derry captain, Henry Towney — who had an outstanding match with young giant Anthony Tohill ever present too, — spoke as he held the trophy aloft.

You'll not find this in soccer: 'Congratulations to our opponents from Cork,' he said handsomely. 'Let's have three cheers for the losers.'

Later I'm in a pub near Kelly's Corner. Two Derry lads are buying bottles of malt. 'Have one yerself Jock,' they said. 'It's not every day the wee nations win.' I don't sort of know what they mean, but I sort of do.

Just before I phoned this through, I'm talking to Bernard Corrigan, Glasgow's legendary fish merchant, across for the game. Tony Gallagher, my chum, is here too. We are all deep in conversation.

'Enjoy the game?' asked Bernard. 'It's the afterwards,' says Tony. 'We're all here to enjoy.'

I'm looking forward to the afterwards myself. And signing off right now.

THE GREAT GAME OF LIFE

January 31, 1994

THERE is always something about Ireland which makes you want to sing like Daniel O'Donnell, or even look like him, a bit. And there is nowhere but Ireland which makes you feel as if you come from somewhere else. I am not entirely sure what I am talking about in this paragraph but I know it is a paragraph at that.

And Irish Football is as different from other footballs as you can imagine. It is not rugby or soccer or — actually it is rather like Australian Rules. You run with round ball; you kick it, you knock the bejasus out of your opponent.

Nobody seems to win at all. Just like rugby. Also it takes a long time. But not yesterday in the Pearse Park Development Cup thingymyjig, at Clarkston Rugby Club, just outside Glasgow.

It took no time at all for Donegal to see off the current owners of the Sam MacGuire Cup, Derry itself, in a glorious game at the Glasgow ground, and Donegal winning — in their gold and green and glory to boot — one to nine which gave them 12 points and Derry, rivals beyond belief, with nothing to 10 which was 10 points.

How you score things in Gaelic footy is beyond me but it is not beyond the spectators, among whom was none other than wur ain Billy McNeill who was loving the game, the first Gaelic he had ever been at. 'It's a great atmosphere,' said Billy, 'but even at my worst I never fouled anybody like that.' I told Billy that the boys weren't actually fouling — they were just enjoying themselves.

Beside William was just the nicest and prettiest girl you ever saw, Maureen Dowds, PE teacher — what else. She had hair the colour of cornfields and eyes like dollar bits. I made wur snapper take snaps. A cold day it was, and all it takes to warm it up is a pretty girl, an ex-Celtic manager, and a nice wee bar, and all three were there. Aye, and the clergy to give us all a blessing. For a start there was Bishop Rafferty, from Derry but auxiliary Bishop of St Andrews in Edinburgh, and Father Healy from Kerry. Now I have to tell you that the pair of them were awffy keen on Derry and I do not blame them.

And after all Derry, last year's winners, were the likeliest candidates, but my chums were all for the green and gold of Donegal and thus victory was sweet.

The match itself was perhaps best summed up by Father Eamonn Sweeney, the Moodiesburn priest who acted as public announcer on the Sunday event in Clarkston. 'Some people think there are no rules in Gaelic Football,' he told the four-and-a-half thousand crowd, 'but there are one or two — if I could think of them.' Certainly referee Des Slater, from Tyrone, didn't have to think of too many, for yesterday's game was, though certainly vibrant, clean at that.

But Gaelic Football is rough. This was no friendly, this Willie Dowds Challenge Cup. And each team was decently parochial enough to want to beat each other.

The game itself seemed to go Derry's way and the reds had most of the first 15 minutes. Later still, despite Donegal looking increasingly dangerous, the somewhat portly Geoffrey McMonnigle of the westie team sneaked a splendid wee free. Derry came in with a good scoreline at the interval. The points, however from Donegal's Marty Carlin, Noel Hendry, and lissom forward Jim McGuinness, gave Donegal the trophy. A hard-fought match with but the one goal, from John Gildea of the Rosses.

Most of the credit has got to be given to the man of the match, goalkeeper Gary Walsh. A youngish fellow, he played like a veteran. Gary is an accountant. His keenest opponent, John McGurk of Derry, is an accountant too. I am thinking of employing the both, they are that competitive.

There were a lot of people there because there are a lot of Irish people in Scotland, well, sort of Irish. There were quite a lot of folk who were very Irish indeed. Colm Mohan, who owns the grand Hutts Bar in Dublin and him from just next door to Daniel O'Donnell, was in attendance at the Clarkston Rugby joint along with chum Dave Gallagher, also from Donegal and living now in Rathgar near Dublin. Across the Irish Sea, to look at their own game at that. There was a goodly group of chaps from one-time Irish backgrounds. There was Tony May, who we all know, and he was just there because, well, you would expect him to be.

John McLean, nae relation, and working himself daft as a journalist on behalf of Scots-Irish relations, John McNally of the housing assoc — och a hell of a lot of people doing their best for a smashing sport and one I am ever glad to report upon. This is me off to the celebration dinner. Packy Bonner is going to give a speech. It'll be grand. Just as well it's no' a Celtic director. Youse never know, I might just dae the moothie as well.

FUN AND GAMES IN THE PARK

June 29, 1992

THE Glasgow Show happens every year, and every year thousands of citizens turn up for it. This year there were about 45,000 of the denizens appearing. And what a grand occasion it is. For a start admission is free.

Saturday was great and there was a considerable increase in the turnout. Yesterday was not so well attended at Bellahouston Park because, in their wisdom, the city leaders decided to allow the Orange chaps to go walkabout in the same area. Many a parent must have promised a visit to the Show and had to turn back in disappointment because of ill-considered grievances by people who add no lustre to our civic life.

But I was there on Saturday. The sky was a little overcast, but that did not stop the sunshine of what is a splendid celebration. As I stated before, the Glasgow Show is free. I do not know how — or even why — the Glasgow Parks and Leisure department do it, but do it they do. They open a show in a situation of a stretched budget which this government cannot even guess at.

The parks people have a budget of £50m a year. They have 2000 workers. They have 10 people working in the public relations set. Cathy Young spoke to me along with Debbie Murray, leader-aff of the PR department. You never met so much enthusiasm outside of a Sammy Davis Jr concert.

Said Cathy: 'We have a great product here — more parks per square mile than any other city in Europe, and beautiful parks at that.' Cathy has taken to speaking like me. She pinned a lovely red carnation on my lapel. Some of the girls didn't have expertise with male concerns, however. Not a one had the slightest idea who the ex-Scottish international goalkeeper was letting wee bits of weans score against him in a penalty competition. It was, of course, Alan Rough, a chap who represented his country for a decade.

Take the most professional PR lassie and let her loose on football and she will still be charmingly oblivious to the national game. Or how about young Ruth, a slim and lissom girl clad in a magnificent champagne-coloured costume who moved back and knocked over young Frank the barman with expertise. It does not do to tangle with girls.

I mention all these PR people because the Glasgow Show doesn't get off the ground without their efforts. The councillors turn up for the politics, the crowds for the fun, but the sponsors — including the hard-working parks punters — turn up for both.

Peter McLean of the parks department was out and about making sure that everything was going smoothly in a two-day event which needs more organisation than a Rio summit. Peter believes in it all. Parks and leisure means more than flowers, trees, grassland, and maintenance: it also means leisure.

At the Glasgow Show we had displays in the environment tent, advice on gardening, a BBC Radio One Road Show, showjumping contests, half of the British Army, and the most frightening display of motorcycle skills I have ever seen in my life by the Flying Gunners. It takes 30 grand a year to keep the Flying Gunners on the road and they were sponsored by, among others, Duckhams the oil people and Kawasaki. They will need more sponsorship next year if they are to continue entertaining the public.

Then there were the parachutists. The para regiment had provided facilities for visitors to do practice runs of parachute jumps. A young para officer asked me if I would take part. I told him I would resign from my job if I had to do it. The kids loved it. Of course they did: fear comes from experience of life. Youse should have seen the household cavalry. Prancing about the horses were and the gleaming breastplates of the horsemen. It was a stirring sight.

The young officer in charge of the announcements proved to come from Edinburgh, an ex-Fettes chap called Valentine Woyka whose parents hailed from the same town as my grandfather in Hungary. See the coincidences. Another coincidence was meeting my doctor's partner's wife. An even better coincidence was that we were both partaking of a small libation.

One of the best things about the Glasgow Show is that you can take your wife or husband and children and still take a dram or a hamburger with the best of them.

I never mentioned the highland dancing. Every year I get ribbed myself for being a former champion in the highland endeavors. My editor loves this. Every year, too, I see him salivating, looking at the horses. The Ingliston Show just the other side of the country was so hard on the turf this year that the horses came across to Glasgow where their wee feet would not take such punishment. Eddie is awfy concerned about the horses, but it doesn't stop him making ribald remarks about the idea of me in a kilt doing Highland Dancing.

But what is there about sport in the Glasgow Show? Everything. Everything that is best in sport is there. The fun and the splendour of ladies all dressed up for the day would do credit to Ascot or Henley.

The sheer enjoyment of sponsors like Joe Dunn of Dunn and Moore, the soft drinks firm, who doesn't actually care about the money on a day like this because his wee girl has eaten his VIP badge, the athleticism of so many of the entertainers, the kids mingling among the gypsies of Glasgow, like a scene out of Frith's Derby Day painting, the effort of the Parks people, the cooncillors with a drink in them, the colour, verve, and sheer Glaswegian chutzpah of the whole event. That's sport, the way it should be.

A REAL SHOW IN THE NAME OF SPORT

June 21, 1993

AFTER all these years I am still asked why we think the Glasgow Show is a sport. It doesn't have international recognition, some say. Yer right. But it does have recognition in Glasgow itself, doesn't it? Like more than 60,000 turning up on a wet Saturday, over 75,000 on Sunday when the sun was splitting the skies. Saturday had intermittent rain at Bellahouston Park and there was wee Denis Mooney with his famille, and him once the supremo at Scottish Television sport.

Says I to him: 'Is this a sporting event?' Says he to me: 'It wis when ah covered it for Scottish.' Eddie the sports editor turns up every year at this event and if the sports editor says it is sport, it is.

But it is more than that. The Glasgow Show is the major event of the year for the Glasgow Parks and Recreation Department. It cost a lot of money and we ratepayers are paying for it.

A lot of them were turning up to see what they were paying for too. They were paying for a splendid celebration and a gala day.

On the very day that we celebrated being Glaswegian, there was another little fiesta taking place at Queens Park, right opposite my own house.

There were hundreds of polizei across the road from me making sure that flute-playing didn't end up with tears before bedtime. There were precisely twelve at the Glasgow Show, eight of them special constables.

The chap with the scrambled egg on his bunnet, boss polis Gerry MacKenzie, wis enjoying himself and told me the only difficulties he had were lost wee boys and girls, though he had one which was a stoatir. One little girl had tearfully turned to a lady gendarme and claimed that her mum had 'been stolen'. The stolen mum, as tearful as the wee girl, finally got reunited with her daughter. In the beer tent actually, and quite right too.

The Glasgow Show has always had high spots. This year it was, undeniably, the display of the King's Troop, Royal Horse Artillery. Queen Victoria should have been living at this hour. I found myself enthralled at the horsemanship of this gaily attired soldiery. I also wanted to know how these lovely chestnut horses could be persuaded to stand at attention when neither myself nor wur Lord Provost, Bob Innes, found such a feat possible.

Actually, Provost Bob and the lady Provost, looking wonderful in a Glasgow tartan skirt and lace, were very still indeed, and still there the next day, and it was myself who was wandering a bit which, considering the hospitality I encountered, was hardly surprising.

Oh, by the way, it is said that the King's Troop cost seventy grand to bring up here and one of the lady grooms suggested that the cuddies were better fed than the troopers, or even us.

But, wandered as I was, I also encountered lots of wonderful people. The most wonderful of all were the children.

Denis Mooney, see above, had two engaging children who were bouncing basketballs. Fiona told me that basketball is better than netball, an assertion I challenged. I was put in my place. 'Basketballs bounce' she said. The wee boy is called Jack. 'I thought you'd know that' he said.

Later, I encountered a nice wee lassie who was the daughter of Councillor Yvonne Anderson, a noted Labour lady. Stated this doughty little girl: 'The best bit, I thought, was the talking. My mum,' she revealed engagingly, 'likes talking. She does it all the time.'

Do not be a mum to a seven year-old daughter with brains.

But the Glasgow Show may well be funded massively by Glasgow District Council: it is also very well sponsored indeed. The Woolwich Building Society sticks a right few quid into the children's entertainment part, as does Abbey Life. The rugby demonstrations, especially important for the young children, are sponsored by Nu-Line Partitions. SPECTRA hosted the showjumping.

I always mention sponsors beause I want them to do it again. Perhaps I should mention the armed forces most of all.

Speaking to colour Sergeant Lewis, a chap from Ayrshire, though based in Glasgow, and in the recruiting office many years, he told me of the Army involvement, and why.

'We have the Highland Fusiliers here, and the Scots Guards, and the Army Air Corps, and the Pioneers and Catering Corps, and Ordnance, and Transport, and Household Cavalry, and Royal Logistics ...' I stopped him at this. Because I haven't a Scooby what logistics are. The Glasgow Show is a focus for the forces, and they know it, which is perhaps why one should wonder why they are charging quite so much poppy for their displays. Considering that the Royal Corps of Signals motorcycling displays cost next to nothing. (An admission here: my daddy was 20 years in Interflora).

But is the Glasgow Show sport? The answer is — yes. It's not just the Highland dancing and the strong man shows and go-karting. There is also the bungee jumping, the daftest sport of all. I refused myself on the basis that it would ruin my cover-up hairstyle.

Provost Bob Innes went up to the platform but baulked at jumping. Said he was wearing the kilt and didn't want to reveal the final secret. That would be sport at that.

AWASH WITH SERIOUS HOSPITALITY

August 17, 1992

FOR all you sports chaps out there who want a nice day for your outside sporting event I will offer you a wee piece of advice: do not invite the Urban V to it.

Cardross Golf Club was the soaking venue for the Scottish Professional Golf Championship which took place over the course of last week. For any real information about the championships you will have to turn to my colleague Mr Jacobs, because I know nothing about the most famous Scottish game ever, though I may say I have always been attracted to the gowf quite simply because I could get to wear splendid gear and swan about with that Michael Jackson-style glove which some players affect. Also I like the idea of dirty bars and every sort of recondite nonsense which golfers go in for.

Golf remains an enigma to me. All this stuff about birdies and eagles and such sounds faintly poetic but I do not know what the terms mean. Some of the chaps at Saturday's final show tried to explain them all to me but I kept on getting mixed up, especially after the hospitality got to me. And they have rare hospitality at golf affairs. This is, of course, because while golfers take their sport very very seriously indeed, they take their hospitality even more so.

My first encounter on Saturday was with the Clydesdale Bank who had a hospitality truck there. Mel McDonald, manager of the local Cardross branch, and Patricia entertained me for a spell. Mel also knows nothing about golf, him being a fishing man. I started jotting down some splendid notes about the fishing until I remembered what I was there for.

Later I encountered lots of chaps I knew in the quiet beer tent, including Alastair Brown, Cardross club member and ex-assistant professional himself. It was quiet, Alastair explained, mainly because the weather on Saturday was so bad, (though there had been sizeable crowds on the previous day when the sun was splitting the skies). They had rather been expecting some 6000 spectators but it was a mere hundred or so fans I saw.

What does a pro do was what I wanted to know. Alastair told me. As far as I can see a golf pro has the hours of a taxi driver and a barman combined. Lessons, organising tournament games, running the shop, ordering the gear. 'The worst bit', said your man, 'is having to repair 40-year-old clubs for members too bloody mean to buy as much as new underpants let alone new clubs!' One of the facts which emerged was that the top prize of £6000 did not attract the big Scottish pros such as Sandy Lyle. Scottish Brewers had sponsored the Championship to the tune of nearly a hundred grand but the championship could do with more sponsors like the beer baron. Yet it has to be said that Scottish golf is still extremely healthy. This country is the cheapest in the world to get a game. Indeed, Cardross costs a mere £300 a year for membership and the waiting list is not much longer than a year.

While it is true that it is also a game in which your social class is not important if you want to play — it is a game which transcends class — it is also true that one rarely hears of a club captain or secretary who is the 'proverbial ordinary working chap' oft quoted by golf fans, though Cardross seems to be different in that respect.

Certainly, it is true that I found everybody to be wonderfully approachable from the club officials to the club pro Robert Craig. Mr Craig is a young chap of 31 who was a little disappointed at himself for his score of 77 — the par for the course is 71 — but he didn't burst into tears like footy players do. In fact he rather bemoaned the over-seriousness of some of today's players, recalling a certain Brian Barnes who was wont to finish a can of lager at the last hole.

The chap who won at the last hole had been playing a blinder even without the can of lager. Paul Lawrie, of the Kings Links club, was holing everything on Saturday and was a worthy winner it was said. He made a very nice wee speech at the trophy ceremony which was held out in the lashing rain. By the time the thing was finished he could have bathed in the contents of his commemorative bowl.

Actually everybody was wet but not caring. Local youngsters Lorna Borland and Caroline Craig, (who had of course been roped in by local minister, the Reverend Andrew Scobie, who himself had been appearing every day at the championships), as scorers, were soaked but flushed with excitement. The Scottish PGA officials wore smart maroon blazers. It was like Princes Street awash with Edinburgh buses.

It was awash anyway, but, you know, curiously, it didn't matter. It is a lovely course, said to be one of the best kept in the country, due to the ministrations of David Gall and his greenkeeping staff. I might just take up this golf at that.

THE LISP-ALONG OLYMPICS

August 3, 1992

THE Olympicth Gameth, I don't like, even in, ethpecially in, Barthelona. For the Olympicth hath, by its very ethenth, a lithp.

In short, to end the tiresome notational rendition of the Spanish speech defect, there is a serious flaw in the Olympics, and most certainly in the world-wide perception of the event.

The Olympic games speak, but they do so at best with a lisp, and at the most serious, in tongues. The Olympic Games are crazy.

The original scene of the Olympic Games was Olympia of course, a spot in Greece, in the Western Peloponnese. It was a Greek architect called Georgios Averoff and the five-foot three Baron de Coubertin who thunk it all up in 1896.

From the start, the Olympics, by neccessity, were commercialised — funding was by the sale of medals and stamps. Back then, of course, the Olympian ideal was amateur. Today the Olympics are still amateur, and if you believe that, you will be prepared to take the likes of Charles Manson in as a lodger for the night.

Back in the days of ideals, people just competed. Then came the times when the Games were about political and national pride. I spoke to a couple of young fellows recently who had never heard of Jesse Owens and the Berlin Games where Hitler had Leni Riefenstahl filming the god-like creatures of the Third Reich and Jesse — considered an 'uppity nigger' — somehow was uppity enough to win everything in front of the blonde Teutons. They had never heard of Teofilio Stevenson, the Cuban boxer who was probably the best heavyweight outside of another Olympian fighter, Cassius Clay. None of them remembered Scotland's own Dick MacTaggart.

Why should they? Nobody remembered any of the great amateurs of tennis or golf. They only remember the professionals of the last two decades. Then the money came in and the sponsorship, the hype, the TV companies, the multinational advertising and the entire bread and circuses to keep the lumpen happy with what Marx called false-consciousness. When that came in, sport went out the open portals.

I don't like the Olympics for several reasons. TV commentators sound demented at the best of times. When it's the Olympics, they sound as though they are describing the birth of Jesus on the spot, the sinking of the Titanic, the start of the Second World War, and Ar · ageddon viewed from Main Street, Larkhall, on a Tuesday night and ho ing for a repeat

fee. Today's Games are a far cry from what the Olympic motto states —
that the important thing is not winning, but taking part. The essential
thing is not conquering but fighting well.

The important thing once was to have the Yanks beating the Ruskies
or the other way round, and the other wee countries thought that, as
long as some beef-witted runner won a medal, the country would be
okey-dokey.

The reason why the West is doing well this Olympics is because the
eastern European countries, so long dominant, finally have realised that
feeding their people and getting ethnic violence sorted out is more important than some steroid-bulked automaton winning a meaningless
medal.

I love sport and praise the values of it every week in this blatt, but
not at the price of an intelligence. It is no coincidence that the Communist dicatorships spent so much effort and money on the promotion of
sport. It is no coincidence that the fascist regimes in Suid Afrika went
for sport. The more the young ran about senselessly, the less time they
had for reading, and the consequences of reading are anathema to communist and fascist hegemonies. Even in this country, it has long been
thought that sport was a safety valve for the dispossessed.

My experience over the last few years of covering diverse sports is
that the nature of physical activity provokes the brain; that young people who are physically active are more often than not more active in the
brain cell department.

My experience of the kind of sports commentators and the kind of
competitors who make their actual living out of professional sport is
otherwise. The truth is that the obsession with winning, or even with
sport itself, which characterises the Olympic Games, is next to fas-
cism.

There really is no value in jumping over a higher stick than your
neighbour, or running quicker than the other chap, or riding a bike
designed to go faster than the other fellow's can manage.

I am sympathetic to the athletes who are intent on crippling themselves in the years to come by injecting drugs into themselves. All it
takes is the sort of crap which coaches and commentators, a gullible
public, and a cynical manipulating collection of government ministers
knowing full well that they can take votes out of triumph from afar.

The Olympic Games are a far cry from the fun I see week after
week at some of the, admittedly, silly pursuits I cover each week. The
silly games have spendid people doing sport for fun.

Despite my undeniable pride in some people I know who are going
to win Gold, (and I pray for Liz McColgan every night), I know what
the Olympic Games really are now. I deplore them.

TOPERS ARE TOPS

November 11, 1992

YESTERDAY saw me not only in my part of the woods, but practically lifting a leg against my tree. Heraghty's Fun Run it was; the ninth year of it.

Fun Runs have been around a long time and very welcome they are. Little can be more dispiriting in sport than the sight of the grey-faced jogger, resolute in his or her idiocy. One of the more wondrous views from my window is that of fat girls with bouncing mammaries and emaciated 40-year-olds flitting down the avenue like daddy-long-legs who have just joined the Mormons. But Heraghty's Fun Run is different. For starters, it is largely fun.

For starters the Run had wee Phil McCall, standing on a soapbox and dressed like a bookie, giving his Thespian all and kicking off the race. McCall stood aside as the runners began the five-and-three-quar-ter-mile run.

Starting first were the ones clad in the fancy dress. There was Dopey and Bashful to begin with. Dopey is George Quar, who presides over the Tasha Blankit Cafe, an upmarket bistro on Glasgow's Cathcart Road. Bashful was the least bashfull barman I have ever encountered, Heraghty's own John Strange. Dressed as an Arab was Tam the Taxi (he drives your Urban about a bit), and then Bishop Casey, complete with vestments, took up the front line along with the other exotics.

Bishop Casey is, in fact, locally known as Del Boy. He is a school-teacher. The good bishop was to prove a wonder to us all. Can of lager in hand from start to finish and with a language salty enough to embar-rass a sports editor, he probably did more to abjure the assorted chil-dren from the religion of the Church of Rome than the real bishop ever did.

But the Fun Run is not simply a daft exercise: there is more than that. Heraghty's Fun Run started off as a result of a chance remark by a customer to John Strange, one of the most irascible barmen in Europe. The customer had a child in Langlands School, a school for profoundly mentally handicapped children. Strange thought of the runs which had happened in the US and went for it.

The result has been that not only Langlands, but a lot of other chari-ties, have benefited from this annual event, and, indeed, other activi-ties, including football matches, hill climbs, etc.

In the last eight years the little pub on the south side which I inhabit

129

has made £20,000 for charity. One year it produced a wee cheque for the sum of £1690. That was the year of the tercentenary of the Battle of the Boyne. It is widely rumoured that Mr Strange, a Rangers shareholder and fan, had made up the difference to such a figure.

Yet the Run is serious enough, too. There are always runners of rank taking part. Last year's winner was Hugh Gallagher, a formidable runner from Bellahouston Club. Hugh came in second this year in 28 minutes. 'I always come in second if Jack Brown is running,' said Hugh, who is 38.

Brown was first in a remarkable 26 minutes, less than five minutes a mile. Jack is with Cambuslang Harriers and ran in Saturday's Glasgow Yooni Road Race where, he told me, he came in just after Liz McColgan, which is not bad racing. Next week he runs in the prestigious Edinburgh-Glasgow Relay.

Brown is a computer expert and son-in-law of coachman Tony Gallagher who runs the Scottish end of Doherty's Coaches, which drive our own Anne Simpson across to Ireland regularly. There is a reason for mentioning this fact. The reason is that I, too, ran the race — after a fashion. I travelled by Mr Gallagher's sleek, dark blue Jag, driven by young Anthony. We were first, really, even though disqualified.

But there is more than money sometimes, and there is in this Fun Run. The entrants were in the bar, getting dressed, at an unearthly hour. They ran through some of the most splendid suburbs of which the entire country can boast, leafy and dappled, with huge, stone-built houses.

Afterwards the bar was awash with the same entrants. Their wives were there (there was a distressing lack of female entrants this year with Sandra Bogan coming in first and Rena Morris, who has run every year from its inception, doing well too). And the children. There were little ones everywhere.

Manager Danny's three angelic children were angelic in behaviour, too, despite the efforts of a now fallen from grace quasi-Bishop Casey (the lager had it's effect: he had fallen into a hedge). Little Rosalleen, Siobhan, and wee Damien had the time of their lives. Dopey and Bashful had ended up at Ibrox Park, where they were videoed by Vincent along with Ally McCoist, in for treatment.

Back in Heraghty's there was soup and grub, some of it provided by Michael of the Taverna and the rest by the redoubtable ladies who have been doing it for all these years.

At the top end we are seeing real athletics. At the toper end we are seeing real people as well.

HAVING A RERR OLD HIELAN FLING

June 7, 1993

WELL, there ah wis, so ah wis, in Shotts at a Heilan' games. Hannah Park wis the venue. Therr wis a beer tent, as youse wid expect at a Heilan games, though why Shotts thinks it is the Heilans is beyond yer correspondent, like.

The sun wis splittin' the skies, so it wis, in Shotts, and therr wis Celtic wrestling, which is nothin' but big blokes pullin' each other aboot werring kilts, and merr kilts on the pipers who were therr in force because therr wurr 60 bands oot. Wan o' them wis the Linwood Caledonia whit hud some o' the nicest looking lassies in it whit youse huv ever seen.

Karen wis a stoatir, and hersel' a nurse fae Bathgate, and Kirsty wis just sublime, and her working in a chemists. Their pal, Lesley, wis a lab technician. They are an awffy fit lot, the pipers. Ah asked therr pipe major, Sammy Black, aw aboot it. He tell't me that they practise twice a week and huv 30 pipers, and that therr gaun tae Islay next week. Ah waanted tae go as well. Well, Islay hus goat tae be merr fun than Shotts. Sarajevo is merr fun than Shotts.

But Shotts Heilan' games hud merr than that. Fur a start it hud the British wrestling championships. Therr wur 12 of the boays turned up, though therr hud been a bigger entry originally, and the final wis the wrestling in Cumberland style, which wis jist great.

Anither wan fur the record wis that therr wis a record 56 pun weight thrown ower the bar. Ah didnae huv a scooby whit this wis but it wis dead good, ah'm tellt. The only thing ah seen thrown ower a bar wis drink, tae be honest, and that wis in the company of an auld china plate, and him the chieftin o' the Games.

Ah mind when Dr John Reid M.P. wis a styoodent revolutionary like masel', an' noo here he wis cavortin' aboot in a braw bit o' tartan skirt and a bunnet wae feathers stickin' oot it like a red Indian wae a drink in him.

Dr Reid wis the same boay uz ah remember him, and wis therr wae his entire faemely, includin' his smashin' wee maw, an' he wis tellin' me nuthin aboot thae Monklands Cooncil blokes, but tell't me aboot Sir David Steele, who wis a chieftin furra games before. Reid sez Steele werrs a kilt like a lassie. He tell't me merr but ah'm no tellin' youse the substance o' it. Needless tae say, he bribed yer reporter wae a big amber. And aboot time tae.

But Shotts wis a grand day oot, and the locals were dancing alang wae the ubiquitous Hielan dancers (some of youse will recollect that yer Urban V wis wance a bit o' a star in this business himsel') and the local St Patrick's Primary won baith the boays' and the lassies' relay races, which teams Jan and Alan Dearie hud coached.

St Pat's beat aw the ithers — schools fae Harthill and Kirk o' Shotts, and Dykehead and ither unlikely places. Even the polis wurr cheerin'. Therr wur eight gendarmes therr, ivery wan o' them chattin' away like linties. Inspector McAllister wis huvin a field day. Beats bouncing idjits oota chip shoaps at midnight any day.

Masel'? Ah hud merr cheeriness than ah've seen in years. Disappointing it wis, a bit, that merr folk hudnae turned up, being a smashing day, but we aw enjoyed it.

Doacter Reid done a good speech, and therr wur girls in kilts and weans eatin' aw the time, and aw ah kin say is ah went tae bed early wae a smile oan ma coupon. Ah'm gaun next year, so ah um.

But, my dears, thet was Setterday when I went to Shotts. On Sunday, I wis aff, sorry, off, tae, sorry, to, Newton Mearns where I seen, sorry, saw, the Eastwood Hielan, sorry, Highland Games.

It was rerr, sorry, rare. Blue skies, too, for the organisers of this day out in the beautiful grounds of Parklands Country Club. As Don, PR for the event, admitted to me privately, a rainy day would have meant a washout. But the sun shone on the Highland dancers and the crowd of 5000, and was it not the sheer artistry of the Rose Galloway School of Dance, with Fiona, Denise, Jaqueline, Donna, Pamela, and Lesley, kicking it all off.

Setting the tone, too, for the wee Irish dancers from the Shamrock School Kilburnie Branch. Young Karen from Dalry has far to go if I'm a judge, and I am at that a bit.

Just to balance things a little with the rather ethereal little dancers were several absolutely huge things as well. Douglas Edmunds, boss of the show and himself a weighty figure, introduced me to Manfred Hobert, who hails from the same village as Arnold Schwarzenegger. He claims to have the biggest biceps in the world. What he most certainly has is a bigger forearm than your correspondent's chest and I am 45 bloody inches.

He shook my hand. Gently. I got it back.

His pal from Holland, Ted, was seven feet tall and is the strongest man in the world, or at least he was last year in Iceland. This year both chums are competing for the title in France.

'How do you like Scotland?' I inquired in my best pan-loaf accent, (it wis Eastwood efter all). Both said it was great, liked the whisky, wanted to meet our beautiful Scottish girls, and both said they liked the money. I'm coming back — big.

PIPERS PLAY THEIR TUNES DAMP WELL

August 16, 1993

IT always pours down at the World Pipe Band Championships in Bellahouston Park. This is because God is a Philistine and only chose the Israelites out of badness.

The pipers struggled manfully at the Bella Highland Games on Saturday, but it is a right scunner to have to go jouking about in waterproof capes when underneath lies enough colour to make Norman Hartnell's designs look insipid.

Has it occurred to you that Scottish pipers are the original punks. And most elaborate of all was Drum Major Alberto Donati MacDonald, who appears at the Park every year from his native Italy. Alberto has contrived to adorn himself in the fashion of both countries and looks wonderful enough to pass for a gelati in Sicily. The world championships have been held here for some years, and successfully too, despite the drizzle.

There were 25,000-plus spectators during the day. And one of them was me, back again. This year the winners were the Irish band, the Field Marshall Montgomery, who retained the trophy against final opponents Shotts and Dykehead Caledonian. They were rather expected to win anyway.

But there's more than winning of course, though Joe Young from Tyrone was delighted with the victory. So was young Mildred Young as well.

Actually, it's amazing how many girl pipers there are these days, and a lot of girl drummers too. Colleague Alastair Simpson, a neep from Aberdeen originally, and once a mean side-drummer with a British Legion band, told me that the girls are creeping in solidly and getting better than the lads at that. 'Better looking too,' he mused.

But there were 193 bands taking part. I spoke to Campbell Gillies, a joiner from Rothesay, and drum major of the Caledonian Airways band. He was there with his eight-year-old daughter Jane, resplendent in our national dress, and his wee Lindsay, only 18 months. 'We had a good run in Class One and no complaints. Mind you,' he said blithely, 'there is always a wee suspicion of favouritism among the RSPBA.'

At first I could not understand what the birds protection mob had to do with the drones game, but then worked the initials out, as I am sure you can too.

This suggestion was echoed, however, by many a piper present. Victoria Police from Australia were said to be somewhat favoured, though myself, I couldn't see it. I thought they were just damned good, and they didn't win in the end anyway.

But there is more to the Bella day out than the piping championships, important as that is. There is sport too. You know my views on what constitutes a sport, and if cavorting about in the rain wearing all that gear and putting on a show and doing it with verve and colour and class isn't sport, then I will swally my sporran.

But there was also the heavy sports. These are big lads involved in what for centuries were the main sports in Scotland. And the same heavy lads seemed to figure in each one of them. Tossing the caber was won by Kevin Thom, with Eric Irvine from Musselburgh, with a score of 26. Runner-up was Mark MacDonald from Dumfries.

Irvine figured again in the 16lb shot putt coming in second to Hamish Davidson, (incidentally strongman and Sassenach Geoff Capes holds the world record in this event, as he does the 22lb and 28lb competitions). Eric Irvine cannot keep away from winning. He came top in the 22lb shot.

My favourite is the caber-tossing because so few competitors ever quite manage it. The ideal toss is the 'twelve o'clock throw.' The Bellahouston programme notes explain this to ourselves, but it hardly needs to do so. Cabers are normally about 17 feet long and weigh 120lb. I can barely toss a cigarette.

And then there is the national tug o' war championships. A surprisingly large number of women now take part in this and great fun it is too. The women's title was taken by East Kilbride, the men's was won by North Fife, and it is of course teams which win: there are no individual stars in such a sport. But all the same, the ladies did outshine, I thought, the men.

This was not entirely confirmed in an interview with a young lady called Fiona, aged four, who was clad delightfully in a bonnet with a feather and a velvet bodice and a wee kilt, and who energetically scratched her bahookie throughout our conversation. (Why do small girls upset the intended elegance of their costumes by such practices?) I asked what she liked most. 'The fat men with the ropes,' she told me with aplomb.

What I liked most was the refreshment to be honest, if you don't count the Highland dancing, sponsored by the Bank of Scotland. Dunn and Moore, and Grants, the whisky people, sponsored well too, though of course Glasgow District Council are major givers.

Once again, a lot of the Parks and Recreation officials were out, doing it for nothing. Provost Bob Innes was there too, grand as ever in his kilt. Not as splendid as Mrs Bob, though, wearing an outfit which would shame the wildest fantasies of Winterthaller painting Bonnie

Prince Charlie, if he'd been alive. A glory to us all every time I see Theresa at the Games. Next time I'll wear my own kilt, and shame the lot of them.

The Young Ones Take Second Place

March 30, 1992

WHEN you cover minority sports, you sometimes find that the word 'minority' is somewhat of a misnomer. Naturally, the footy takes up most of the space in the blatts, and the space in the heads of the readers too.

But there are a lot of sports out there which are followed by thousands and *The Herald* is one of the few newspapers in Britain which seem to recognise this fact. Why they send your Urban Voltaire out to cover these specialist activities is a mystery to all, but cover all the sports we do.

This week it was hockey — a minority sport I don't think. There are more than 200,000 hockey players in this country, and about 9000 of them are men.

Needless to say, the men's game gets the biggest subsidy from the hockey associations, much to the chagrin of the girls. Elaine McAra, former Scottish internationalist, and a prominent hockey coach and one-time PE teacher, admitted that this annoyed her considerably. 'It's time that the ladies stopped being quite so ladylike,' I remember her telling me last summer. But Elaine is still at the hockey, and yesterday she was in the rain at Strathclyde University's playing fields, witnessing the Scottish Cup semi-finals.

Clydesdale and Kelburne were matched against each other. The other semi, Civil Service versus Torbrex Wanderers, resulted in a victory for the Dundonians on penalties after what I am told was an exciting match.

It was certainly vibrant enough in the match I witnessed betwixt Kelburne and my old cricket club, Clydesdale. The excitement was perhaps due to the struggle between an experienced club and a young one.

Clydesdale are the young ones and it showed. They lost 2-1, and deserved to lose really, but this does not take away from their astonishing achievement this year. Although Kelburne are top of the first division, Clydesdale have just managed to lift themselves into that company after 10 years in the doldrums of the second.

By the look of the play, Clydesdale have yet a long way to go. Said cricketing doyen of the Titwood club, Mike Stanger: 'You can see the experience of the Kelburne players. They are that bit faster than ourselves. But we'll learn, and just you see us this time next year.'

Another problem for the Glasgow club was the artificial pitch. Grass slows the ball down considerably, and the 'Dale are used to the vagaries of turf. Kelburne clearly benefited from the sheer speed of the ball off the astroturf. Mike Stanger again: 'We knew we would be at a disadvantage but just getting promotion yesterday has lifted our morale to the extent that we might just have a chance in terms of sheer enthusiasm.'

Mike is at all times an enthusiast. You sort of have to be as Michael Kelly's front man, and there is something demonically decent about a chap who turns up to watch his club's hockey team in the rain the day before he is handling the public relations for Celtic Football Club's AGM the day after.

But hockey is nothing if not decent. The Kelburne coach is none other than ex-Clydesdale star Derek Forsyth, now Scotland's national coach, and the Clydesdale coach is the famed ex-Kelburne player Stuart Gilmour. Both are respective manager and coach of the under-21 Scotland hockey squad. You meet a better class of sportsman at the minority sports.

Thanks for the two large whiskies as well, boys. It kept out the cauld full well.

Thanks, too, for the welcome from Strathclyde Yooni playing fields club manager, John McBeth, who has long been a fixture in the club scene, having been manager at the BBC Club for some years and then manager in the Strathclyde Staff Club. He agreed to take over this venue just after it opened about a year ago. Sadly the Tech, (I still call it that out of working class snobbery), has decided to close the bar and catering facilities as from a fortnight's time.

The fact is, as Elaine McAra told me, and as I hear at every minority sports event, that the teachers' strike and subsequent municipal vendettas against staff has resulted in a withering away of teacher involvement. That universities are no longer meeting their responsibilities in sport is very saddening indeed. Mike Stanger again: 'I know it sounds crazy, but my belief is that the extra amount of oxygen going to the brain when you take part in sport increases the brain's ability too.' It doesn't sound crazy to me and the spin-off benefits of sport for young people cannot be contested.

For a start, and I have said this many times before, the relationship between old and young, and parent and child, is splendid. The auld yins benefit from seeing the young players go out there and do better than them, and the kids get a chance to speak on equal terms with their mums and dads, uncles and aunties.

And there were plenty of them at Strathclyde's Millerston Park yesterday — including the mother of Graham Dunlop, who was making his debut for Clydesdale's first team.

Graham, who is only 16, had a good game, and he should go on to full international status — he already plays for the under-16s. That's what his mum said and she should know. Graham, a pupil at Shawlands

Academy, learned the game at Clydesdale, not at his school. I remember when Shawlands had a thriving hockey team. Not now.

The final, the week after Easter, will have Kelburne and Dundee Wanderers showing their class. It is hoped that television may cover it, if only to get more interest in the game. But it is to the schools we still have to look for impetus. There are lots of young Graham Dunlops out there, and it is time the potential was realised.

BREATH OF FRESH AYR AT THE RACES

July 20, 1992

MY dad once asked me how the race was. 'What race?' I asked. 'The human race,' he replied.

I was five and at the age when adults, especially fathers, thought it appropriate to twit you a bit. Idjits, adults are. But not as much of idjits as you can find at a real race, and one with horses at it.

Thus your man here found himself at Ayr on Saturday, courtesy of a drive down by Mr Charles Harrigan, a doyen of the folk scene in Scotland and generally to be avoided on a Friday due to his unique capacity to get you appearing at folk festivals for no fee at all.

My brother Brian joined us on the trip. I could not have been in any worse company. Suited and booted, and with a drop off on the way for a wee libation, we would have done credit to Regret The Horseplayer and the Lemon Drop Kid, and anybody else who has been immortalised by Mr Runyon. With hats on, we three looked like the actors who should have been chosen for *Guys And Dolls*.

Ayr is a splendid venue, and there is always lots of fun. There are bars and restaurants. Down the sides of the various fences are planted flowers; pansies for heaven's sake. The ladies dress up and so do the men. At Ayr, there were pansies everywhere. I felt a bit of one myself when I discovered that two well-dressed lasses didn't want to talk to *The Herald* on the basis that they had never heard of me, *The Herald*, or anything which represents the written word.

Racing is raffish: that's the splendour of it. Do I not see all sorts of nefarious characters here? Do I not see many a worthy of my acquaintance?

Well, I see Roger Church who gives me good advice. 'Don't drink in the cheap bars. The expensive ones are better value. Don't order the steak pie; take the smoked salmon.'

And best advice of all: 'Don't bet, even with me.' I bet, with an old chum, bookie and boxing promoter, Matt Sawyer. Matt has been a bookie, boy and man, and his father before him. He gave me a long-odds tip, and told me I was daft anyway. Later my horse won. Even later, I stuck the stake on a horse called Ebony Isle, which fronted the course for most of it and came in fourth. Matt got his money back. For £10, I had enough excitement to cause heart lesions.

A lot of chums were there. Jackie Connors, about whom I penned a wee profile a while back, was doing what people in the bookmaking game generally don't, and out of decency. 'Stick a quid on.' I am not telling you the name of the animal. I stuck a quid on. True to form, it came in second but I was betting on the nose. When it comes to betting, I am an idjit incarnate. When it comes to betting at racecourses, I am not caring, because it is a great day out. Nae wonder Damon Runyon spent half his life on course.

Other nefarious characters turned up. I bumped into another chum, none other than Bobby Shearer, him ex of the Rangers. He is with a party of publicans and also his colleagues in the Thermal Care Windows firm. They had a box all to themselves. And me in it, rattling down the whisky and grub. Racing is about lots of whisky, grub, and camaraderie. The company I find myself could get taken up by Central Casting for any movie with Robert de Niro in it.

But there was more than that. How about Zoe and Laura, and David and Megan who are wee ones just there at the track and having a great time. Saturday was quieter than it will be today when there will be almost mobbing to get in.

But the adults who took the kids to the Ayr course knew what they were doing on Saturday. A day out with food and fun. The kids loved it. And so did myself. I always do. My brother and Charlie enjoyed it. They would. They won enough to pay for the champagne, which is more than I did.

But there is also the human race. Yesterday, I found myself at the Mileathon at the Kelvin Hall. The elegance of horses was supplanted by the bestiality of humans.

The Mileathon was part of the Telethon event. Sadly it was not particularly well attended. Sadly because the Parks and Leisure Department of Glasgow, for which I have oft-expressed an unreserved admiration, had funded this event.

Horse-racing is fuelled by fun and greed. The tendancy in amateur sport is otherwise and is fuelled, if at all, by an egotism which reflects no credit on many professional athletes.

A lot of celebs were meant to turn up but didn't. Not enough people turned up at all which is disgraceful, considering the number of employees who did, and for nothing. The disco and the Karaoke — both run by national organisations — were free. Athletes do damn near anything to run for money and then claim amateur status.

Two amateurs who ran were Tom and Katie Horne from Langside. Both were splendidly polite youngsters. Also running with them were a collection of grisly youngsters from Partick, who were as polite as Harry The Horse on a bad day, which is to say that they are not going to get their photies in the paper and no mistake.

I was brought up to be quiescent and courteous. The brats whom I encountered were largely rude and unashamedly egoistic; the equivalent of the sort of weans who bugger up filmed interviews by waving at the cameras. The polite children were polite: the difficult ones were clad in expensive shellsuits, trainers with tongues on them which could put out their eyes, and sported diamond stud earrings and gold necklaces. And that was the boys.

The difference between nice children and brats is made even more evident in sport than it is in a street. I have said it so often, but sport is good for kids, especially nice kids. Let me give you two other nice children, Joanne and Claire, whom I met with their aunt. The children came from Wishaw. If you can be nice, helpful, pleasant, and come from Wishaw, so can anybody, even in Partick. There is a lot of commitment from people in such events. Manager of the Kelvin Hall, Peter Eadie, like many of his colleagues, a former PE teacher, tries hard to make the centre go well.

'The Kelvin is busy but it's so big that sometimes it might not look so,' he said. The Kelvin is massive and possibly over-used in the summer months. It, and other places like it, are assets which the city often does not understand and are at least as important as the arts centres which have been burgeoning.

Then how about David Morrison who looks younger than me and is 78 years of age. He is running like a greyhound before it eats and has already done six miles. I couldn't run the length of the Press Bar. I liked David immediately. A lot more than Ebony Isle who took my winnings to the cleaners, I can tell you.

Yet racing, whether it be horses or humans, is much the same. I bet on David. This time I won.

THE GOVERNMENT'S ON A WINNER

January 4, 1993

JOCKEY Scroon is the sort of wee Shi-ite you would want to send to Bosnia or Lebanon. Jockey Scroon is, of course, the horse-riding villain who causes so much pain to Damon Runyon's never-named chronicler of race-track stories.

Those who bet will give you any amount of Jockey Scroons. You should hear them on trainers, or owners, or the racecourse aristos. But you should especially hear them on bookmakers.

Punters on bookmakers sound like Orangemen on the IRA, and maybe vice versa, at that, on both sides. Bookies now are not just anathema to punters, they are worse. They are necessary. Without punters there would never be bookies. Bookies are, in legend, ever sporting yellow checked suits and bow ties and large coarse banknotes and are raffish characters all round.

Anybody who has ever been to a racecourse knows that this is not mere legend. You would be right at that. Thus it is in betting shops.

When the Government in its wisdom decided, in 1961, to legalise betting shops it little realised what a disservice it did to an honorable profession. Prior to this there were lots of betting shops and all of them utterly illegal.

Street bookies were earning of course and the Government wanted to get into the action — and it did. In the old days you had Homeric chaps like, say, Corry McGowan. 'Don't Be Sorry: Bet With Corry' the line ran in Govan.

Corry started running lines during the War. His first shop was up a close. Between 1945 and '57, when he went semi-legit, he had 19 convictions, a regular felon altogether.

As his son, Benny — a yooni lecturer — says: 'He got arrested every five months or so. The police used to phone him up and he'd get a carry-out in for them. They'd come out bevvied and he'd be fined by a magistrate who'd placed a bet with him the day before.'

Other old hands remember those days with considerable affection. Says Roger Church, himself a bookmaker on course and whose father was a bit of a legend himself: 'The business was ruined by legitimacy and is not nearly as much fun.' Church claims that the only people making real money now is the Government itself. 'The eccies for a bookmaker are appalling. Running a betting shop is damned near ruinous.'

To a great extent Roger's impressions would appear to be correct. The old days when a betting shop operated with a couple of bits of chalk and string, are over. Today's shops are lavish affairs with rows of television sets replacing the old lag who used to write the names and numbers.

Ladbroke's, for instance, have closed their entire operation in Belgium. They have diversified into more lucrative areas, such as hotels. Ladbroke's was one of the big companies, headed by a Jewish family, and especially by Cyril Stein, and which owns, most lucratively of all, Vernon's Pools.

Other Jewish bookies were Joe Coral and William Hill — started by Charles Clore and now owned by George Walker, brother of ex-boxer, Billy.

But Scots have figured high in the betting business. Most particularly those of Irish origin. The old fellows like Tommy Marshall and the still well alive Tony Queen had the biggest businesses in British bookmaking.

There are still old hands about like Jackie Connor, clerk of the course and sometime cyclist whom you have met before in my columns.

Billy King is still about doing business wherever there is a horse or dug or anything with feet, if it comes to that.

There was the amazing Harold Brown who regularly shot the craw when the result went against him. It was okey-dokey for Ladbrokes who serviced the gentry, (the gentry got around the betting laws by placing credit bets rather than cash), but your average bookie was often in dire straits himself.

Dire straits or not, the proletariat regarded the street bookie as a bit of a local hero. Corry McGowan was renowned for giving the dafter punter's money back if the idjit's family was wanting.

Raffish character he was, like the famous Eddie Treanor and James McLean, great exponents of the old McFarlane-Lang, (slang that is to youse). You should have heard Ownie Cryan's on the MacFarlane.

Today is different, though. I visited Coral's establishment near my little, south-side club. Chairs and carpets. Some places run to coffee and biscuits, and big leggy girls calling you 'Sir'.

A far cry from the bleak, Bosnian clearing houses of old. Behind the counter, (no grilles or barriers), were Gillian, a Glasgow yooni student whom I last encountered captaining her varsity volleyball team, and Louise, a student accountant.

Mangeress Janice was cashing up. 'We don't get any trouble or hassle here,' said Janice. 'The customers regulate everything.' I was a touch sceptical. To be honest I don't think three lovely girls would be likely to see off rank bajins, but then in betting you don't see much of that anyway.

I was the only bajin that day, apart from the Jockey Scroon who was obviously riding my horse. Newbury it was. My tricast didnae work or anything like it. I blame the rider, not the girls. Mr Coral got a few quid, too, but I hope the girls get paid well.

KIDS ON THE SKIDS

April 5, 1993

THE Summit Centre has been there in Finnieston for six years and it is lovely. There is no funding for this piece of art and sport. Margaret Murphy, resplendent in dress and demeanour, knows full well how hard it is to run a business, and runs it well.

There is curling from September to April and the Summit is a major venue for this sport, which managed to make Scotland into a world power over the past few years. Indeed, Scottish men and women curlers won the world junior titles last weekend, and yesterday, although our men lost to the Canadians in the senior championship in Geneva, they were in the final.

We are the very berries. But Olympic-sized Summit does more than curling. Ice dancing, skating, ice hockey, you name it. Professional this is. Fiona Mackenzie, from Paisley, trains here, and also gives tuition to wee ones.

The schools come in, from 2 to 3pm, and the next hour as well. Saturday is set aside for junior hockey. The majors play on Saturdays, with large audiences, some of which are likely to engorge the bar profits-wise, for the Summit has a splendid bar and restaurant.

Schools are well represented at The Summit, and looked after by the redoubtable Peggie Smith, whose own two daughters play the ice to some distinction. She is the chatelaine of Partick Bell Curling Club, a club of 150 years' standing. Says Peggie about the ice scene: 'Good to hear that Torvill and Dean are going back to amateur status: it will build up this smashing sport, and TV coverage will bring in the money!'

The Summit is something else, though, and grand. Elsewhere, it is not quite thus. Elsewhere in Glasgow is the St Enoch Centre Rink. Take a squint at Summit and you will find curling, figure, individual, leisure skating, and ice hockey. St Enoch's, set in the middle of a shopping centre, is small and drab. Skating here consists of doing exactly that, just round and round, like shopping. Parents would be discouraged from here. Their children are searched, like something out of an American police movie, by bouncers. I am sure it is necessary, but it is not what I would want my own children to encounter.

The ice is scrappy and ill-looked after. Facilities are minimal. There is no bar for the parents. There is not anything for the parents. This is, after all, the City Centre. My greeting from the St Enoch was hardly welcoming: it smelled like the hand of a local authority behind it.

But local authorities are behind other ice rinks — perhaps the most famous of all in Scotland being Paisley. When I was a lad, there was Paisley and there was Crossmyloof. Paisley still has the Pirates — the most famous ice hockey team in Britain, for heaven's sake. It has changed venue and now possesses the most beautiful home ice in these isles.

Caroline is 14, and a pupil at Trinity High, comes here with her friends several times a week. It costs her two quid for two-and-a-half-hours' skipping across the ice. Paisley also has the Lagoon Leisure Centre, and it has more than ice: it is really a leisure centre. Margaret and Liz preside over the magnificent bar. Lunch costs 95p for children, and not much more for adults.

Lunch is grand. Richard Harding, curling writer and commentator, is manager. I had lunch and a brace of whiskies, and watched the wee ones skiting as well as skating across the white menace. Oddly enough, The Lagoon Centre, which opened last September, is owned and operated by Renfrew District Council. You would not know this by the sheer enthusiasm of the staff. Sonny's Bar has got to do one of the best menus of any local authority venue.

East Kilbride, too, has a splendid rink, with lots of fun for us all. Irvine's Magnum is Olympic-sized and facilities are marvellous. These are places to take your children to and allow yourself to disappear in the bar and restaurant for an hour or so.

But there really is more than that. What was so disappointing about the St Enoch Centre, right in the middle of Glasgow, is that nothing was there. Not just the absence of facilities for parents, but for children and adolescents, too.

The Summit, for instance, advertises birthday parties for the little ones and older ones, too. Irvine's Magnum would knock you out with the size of it. The Lagoon in Paisley has a bar which would do credit to Geneva. Try as I did, I never saw a lassie in a short skirt, though. A real disappointment.

THERE'S NO MORE CHILD'S PLAY

July 6, 1992

YOU started at the crack of dawn and finished at sunset. It was called the school holidays. Sometimes you turned up for your tea. If your mum was perspicacious enough, she had made enough pieces to last you till bedtime.

The school holidays were great. You played all day.

I have written this before, and I am doing so again. All sport is based on play and on children, and if there is less play in sport now, there are more children in it refusing to grow up. Peter Pan is still with us, and he has lost his shadow. That was called Responsibility. But the shadow has other names.

One of these is Fun, and I keep on coming back to fun. I have been watching the Wimbledon tennis championships on the television this last week and there is no fun in it at all. The girls all look as though they have been injecting steroids into their heads, for heaven's sake, let alone their over-developed muscles.

John McEnroe is as unpleasant as ever he was — and he was extraordinarily unpleasant — but the crowds now cheer him to the rafters of their cerebellums because tennis has become a diversion for rich idjits rather than a sport.

Cricket is for fat English boys and thin Asians who need the money, and the Long Room is packed with establishment chaps who, sporting blazers and the famous egg and strawberry tie, will willingly join with each other in long denunciatory tales of how things are not what they used to be. I couldn't care less about their whines. Cricket has been able to survive the MCC for many a year, and will long continue in that notion. Even in Scotland.

Cricket is the summer game. Cricket has been organising mini-cricket for a good few years and is bringing more children into the game. But then rugby has been doing mini-rugby, and tennis has been organising a shorter, simpler, game for children too, and so has every other sport. But when I was a child we were out from dawn to dusk, and we played every imaginable game without clubs or associations or sporting bodies at all.

Cricket we played in the middle of the slums in which I was brought up. You chalked three lines upon a warehouse wall and, armed with a bat, you skelped the rubber ball as far as you could and to hell with boundaries.

Later still, in the deepening dark, you fought each other over the final score. That was a kind of sport in itself. You played tennis in the streets, sometimes with girls. Sometimes the girls played tennis with you. You played all summer. Children were everywhere, except in the house.

Today it is different. Children are nowhere to be seen. They are inside. Computer games, videos, at the disco till late, gorging themselves on MacDonald's: they are not out on the streets. They don't play any more. The only children I see playing outside in the park are little ones. After they are 12 years of age, they are more adult than I am.

Sport starts as play, of course. It starts out with little ones wanting to get their energy worked off. Playing turns into sport. Marbles is only a game, but it turns into snooker. Endless hours of keepie-uppie is only a game, but it turns into Pele.

Girls, in particular, no longer seem to be doing anything on the streets of our cities except dress up. I remember all those wonderful games girls played. Peever, ropes, that amazing set of ball games girls could draw upon — I never managed to do that, bouncing the balls against the wall and chanting wee daft rhymes at the time — all these games are of the past.

Many times I remember the summer holidays when, like somebody out of *The Famous Five*, I went to my Kirrin Island, travelling 25 miles off to Largs and elsewhere out of the city.

Children cannot do that any more, and I realise that. Parents are right to be concerned about their children today. Out in the street in my childhood days was a blessing to my parents, not an anxiety as it is to modern mums and dads.

Other pressures there are. When I was a child, every little girl wore a summer frock and every little boy spent three months in a pair of khaki shorts. Oddly enough, today's 'leisure wear' is a lot more restrictive and a lot less healthy.

Lasses and boys are now clad in expensive shell suits and trackwear and the sort of sandshoes which were once worn only by astronauts and cost the same. They sit about houses in this exotic gear. Khaki shorts and a pair of black plimsolls somehow managed to produce more physical activity.

I turned up for the first day of the school hols — at the Haggs Castle Museum of Childhood, it was. Young Meg and Laura are still working there, a year after I interviewed them last. Once again they told me how few children know how to play.

Said Meg: 'We get 100 and more children a day. The ones who know how to jump about best are the tourists. We hardly ever see ordinary working class kids, and they're the ones we want to see more than anyone else.'

As if I needed a testament, American dentist Ed Thibodeau and wife Gail were there along with their two children, Allyson and Bryan. Both the kids loved the day out. Both were healthy and both were polite in a manner you usually find only in healthy kids.

Meg also told me about how awful some of the parents and teachers are. 'Children are OK, but sometimes you get parents and teachers who don't seem to see past their own ones.' She told me of parents who disappear to Safeways down the road for the shopping, or dads who nip off to the pub, leaving their children at Haggs Castle. 'Children don't play much any more,' she said. 'They need that as much as they need to read and write.'

Children are the start of sport, and without them there won't be a single one worth writing about. The school holidays are when the weans should be out and about. In the school holidays, that should be from dawn to dusk and happy days.

MINORITY MAYHEM

January 28, 1991

A 46-YEAR-OLD man was being held in custody in Edinburgh at the weekend following an incident at a schoolgirls' lacrosse tournament on Saturday ...

Such was the prediction of my chums and colleagues when it was discovered that my assignment this week was to cover the Scottish Schools Annual Open Lacrosse do at the august St George's School in our capital city. But I'll tell you this: it was that freezing on Saturday at those splendid playing fields right in the middle of the best of the well-set Edinburgh suburbs that even Errol Flynn's famous ardour would have been cooled. Cold it certainly was.

Not that the girls seem to notice. What is it about young people that they don't recognise the cauld? If Captain Scott had taken along a collection of lacrosse-playing schoolgirls, he'd have got back from the South Pole nae bother. Jimmy the photographer had fingers on him the colour of a Manchester City shirt. The lassies didn't feel the chill. They didn't seem to feel the undoubted physical knocks they took constantly in this amazing game.

Lacrosse, as everybody knows, or should do, was invented by the North American Indians, but it is very much of a minority sport enjoyed especially by the girls at posh schools. There is a certain involvement in the men's game, though it it is largely a ladies' sport. There has been a considerable development recently — the Scottish Sports Council is increasingly promoting the game, especially, oddly enough, in the Lockerbie area — but as a sport it is mainly confined to girls at what toffs invariably refer to with the euphemism 'independent schools'.

It is a pity therefore that the game does not seem to be more readily available to the girls from the state sector. I have never understood why hockey is the girls' game. It is flat, uninspiring, full of rules, and damned dangerous, as anybody who ever watched wee lassies limp into a classroom after a half hour on the playing field would know.

Lacrosse is different from hockey. It is an aerial game for a start. The sticks have little nets at the top of them in which the ball — somewhat like a hockey ball and just as hard — can be caught. It looked easy when I saw the teams, but it clearly is not and, though physical contact is prohibited in theory in the women's game, the speed and the dexterity with which it is played means that injury is not infrequent.

Considering the astonishing speed at which the sport is played, it is a wonder that there aren't more injuries at that. Those footballing jessies who writhe dramatically about the pitch because their garter has snapped would be put to shame by the lacrosse girls. Young Kate from St George's School was to be seen in the interval holding an ice pack to her face after a collision with the ball right in the coupon: seconds later she was out there playing like a demon. Or how about the young fair-haired beauty from England's Moreton Hall who got skelped good and proper on the back of the head with an opponent's stick (her adversary gasped and held her hand to her mouth in horror), and immediately ran the full length of the pitch to score a quite marvellous goal. As it happens, Moreton Hall won the St Leonard's Centenary Cup and so they should because they played superbly. As did St George's second team, who won the Quaich. This is a high-speed game with considerable skill. There are twelve players and something very odd: no boundaries to the pitch. I got the fright of my life as I casually strolled across the greensward to discover two bloody great Amazons hurtling past me with their sticks not inches from my fedora.

Naturally there were plenty of fond parents in attendance, all blue with frost like myself. Mrs Hatfield from York was there to overlook her internationalist daughter Sarah. I saw Sarah. She looked willowy enough off the pitch, but on it she made Mike Tyson look a wimp. Dr Willie Pollock was clearly bemused at the transition from a nice wee slip of a daughter to a hurtling jet who would make mincemeat of any athletic pretensions he may once himself have possessed.

There is something strange about girls' sport, at least to a male chap like myself. The politeness of their behaviour is nearly as weird as hearing bits of girls shouting for their pals. Julie and Caroline and Pippa are not names you normally hear shrieked out over a playing field on a cold day. There was even a girl called Barbie. She was a doll, I can tell you. Here, this is ending nearly as sexist as it started off. But kidding apart, I have not enjoyed an actual sport as much in a long time. Incidentally I won my wager over St George's second team. Thank you Becky, Charlotte, and Alice. You scored the goals in the match that won me a tenner from Jimmy the photographer.

LACROSSE CAN BE PLAYED FOR EVER

April 19, 1993

WHAT is it about lacrosse that it has to be played in Arctic conditions? The North American Indians invented this splendid sport, but I'll bet they played it in the summer. The last time I covered it, me and Jimmy Millar, the photographer, had frostbite worthy of a Russian mountaineering expedition.

This time Harry and me ended up at the Scotland v Wales women's international at Edinburgh's Riccarton playing fields with fingers that could hardly hold a hot toddy.

The Scots and Welsh girls didn't seem to notice. They were jouking about in skirts short enough to have your Urban salivating.

I may say that the Scottish A and B teams were resplendent in tartan kilts. Sadly, some of the girls had resorted to those cycling shorts things. They look silly on men and unattractive on girls.

But they are not all girls in lacrosse. The Scotland B team is, indeed, very young. Scotland B coach Tony O'Connor, an advertising mogul from England and married to Scottish A team player Jackie O'Connor, told me that 11 of his 16 players were under 21.

It rather showed in the B match, which Wales won 9-3. Mind you, Wales had nine internationalists in their B team as a run-up to selection for their participation in the forthcoming World Cup at Riccarton in August.

Scotland were younger and slighter but had used the B team for diagnostic purposes. Many of the Scottish girls are going to hit the senior squad within the next year. Ali Reid, ex-St George's (an especially renowned lacrosse school) showed speed and dexterity, as well she might. Her sister Fiona is an A player. But some of the ladies are rather more elderly, and nothing wrong with that. Jackie O'Connor, at 34, was easily the fastest player on the park on Saturday, and A team captain Val Houston is in her thirties and a world-class player.

Val scored two goals in Scotland's 10-5 win against a much weaker Welsh side (Kirsty Barber and Susan Warren also scored two each).

Welsh coach for A and B teams, Viv Jones, has got hair whiter than mine and is of the sort of age one calls indeterminate when speaking of ladies: she plays for Wales and has enough speed and skill to shame Eoin Jess. Lacrosse is a game for people who want to play for ever.

There are reasons for this. It is not, strictly, a physical contact game, so injuries tend to be strains (though, believe me, these are fit ladies and contact would be injurious indeed). The speed of this essentially aerial game is stupendous, and the level of tactical play demands a mental effort. Scottish lacrosse would seem, despite being a minority sport enjoyed mainly by girls from the independent schools, to be doing very well.

Scotland currently run about fourth in world rankings, with England, USA, and Australia ahead of them. The World Cup may see Scotland forging ahead. Certainly, the Scottish coups of the last wee while have been remarkable. They beat Canada twice at the beginning of the season and toured the States, where they won 10 of their 12 games.

Scotland does remarkably well in this marvellous sport and, in the circumstances, they really shouldn't. As I have been saying ever since I encountered lacrosse, we must have more schools starting up the game.

There is no reason why it should be confined to the posh schools, and that is what the girls from the posh schools say as well. They rather resent the implication that it cannot be afforded. The only sizable item is the stick, which costs about £30. That is peanuts to what many a state school pays out for other sporting demands.

Mind you, like other specialist sports, lacrosse makes horrible demands on travel costs. It is reckoned that it can cost as much as five grand a player per year just to get about and train and things.

Zoe Tabraham, a nice blonde girl studying at Birmingham University who played on Saturday for the B team, spends a great deal of time and money travelling up to train with the Scottish squad. She supplements her income by working nights in pubs.

Surely we can manage rather better than that in Scottish sport.

Scottish sport needs these athletes, especially after our showing against the Welsh A. We won well.

Roll on the World Cup.

WHY THE SUN IS RISING ON LACROSSE

August 9, 1993

SCOTLAND beat Japan 13-5 on Saturday. That's the first time I have gave a score, and damn near the first time I got it right. But Scotland didn't get the score right at all. I think I know why.

The ladies in lacrosse in Scotland have an enviable record. For such a small country, we have done well over the years. The United States, Australia, England, Canada, all of them are winners and hardly surprising that is, but Scotland is rated fifth in the world, and indeed took fifth place at the last World Cup in Perth, Australia in 1989.

This week has seen the World Cup in Riccarton, Edinburgh, which goes through to the August 14. The Scots may have won against Japan, but should have done so by more.

For a start, this is Japan's first World Cup tournament. The game was only introduced to Japan, by students from the John Hopkins University, in the last six years. Yet lacrosse is the growing sport for Japanese women — there are now 8300 registered players in those islands, with more than 50,000 fans. Scotland has a few hundred players.

Women playing sport are dreadfully wonderful and nice, but if they were cleverer they could just be a touch more ruthless. And a touch more they will have to be.

Scotland are fifth and that is remarkable. What is even more remarkable is how they continue to be quite so successful considering how old the players are. The ladies may feel this is ungallant, but it is true. The Japanese took two extra goals because they were younger and, in the parlance of men's sport, the Scots' legs gave out.

The Japanese team were all around about 20 or 21. The Scots had veterans of 34, the age Jackie O'Connor is, and Georgina Marshall, both Anglo-Scots. The youngest is Emily Salvesen, an office administrator, at 22. Almost all of the players came from the private school sector.

The Japanese are young and are going to get much better. The Czechs, for heaven's sake, have an average age of 18; their youngest girl is 16, Lida Cechova. Their interpreter, Lucka Ruzkova, is 17 and would break your heart with a swish of her blonde hair, and Scotland doesn't have a language person at all. Why?

What is surprising is the age of these participants and the attitudes of the young girls who should be taking over. Caroline from Fettes, Alyson of St George's, Briony Croall from St Margaret's were there at the Saturday international, working as ball-girls. All of them were rather engaging because all of them were just in receipt of their A level results. Yet all of them thought the Scottish lacrosse team were splendid and, said Caroline, 'very experienced'. Well the ladies are. But boys would not put up with that: they'd be challenging for the place in the national squad.

You should have seen the Czechs. Caroline and Alyson and Briony should be thinking of an international place and nae danger about it. There is a definite need for younger legs and young blood to boot.

The Czechs were very young, and I may say, beautiful — this is a real spin-off in my job — but they were also very enthusiastic. Coach Leslie Why, a 23-year-old from Philadelphia, and an all-American International, was bringing the Czech girls' enthusiasm to a pitch the Scots girls should have had.

She was also exercising a discipline impossible for a British coach. When she told the girls to sit down they did; when they had to run, they did. When they were told they were going to win, they did — three years since Czechoslovakia first encountered the sport at all.

It is undeniably an expensive sport initially, which is why it is exclusive to private girls' schools. STX had a tent at this World Cup tournament in Riccarton, selling sticks and tee-shirts and caps. An American-based company, they are the biggest lacrosse firm in the world. Wooden sticks, with nets, go for about £45. The plastic sticks are cheaper but you will develop better ball skills with the wood. I haven't told you what these ball skills are in lacrosse. I will tell you now. This is the fastest game outside of ice hockey and it is aerial. The ball goes not only through the air, but the 12 players are constantly running. As they are also constantly very lovely this is a bonus: I did not say this it just slipped out. Youse have the best sport in the world.

Incredibly this sport, an ancient game originally designed to train the warriors of the indigenous North American tribes and now largely a women's and girls' game, only had a world cup tournament in 1982, in Nottingham. Amazingly Japan will hold the fifth World Cup in 1997. Astoundingly Scotland held it this year. Four years from now I expect to see Caroline, Alyson, and Briony playing in the tartan skirt of Scotland, (Japan played in tartan skirts too).

I'll bet Georgina and Jackie will be there as well at that. And they should be because lacrosse is a marvellous game and one which girls play very well: better than they think they do. Boys don't play it, even the Red Indian ones, and girls do it better.

Well maybe they do at that. They most certainly look better, and that is my last word. Not quite. I have got a last sentence. I am 50 tomorrow. This weekend's Lacrosse World Cup has made an old man very happy.

THANK HEAVENS FOR ALL THOSE GIRLS

January 6, 1992

THE year 1991 was rather grand for Scottish sport, at least for the ones I cover. It was miserable for football, and I am not surprised. What can you say about a sport which allows so many people to disappear — Mark Walters, Mo Johnston, and Billy McNeill come to mind instantly.

Look on the bright side — so did Graeme Souness, now enervating his new club at Merseyside. Possibly the most depressing element of the football year was the Scottish international team. No more risible sight was there than the televised scenes of those chaps up at the SFA celebrating getting into the Euro finals because two Ruritarian teams let us in, courtesy of a missed penalty by a Mr Hagi, one of the best players in Europe.

Far from celebrating, the lads should have been scourging themselves with barbed wire and apologising to us all.

But why dwell on this. Elsewhere, we had Liz McColgan winning everything, and what a pleasant girl she is. I rather deplore athletics, to be honest with you, but I approve of our Liz.

I approve especially of all the people involved in the specialist sports who work so hard for nothing but dreams and decency. Some of them don't, however, approve of me. I had the lady who complained about my coverage of the Scottish Schools Cross Country Championships at Irvine because I had failed to give all the results.

As there were about a squillion races with three placings in each and this would have taken up about two pages of this blatt, I thought this criticism a touch unjust.

Then the Scottish Sports Council got annoyed because I attacked the notion some of their members seem to have that sport is really a kind of outward-bound programme to be thrust upon bad lads instead of borstal training.

Symington Primary School were especially upset because I disdained their winning entry to an 'Invent-a-Sport' competition. I care not. Most of the sports I covered were happy to get a mention at all.

One of them, at least, was not really a sport, though my editor thought it was. Chess might be a mere pastime, but damned good it was too, and you get a dram at it as well.

Synchronised swimming might be the same, but it takes a lot more effort and physical fitness than most footy players can summon up, believe me. Also, they are all girls, and that always seems to interest me a

155

touch. I like girls, and I like them to be involved in sport. Sadly, most lassies give up games after they leave school, and it is no wonder, considering the lack of investment by sporting bodies in women's sport.

My investigations in this matter over the last year or so have turned me into a damned feminist — well, almost. For a start, I witnessed a splendid 5-a-side football match in which Pentland schoolgirls won, with little Elspeth McPartland playing her heart out.

She was the first girl to get a trial for Edinburgh Schools — under-12s that is. Girls football has a long way to go before those male football officials can be prised from their prejudices.

Also witnessed was the women's match betwixt Clydesdale and Glenrothes in which keeper Miss Ann Stevenson was sent off in the last minute of the game for the gentlest professional foul I have ever seen. Miss Stevenson, a nurse by profession, fled from the pitch in tears. The week before saw some of the most appalling fouls from the big men of Rangers and Celtic and damn-all the sending off they got.

I saw a lot of girls last year. Rachel McFaddyen impressed at the fencing. I enjoyed that — and once again met the ubiquitous Norman Mortimer, a PE teacher. I met him at all sorts of sporting events. It is people like himself who are the lifeblood of sport.

Girls at the Scottish National Trampolining Championships in the Bells Sports Centre at Perth were splendid. I may say that it looks like there will be some funding from commerce for the bouncers to go to the world championships later this year as a result of my wee report; it is not often I do good. There you are then.

In the course of the year I have covered karate (when I encountered world expert Mr Harada from Japan, and one of the nicest people I have ever met), squash and volleyball, at which Celtic Football Club sponsored the women's Powerhouse squad against Spain's CV Murcia, and all credit to the Bhoys for it.

I also went to and enjoyed the Curragh races in Ireland, where I lost my shirt but gained a friend in Dublin, lawyer Pat McShane, was talked at by Sir James Saville playing Pheidippides at the Great Scottish Run in Glasgow; went go-karting, bowling indoor and out, and looked entirely daft at the yachting at Rhu (I turned up dressed like Captain Birdseye in the full blazer and white duck ceremonials only to discover that the last person to dress like that at the sailing was Sir Thomas Lipton).

I met a lot of grand folk last year. Jackie Connor, the septuagenarian cyclist who still does 25 miles a day and still contrives to be a lovely man who doesn't look down his nose at unfit chaps like myself, was one. A mention must be made too of Peter McLean and his colleagues at the Glasgow Parks and Recreation Department who do so much to promote sport.

There was tennis at Newlands and cricket at Titwood. Rowing at the Clyde Regatta — come in Dr Cherry Wainwright, your time is up — dog racing at Shawfield. Weightlifting at Easterhouse, and lacrosse at Edinburgh. I liked the last one especially: there were more pretty girls there than you would find in a Hollywood director's Christmas party.

Grand folk I met too during the Rugby World Cup, where sportsmanship still exists (for how long one wonders). The most bizarre report I did this year must be the one I did on peever. I was rotten at that, too, but at least I tried.

SKILL ON A FLYING MACHINE

July 12, 1993

I CAME off a Triumph Tiger Cub in the middle of Newlands Road when I was 16. I was wearing a pair of ice-blue jeans, a tee-shirt, and grey, suede winklepickers with double buckles. When I got out of hospital I was also clad in enough bandages to pass for the Invisible Man.

Ever since, I have wanted to be Bob Dylan or maybe James Dean and most certainly Marlon Brando from *The Wild One*. But so does every middle-aged halfwit with a cover-up hairstyle.

Actually I am quite glad that I am incapable of going a pogo stick now that I am an elder statesman on this blatt. Any attempt of mine in motorcycle sport would end in disaster, for me at any rate. A motorcycle death might be dreadfully romantic if youse are a star, but you're still deid. The older you get, the less romanticism figures in your life at that.

Yet there are still chaps and chapettes out there who pursue this sport. There is no question that just riding a bike, whether you are competing or not, is a sport. It takes courage, skill, expertise, and, perhaps, a touch of idiocy. That makes it a sport. And there are lots and lots of people with the attributes described above. Iain 'Stone' Hamilton QC is one of them. He can regularly be seen astride his massive motorcycle, dressed in leathers and sporting a helmet the size of that worn by the leader-aff of a Roman Legion.

Others who zoom about on these massive machines include Kenneth MacKellar, who moves round the roads to the Isles more than he sings about them. Or this blatt's photo man Stuart Paterson, who admits that he fulfilled his dream of biking and became 'a geriatric delinquent'. He tells me the grand thing about it is 'frightening the life out of teenagers'.

Motorcycling gets books written about it. A new one, *Wild At Heart*, a volume dedicated to the famous US manufacturers, Harley Davidson, and the riders who wheel them, has recently come out and will be reviewed next week. The company is perhaps the most famous in the world, and the bikes they produce are certainly astoundingly exotic.

But though the company started off at the beginning of the century, British firms such as Triumph, BSA, and Norton had the edge on them for many years. Sadly the Brits stopped research and development at a level which could sustain the native industry and the famous Triumph company (whose product had so nearly martyred me in 1960) went into liquidation and then became, briefly, a co-operative. The company, or at least the name, was re-launched two years ago.

The motorcycle trade was devastated by the increased sales of cheap automobiles in the 1950s and 60s. Victor Devine, who along with his brother runs one of the biggest motorcycle shops in Glasgow, told me that the best ever year for bike registrations — sales, that is, to you — was 1959, with 320,000 that year. By 1969 it was down to a mere 80,000 and lack of diversification in the motorbike firms meant a lot of the British manufacturing industry closed down. In 1980 another peak was reached with sales of 316,000. The current recession meant that in 1992 only 54,000 bikes were sold. And the last 20 years has seen the Honda phenomenon.

Honda started off with silly little bikes which were laughed at, but not for long. Now Hondas are highly prized and go up to a superbly crafted bike which comes in at £38,000. There are only 200 of them in the world. Snooker star Steve James has one. Honda produces three million bikes a year and — a measure of Japan's industrial perspicacity — that is but one-tenth of their other business.

Victor Devine, himself a keen biker, goes back 30 years in the business, his father having kicked it all off in 1924. There has been a motorcycle shop in Great Western Road in Glasgow since the turn of the century. Devine is enthusiastic about more than selling bikes: even more of a passion is that of safety, and he was one of the strongest lobbyists for the changes in the law which now allows a 16-year-old to purchase only a moped with a maximum speed of 35 mph, and a 17-year-old a bike with a maximum 125cc capacity.

Provisional licence holders must undergo a course of training and must pass their certificate of competence within two years. As for young teenagers buying a really heavy bike — he would not get the insurance cover.

The result has been an enormous reduction in motorcycle accidents since the legislation was introduced. But bear in mind that 75% of bike accidents are due to four-wheeled vehicles.

The sport in biking naturally includes all the actual racing. There are lots of venues, Knockhill circuit near Kincardine Bridge, being the best-known in Scotland. Then there is the mud and glaur of motocross, a bit like cross-country running with exhaust fumes as well as exhaustion. Classic racing — for the older bikes — is also popular. And the famed notion of biker gangs of Hell's Angels is a myth. 'Bikers,' said Victor, 'go from 17 to 70 and there really is a tremendous fraternity among us all.'

But sport or not, the aesthetics of these magnificent gleaming machines has got to be a major part of the appeal. Oh, aye, and the gear, which is surprisingly inexpensive. Helmets, compulsory since 1974, come in at between £40 or £50, though brands such as Arai can go up to £300. All helmets are to the kitemark British Standard. As for the leathers; at between £100 and £200 they often sell as fashion garments.

'We've got plenty of customers for leather jackets who never put their bottom anywhere near a bike saddle,' he said. That, Victor, would include me. I am older than as of yore.

EVEN THE KIWIS TAKE IT SERIOUSLY

October 5, 1992

NETBALL is one of these sports which is regarded as simply for girls, which is why, of course, I turned up at the Scottish Club championships in Glasgow's Kelvin Hall at the weekend. If it has girls in it, I am all for it.

Netball is too widely thought of in a poor, which is to say sexist, light. Boys and men discourage sport for women, anyway, and think girls incapable of any activity other than crimping their hair and sewing samplers of an evening.

My sojourns into sport in which the female sex is involved have practically turned me into a damned feminist, for heaven's sake. For a start, women don't play enough sport and they stop it at a very early age. At about 14 girls chuck the gymnasia.

Netball is one of the great girls' games. But today it is also played by increasing numbers of boys. There are reasons for this.

The first is that netball is a splendid game which involves speed and concentration. It is strictly non-contact, or should be, and has therefore been ideal for women, but there really is no reason why men shouldn't play it.

At the risk of being called a Big Girl's Blouse I can say that I wish my PE teachers — in my day they were called 'Drillies' — had introduced me to this fluid and challenging sport. It is a sufficiently challenging game for it to be widely played by men in Australasia.

The land of Crocodile Dundee has taken it to its bosom and, across the water in New Zealand, the Kiwis consider netball to be the equal of their other sporting obsession, rugby football.

The national NZ team, the Silver Ferns, are as highly regarded in that antipodean country as their own All Blacks, and the televising of netball is daily. Despite being a largely amateur sport, netball is big business in that sub-continent down below.

It is also big in the West Indies, where the weemenfolk get to become major stars in the athletic business. Britain's sports organisations are still thirled to male chauvinism. Elsewhere, girls can get a look in, but not here.

Despite all that, netball is going well in this country. Scotland is ninth in the world league and England is fourth.

Scottish team coach Anne Marie Daly hopes that the forthcoming world championships will perhaps generate more media coverage for, like all so-called minority sports, netball needs all the help it can get. It might help things if the possibility of an all-British Isles team gets off the ground, and this has been much discussed. It doesn't get much help from anywhere, really. The sponsors of the Bank of Scotland National Club championships at the weekend were, of course, the Bank of Scotland. They put in a thousand quid for the Sunday event and the girls are very grateful for their support.

Yet the same Bank of Scotland couldn't actually manage to turn up for the event, and, indeed, the participants' medals — which, I may say, were rather grand and even tasteful — were sent by courier and were late; too late for the initial award ceremony. If I were a lassie who had played netball at school and was now working for the Bank of Scotland, I would be a little upset at the cavalier attitude of the company.

Netball is of fairly recent origin and it dates, in Britain, from 1895, when an American, Dr Toles, taught the girls of a London physical training college how to play basketball. The Ling Association of physical training instructors drew up a set of rules different from, though similar to, basketball. The major differences between the related games are that netball has seven players, whereas women's basketball has six, and that netball is an entirely catching game. You can't run with the ball, either, and can take only two steps.

Netball is about aerial space; about relationships between the players. It is also about tall girls putting the ball into the net and quite wee girls chucking the bladder about with consummate ease and decision.

A full match is set in four quarters of 15 minutes each, but the Scottish championships were two halves of seven minutes each way, which I should have thought would be wearing enough for anybody.

One of the unique features of this sport is that some of the girls were really quite elderly in comparison to some of the others. Captain of the winning Scotstoun team, Sandra Frame, has been playing the game for 20 years. Little Maxine, from Coatbridge, who also starred in her team's 9-5 victory over Castlemilk in the seniors' game, is 14. Lesley Anne, a 13-year-old schoolgirl from East Kilbride's Hunter High School, was bubbling with enthusiasm about the game she loves to play along with her chum, Lorraine. Nobody seemed to see any difference in ages as a hindrance.

Sandra, for instance, is the new development officer for the Scottish Netball Association. She is half funded by the splendid Glasgow Parks and Leisure people, and part by the Scottish Sports Council. She has taken, she reluctantly admitted to me, a drop in salary to do the job.

'I do it for the girls and the kids really. I really want to promote the sport.' She clearly does, too, and enjoyed her triumph on winning the club championship trophy. The plate trophy also was competed for by a Scotstoun team (this time the third team), who were beaten 18-11 by a fine set of sonsie girls from Bishopbriggs. I never got to find out why Scotstoun attracts such marvellous ladies to their netball club. I never got quite to understand why so few men turned up to support their wives and girlfriends and daughters. A Sunday afternoon watching nubile young ladies in knickers indulging in an exciting sport seems to me to be an awful good idea for a spot of recreation.

There you are: I'll bet you knew I couldn't get through an entire article on netball without the mention of knickers. I couldn't, either. What I did bet on was the final result of the plate trophy. I lost there, too.

A WEE PIG OF A GAME

May 3, 1993

EVERYBODY in Troon is called Bill. Well, they are if they're playing petanque for the Celtic Challenge 1993 at the Anchorage Hotel. The Anchorage is a splendid hotel, and the oldest licenced establishment in this home better known for golf. Bill Gray of the Troon club, (60 members at least in the club and more), told me of his involvement in the early days.

Troon is twinned with a French town called Villeneuve sur Lot, and their mayor sent off a set of competition boules. The boules, incidentally, are made of various metals, from steel to titanium for heaven's sake. They are of various weights, too, and absolutely unique to each player. Some of the boules are smooth, and some are etched with circles and other patterns, all of them individual, the way clowns have their own registered make-ups.

But Bill, a former art teacher and now art advisor for Ayrshire, saw fit to set up the Troon club — there is one also in Ayr, and a new club in Kilmarnock, though the strongest areas for this game remain in Stirling and Fochabers.

Taylor even created the smashing logo for the Troon club, a wee Highland mascot of a chap with a big Kilmarnock bunnet called Chuck MacCoche — coche is the word for the wee jack at which you have to punt the steel boules.

Coche, incidentally, if youse did not know already, is French for pig. The coche is properly called 'cochenet,' meaning little pig, and is very little indeed. It is not easy to throw the boule near to the wee creature at all.

And throw it they do, for this is not played along the ground like your normal bowls on grass or indoor. You chuck these little steel spheres. It is not as easy as it looks.

Though the action itself is not much different from the pitch-and-toss I remember from my youth, the balls either roll, or do not, on anything but smooth surfaces. The pistes — the pitches if you like — are bumpy and uneven, and can be made of any material.

At the Anchorage, there was red blaes. There were enough pistes at the hotel to accommodate the Irish, Welsh, and Scottish teams — there were two Scottish teams, an A team, and a B to make up numbers really — and the pistes measure 15 by 4 metres. It is an ideal game for pubs what have a bit ground behind them.

There are but 500 petanque players in Scotland, though a lot more play for sheer leisure. Yet the game is worldwide. Similar to the Italian bocci, a game played by thousands in that part of the world, it is played by 486,174 registered French folk. Algeria and Spain probably come next. There are 30 countries playing petanque.

The name means 'tied feet,' referring to the rule that before you throw the boules, you draw a wee circle for yourself and cannot even lift your feet off the ground, let alone move out the circle.

Out of the near half million registered players in France roughly 50,000 are females, and the same again are juniors. The half million enthusiasts, of course, represent only a fraction of French people who play petanque on a regular basis.

But if Bill Taylor of Troon kicked off the game in that town, it was started up really in Scotland a mere 17 years ago or so as a result of a variety of Scottish hoteliers having wee challenges.

The Celtic Challenge match at the weekend was, of course, held in a hotel, for this is a pub game par excellence. It gets all generations playing. It must be one of the few games in which you can find four generations together and bonhomie is the watchword. If petanque is played with a rare passion in France, it is a little more low key in Britain for the fun's the thing.

So is the bar.

T'was in there I found Bill Taylor of Troon introducing me to John Coulthard of Wales, whose club had held last year's Celtic jamboree at Brecon. A wee conundrum was solved over a pint of Stuart Bickerstaff's hotel's real ale. 'Where were the Cornish?' asked Phil, the photographer, who is from Cornwall. 'I'm not taking photos if we're left out,' he moaned plaintively.

The Welsh captain's wife was from Cornwall. Ireland's Jim Ryan is from Cork. It is amazing how Celtic you feel when we lot are all together, especially over pints of real ale. Jim tells me that his team qualified in Kilmailing Hospice's grounds. In fact, he chucked the winning boule on the very spot that James Connolly was shot after the Easter Rising. Irish folk tell you things like that, and you believe them.

Just to make it a bit mair internationalist-like, the Irish had fielded a team of Frenchmen, the Breteche lads, who played against a Scottish set of Italians, the Casinis from Inverleith, otherwise known as The Gamblers. Another Scottish team were named as the Sex Pistols. I don't — they don't — know why myself looked more like a punk than these lads.

But a lot of women play this. There is always a girl in my reports, and thus I introduce you to the Scottish umpire's daughter Catherine Adams. Aged 18, and a student at Queen Margaret College in Edinburgh, she has moved up from the juniors to play for Scotland for the first time at the weekend, joined by 16-year-old Robbie Stronach. The both play every week, and love it.

There's so much more I could tell you about this hugely enjoyable game — what pointers do, and shooters do, and the difference between triples and pairs and — why should I tell youse? Find out for yourselves.

I tried it, and no bad I was either. Mind you, the Welsh won. By the sound of the hooley afterwards on Sunday, everybody had won at that.

Daft, simple, and fun

July 27, 1992

THE opening of the Olympics had nothing on John Inglis — one of the last two miners left in Shotts giving it laldy on the pipes and representing the Caledonian Airway Pipe Band on the procession to Torbothie Quoiting Club, Shotts, on Saturday for the Wales and Scotland Quoits International.

Quoits is simple and a wee bit daft but lots of fun. Quoits is the business of chucking a bloody great lump of metal, usually iron, shaped as a ring, onto a sort of spike called a pin which is set in a rink, or a bed, of clay. Have you got me so far? Traditionally it is a miners' game. Miners play a lot of games because their employment below stairs is so arduous and dangerous and so open to unemployment at every turn that they have to think up diversions which can take their minds off being either entombed or on the dole. Quoits is so deliciously aff it's heid that miners took to it instantly.

The Wales-Scotland match is a major point in the calendar. Scotland now possesses only six teams — Prestwick, Renton, Linwood, Birkinshaw, Stonehaven, and Shotts. What a list. I once wanted to write a series called 'The Search For Scotland's Worst Town'. I wanted to call it 'Shotts in the Dark'. But Shotts Torbothie Club is not like that at all. It is a nice wee place with nice wee people who buy you a drink and introduce you to their chums.

As in a lot of the sports I cover, I knew a lot of the chums already. Pat McGibbon, whom I know of old from the licensed trade, introduced me to many a sportsman. The Welsh president, the Reverend Tom Mudd, was keen to tell me that he rather wanted Scotland to win because, he said: 'Wales has won so often and the game can only benefit in Scotland from a sense of victory.' You'll not find such magnaminity in footy, believe me. Wales Quoits people are on the Welsh Sports Council, but Scotland's members are not, and therefore are not financed by the Scots body. Saturday's event was funded, a wee bit at least, by lots of chaps, but Motherwell District Council showed up well. Councillor Frank Gormill told me that they put in £500 plus the printing costs of the hilarious programme issued to those who turned up. By the way, Scotland always loses to Wales but a lot of fun is had.

Quoits is basically hoopla on the ground but it is by no means easy. The quoiting clubs are trying to interest new members, including the weans, but, like all miner-orientated sports, it is essentially a social game. The 14-manned international teams each received a splendid travelling clock and a dance afterwards; the way sport should be. Nobody greets when they lose, which is just as well because Scotland lost by 208 to 192, despite the efforts of the three Falconer brothers who hail from Larkhall — a contender I should think for the title of Scotland's Worst Town. Ach, I'm only kidding.

A wet day it was and cosy in the splendid wee bar of the Torbothie Quoiting Club. It was so wet I retreated from the rinks outside to the inside of the clubhouse itself. Inside I meet the Welsh lads who are singing as if it was Cardiff Arms Park. Weans are being sick over copious Cokes. The weemenfolk are talking to each other in the patronising way that weemenfolk do when their men are engaged in the serious business of doing silly things like throwing dods of metal onto spikes. The men are loving it. Wales is staying at the Hilton Hotel in Livingstone. A hotel in Livingstone is a revelation to me, let alone a Hilton.

Despite the rain the players play on. Says Torbothie Club president George Fleming: 'Ye cannae interrupt a championship.' I get the final line. 'You should,' I say. 'It would be, after all, Quoitus Interruptus.' Or getting aff at Shotts. I couldn't resist that. Who could?

The Other Boat Race Leaves a Warm Glow

April 6, 1992

SPEAKING as the sort of boater who clads itself in a blazer, white ducks, and a Panama hat and, in short, looks like Sir Thomas Lipton with a drink in him, it is extremely upsetting to discover that somebody else is doing the Oxford-Cambridge Boat Race.

This is a major icon of British cultural life and I have reported upon the phenomenon before. Mind you, speaking as a wee Glaswegian who wants to stay, if he can, in Scotland in the first place, I was awffy glad to find myself reporting on the Scottish Boat Race rather than down at my old university, where everybody who reads my columns knows that I studied Country and Western music at where else than Magdalen College.

The Oxford lads won again, the sixteenth win for the dark blues in 17 years. They might be cleverer in Cambridge but WE have the bigger pectorals. That is a polite word considering that these days ladies are vying for places on the oarie boat.

There was not one lady looking for a place on the oarie boats at the Scottish Boat Race. We Scots are right about insisting on alternative cup finals and alternative Badminton and Boat Races.

The Scottish Boat Race complete with an impressive catalogue and programme notes which could have been written by James Joyce. Nothing would do but your intrepid reporter was sent off to cover this august race upon the waters.

Mike Haggerty was in Germany covering the racing and watching the Blues on the telly. I was at Ratho watching the still waters of the Union Canal and eventually giving up enough to watch the still waters of a large Macallan in the rather splendid Bridge Inn. Ratho has a canal and it has got a pub and it has also got an annual boat race.

Every year the Scottish Boat Race takes place and every year the organisers tell the media about it. This year The Blatt decided that one idjit was enough to cover the Oxford-Cambridge farrago.

The truth is that the most famous boat race in the world is ill-regarded by professionals and even amateurs in punting. The most famous boat race in the world is thought of as for Hooray Henries, and even the presence of all those Americans in the teams or Dan Topolski as coach and 10,000 cameras and reporters and Denis Thatcher with a half-bottle of Gilbey's in his blazer pocket will not make the last vestige of Imperial sportsmanship any more dignified.

The truth is that while the Oxford-Cambridge Boat Race is itself a kid-on, this Scottish Boat Race is even more of a lie. The programme notes informed me that this race was 186 years old. In fact the two teams have been playing the game for 15 years. The two competitors — there are four on each side — come from Edinburgh.

One of them — and they won, in fact, though this didn't seem to matter — was the Honourable Society of Edinburgh Boaters. They beat the St Andrews Boat Club of Edinburgh hollow — well, by a minute.

There were four in each team which was rather larger than the number of supporters, all of whom were women and children, none of whom actually cared very much who won just as long as they survived.

Survive they nearly didn't because two of the eight boaters fell into the water. Ray Green, for instance, didn't just fall into the murky depths, he came out insisting on a photie as well.

You never saw more people more determined on snaps. Jim Henry was wearing a striped blazer which would have done credit to Bertie Wooster. His wee boy, Niall, said he just put up with it. There is £23 in the Honourable Society of Edinburgh Boater's account, and the St Andrew's Boat Club of Edinburgh is 10 years old, and all of this, on the day that the Oxford-Cambridge sailing is on, is a spoof. Except that, of course, it isn't really.

It is a spoof in the sense that the boys and girls (the captain is a splendid girl called Ailie Currie), who enjoy themselves hugely on the punting competition on this old canal, are content to row and happy to have fun. I have written this many a time but it remains true. What sport and recreation is about is having a good time. There were children, wives, girl, boys, and husbands having that. On Saturday we also saw a world-televised boat race on the Thames and an unlikely horse cost the bookies a few quid.

I — *The Herald* — was had. The brochure, which explained to us all about this alternative Boat Race, was very persuasive and we were conned. I am glad we were because sport is about that as well. The fun and pleasure and the excitement was just the same as if I had Alex Ferguson cracking up if Man U had lost. Better though. I ended up in Ratho's Bridge Inn with a lovely meal, a wee hauf, and Lady Weir, of Hermiston, presenting the winning prize of some very seedy antlers to Angus Campbell. Nae danger.

OK Jimmy, the accent's on rowing

May 18, 1992

EVEN the word 'regatta' reminds you of toffs — blazers, white ducks, gin and tonic, girls in swishing dresses and straw hats, upper-class accents, Pimms No.1. The International Strathclyde Regatta this glorious weekend is actually like that, except for the upper-class accents. The first accent I encountered at the weekend's affair in the splendid waterway of Strathclyde Park was that of a lovely chap from Czechoslovakia called Jimmy.

At least that's what everybody at the regatta called him because his name is Jimmy in Czech.

His real name is Jiri Klemes and he was one of the committee which were overseeing this wee burst of sportsmanship on the water. He was an umpire.

Jiri has spent a couple of years in Edinburgh and is now down in Manchester. He is a big lad, a Doctor of Philosophy, and more. He is an East European who has been around Britain for a long time, and right well known in rowing circles.

Oddly enough, you will not find too many upper-class accents at rowing regattas: you are more likely to discover a Jiri Klemes. Rowing is very expensive, but it is well sponsored and is not an elitist sport at all.

The weekend regatta was supported to a tune that could have been written by Cole Porter, and nae wonder. On a day with weather which Mr Porter could have written about himself, and Mr Irving Berlin certainly did (*Blue Skies* for those of who you didn't get the reference), the oarspeople spent their labours with considerable enjoyment.

The skies were more azure than a Rangers jersey and the heat blew across the water like a gas fire left on by accident. Too hot, in fact, for the rowers, and the water was too calm as well.

What I discovered was that when there is not a ripple in the water it is a lot more difficult to row than when there is a bit of a blow.

Rowing is a difficult sport in the first place, and demanding. Most demanding is physical strength, especially that of the bigger sorts of chaps and chapettes of this world. Small people get perhaps to be coxes.

Liz Chick, whose dad is on the Scottish committee, used to be a rower, didn't grow big enough, and is now the Oxford University cox. She is at Christ Church and I am upset that my own old college, Magdalen, has not provided the cox for the first time in some years. Liz won the gold medal in the Junior National championships and I remember her doing it. Not getting a wee bit bigger must have been a little — apt that word — disappointing. Still, Miss Chick is still in the business of rowing, which is more than I am.

Considering that I went to one of the most famous rowing schools in the country, I should know more about it. Did I not meet one of the committee fellows and an umpire who was at the same Alma Mater as myself. Gordon Day, a big fellow, was clad in blazer and flannels like us all. Incidentally, in rowing the officials sport grey or pale blue shirts because they use white flags to steer the crews.

Mr Day told me that rowing was good for you, and it is. It is also more popular than you would think, though still very much a minority sport. Mind you, it is rather well sponsored.

I am not at liberty to tell you who the new sponsoring company is at the moment, though we are talking here of a five-figure sum, but British Midland have been very generous to rowing for some years.

Scotland has done well in the recent past. Scottish team manager, and The Herald's rowing correspondent, Mike Haggerty, informed me at the weekend that there was a trial in Essen on Saturday in which six Scots were competing for the Olympic team, four of them girls, including cox Alison Paterson.

'One of the reasons why Scots are doing well is that this Strathclyde course is so good,' he said yesterday. I was only an aesthete in this matter. It was a beautiful weekend and the river looked lovely. I was told more than that.

Strathclyde Park is apparently the only Olympic water course in Britain outside of Nottingham, and better than that Midlands spot at that. Strathclyde waterway is used only four times a year for rowing, though it is also an Olympic waterway for canoeing and is a considerable tourist attraction in its own right. Water ski-ing — and, indeed, orienteering — is regular on this stretch of water. Oddly enough, Strathclyde's rowing course is the only actual Olympic standard sports facility in Scotland.

This is the occasion when one can't help telling youse out there that 'not a lot of people know that'. Something should be brought to your attention, though. Scotland does very well indeed in international rowing, certainly for a small nation. In Ghent last week, Scottish rowers won two golds and a bronze against international competition, and Scotland is a genuine force in the rowing world.

Rowing is a lovely thing to witness on a fine day. There is something obviously nice about a sport in which the girls dress up in swirling skirts and straw hats, and the chaps dress like Captain Bird's Eye, and it is the only sport in the world in which the participants look backwards to go forwards.

For some reason, I feel I could do it myself.

IN A CLASS OF ITS OWN

June 14, 1993

THE very first chap I met at the Scottish Rowing Championships on Strathclyde Park was senior umpire, and ex-rower, and indeed a fellow from a wee newspaper in that Edinburgh, Jim MacRitchie.

Resplendent in blazer and flannels he was. I wasn't, because I remember last year's wee foxes pass at this lovely venue when I turned up in the full outfit looking like Sir Thomas Lipton, with every competitor demanding instructions about where the lavatories were.

I learned my lesson. Mr MacRitchie sent me to the right tent, which was, well, the beer tent. Ensconced there was the Glasgow Rowing Club, what was running the free-flow of libations because they, like every rowing club in the world, are in need of funds. Well not every rowing club at all, really. Some of them are doing okey-dokey.

How many times do I have to write this? If it was up to the powers that be, they would be having football the only sport and treating them like crap. Toffs go to Ascot instead of the dugs. Football has the money, rugby the Establishment ambience, cricket has both.

But minority sports have a dreadful task of balancing it all. Clyde and Clydesdale Rowing clubs do not even speak to each other, for heaven's sake, and they live in the same damned building on the River Clyde at Glasgow Green where the People's Palace is seconds away and there are more Trotskyists than youse could have found in St Petersburg in the 1905 revolt.

Lev Davidovich would not be welcomed in the rowing fraternity for this sport's boys and girls invariably are drawn from an entirely different class.

The next people I talked to were from the upper division and very nice and pleasant they were too. Here I was talking to lovely, splendid tall girls called Isabal and Faye. They were blonde and brunette and I fell in love instantly. Both had been the winners of Junior 14 girls' races, and it was then that I realised I was talking to two schoolgirls from George Heriot's School in Edinburgh.

I had been warned about this cabal. I was forewarned, really, because coach George Hunter, of George Watson's, had already demanded that I present — which I did — the gold medals to the under-18s eights winners.

Heriot's is a big deal in the rowing because I threw the ribbons over the necks of a Heriot's crew who had beaten a Heriot's and Dumfries crew, (it's known collectively as 'Nithsdale') and it wisnae really fair, for the Nithsdale lads had caught a buoy on the way, and lost out as a result. I suppose, all the same, that a lot of expensive Edinburgh schools get themselves into trouble quite regularly with catching buoys. I withdraw that remark immediately. Shocking.

But Strathclyde Park is a marvellous venue for this, and showed it late in the afternoon with a burst of sunshine. As it happens, it is an ideal place for the Olympics, for the area has every single advantage for water and field sports.

One of the basic difficulties in Scottish, and indeed British, sport is the idiocy of not getting the settings or regulations right. Meadowbank Stadium, for instance, is seconds short of Olympic requirements. Well Strathclyde Park has it all there. It could do Olympics, believe me.

We most certainly could do well, too, because did I not encounter Gillian Lindsay, who was in the Olympic rowing team for 1992. Only five years rowing, she has been four years an internationalist. She is, after all, six feet tall, and played basketball for Scotland as well.

Hailing from Paisley, and an employee of Sun Alliance, (who, she tells me, are very supportive indeed, and good luck to them), she insists that I give a jolly to her former teacher at St Andrews — her home town — and now coach, Richard Walsh. It is not the first time, and it will not be the last that I shall discover these marvellous young people who ascribe their achievements to the help of others, but it is splendid to hear all the same.

And another young person who achieved much on Saturday was none other than the son of my old pal and pedagogic adversary George Warnock, the old buffer (couldn't resist that, George), who won the vets' pairs. His son Alistair, a Hutchie lad, (how well I remember the days when my own alma mater Glen's won every damned thing in sight), won two races and was in spectacular form.

After having won the junior individual sculls, he scored a genuine beauty by beating the experienced Willie Brown in the senior event. I wis told that the contest was reminiscent of the two Searle brothers beating the Abbagnale boys on the line in Barcelona at the last Olympics. I will just have to take my informants' word for that. I most certainly took the large whisky which proud dad George poured out for me.

But one of the reasons why you find me at these recondite sports is that there is a lot of merriment and enjoyment in taking part, even if it is only me in with bad company. Good company it was with the Glasgow club who are currently trying to raise sufficient funds for a new boathouse near Richmond Bowling Club.

They are only looking for seventy grand and Glasgow District Council is sympathetic, but it is a lot of money all the same. Considering what a real 'extra' it is having a bloody great collection of rivers, lochs, waterways, and canals, which Scotland does, it seems daft to make so little use of our wet stuff. Crivvens, we have enough of it.

Then we have the Loch Lomond Club frae Balloch. Two boys' and two girls' crews. Jack Reid has been coach for the last four years. His daughter Sarah, aged 15, and son Chris, 18, are members and keen. Jack telt me the best lie I have ever heard in sport. Said the Balloch-based crew came in second. That's true. Neglected to tell me that there were only two crews competing. I'll give you that one, Jack. A stoatir.

Or how about the two grand lads from the Stirling club, Fraser and Ollie, who hudnae done very well, they agreed, and introduced me to Eleanor, a fine-looking lass from the local area who was, as happens in sport these days, one of the random sportspeople who was to be drug-tested.

I asked what her second name was. It took me a day to realise that she is by no means called Rigby. The boys will have their fun. So will myself at that.

THE GIRLS TACKLE WITH GUSTO

February 15, 1993

EDINBURGH Academicals' splendid ground, in what Auden once described as 'well set Edinburgh', was the venue for the first women's rugby international between Scotland and Ireland. A grand setting, too, with a long terrace of baroque red sandstone houses overlooking.

The middle-classes are out in force. I stand at the start of the match listening to the lovely tones of two young women who are describing their jobs to each other.

Jill — who went to Dundee University and towers above me — played rugby herself and turned up to support her pal, Scottish internationalist Lee Cockburn. Lee is 6ft 3in. and very pretty (stop that). It doesn't matter if she is very pretty: she is playing for Scotland, after all. On the other hand, she is 6ft 3in.

As it happens, most of the girls are very petite and pretty (stop that again), and it shows in the play. The truth is that the big players among the forwards tended to stop the flow of the backs, who, on either side, failed to get the game moving enough.

Nerves must have had something to do with the lack of fluidity. Kicking was excellent and the commitment was wonderful to behold, and I mean that. Scotland's lads could learn a lot from both teams when it comes to tackling opponents.

Thus said Peter Wright, of Boroughmuir and Scotland, himself no mean tackler. Peter said, and I quote: 'It was a pleasant surprise to see such flowing play from the girls. They are a bit gentler than the men, admittedly.' This, coming from a chap who thinks the word gentle means not shaving with a blowlamp, means little. But both teams played at the top of their form.

Sandra Colamartino was brilliant. This is praise indeed, and was echoed by wee Doddie Weir, who was enjoying the game and a pint at the same time in the august Eddy Accies' clubhouse (the Academicals' Raeburn Place ground hosted the internationals long before Murrayfield was founded).

Incidentally, Sandra Colomartino, operating at scrum half, the position I performed in myself once, had a marvellous game, scoring both tries in a 10-0 victory over a decent Irish team.

Sandra scored the first try with a break from a pick-up by her No.8. Her second came as a result of a charge-down inches from the Irish line in the second half. It was an easy score and showed just how the women's game will never have the same level of sheer physical power that the men's game demands.

The truth is that the girls are slight and there is not the chance of power play. Skill is more prevalent than physical strength in the women's game and it would be silly not to admit that.

But there are awful nice things in women's rugby. Like the fact that Debbie Francis has played 20 times for England and has now, as they say, went to Scotland. Scottish women's rugby once offered so little opportunity that Debbie, from George Watson's, was forced to play for the Auld Enemy; now she is back in the fold, for Scotland have an international team.

It has taken some doing. Money is slight and sponsorship zilch, though this historic first international match did get some assistance from Irish brewers Smethwicks, a purveyor of a very decent stout and an even better bitter.

The Irish team was also fortified by the presence of young Joanne Moore, who started playing rugby only at the end of October last year and whose brother, cousins, parents, and half of Blackrock Rugby Club turned up to cheer her, as well as the four other Blackrock women players who were representing the Emerald Isle.

Brother Stephen told me that the Blackrock club were very male and macho. He also said, despite his loyalty to his sister, that the Irish player of the day just had to be Aoife Rogers. I had to agree. A lovely runner with a deft turn of speed and a hip sway which Ian McMillan would have envied. She was also a lovely dark colleen (stop that right now).

There were a lot of men about at the match all the same, admiring the play let alone the legs (enough). There was, for instance, Irish coach Alain Roland and the Scottish coaches, Roddy Stevenson, a PE teacher at Heriot-Watt, whom I have encountered before and who admits he went into the women's game in a weak moment, and 50-times capped Scottish international and British Lion Sandy Carmichael. Mark Francis brings up the rear. Could Mark be related to Debbie Francis by any chance, a lovely girl who has been playing for Richmond for eight years, has a four-month-old son, and represented England 12 times before coming to us?

But there were a lot of men around, including some of the more nefarious Edinburgh advocates lusting after the lassies. One of them at least was with his wife and children. His boys played the pipes before the game. Andrew and Bruce of the George Watson's Pipe Band are too young, no doubt, to notice the rugby, or the girls, either, if it comes to that. Neither me nor their dad were that young, believe me. Och, the rugby was still smashing.

ROUND THE BOOM IN A FAST CANOE

August 10, 1992

ANY umberellas, any umberellas to mend today? Flanagan and Allen got it right in the song if the International Canoe Europa Cup Championship at Rowardennan at the weekend and over the next week is anything to go by. I felt like Humphrey Bogart in *Key Largo* within seconds, it was raining that hard.

Sayeth the letter inviting me to the event: 'The Clyde Canoe Club will be delighted to give Jack McLean a trial on one of the canoes ...' The letter goes further and explains the sport which it invites me to cover.

'The canoes themselves are modified versions of a traditional canoe with a mast and sail added. The crafts move at tremendous speed steered by a canoeist on a roller seat. This means that the canoeist has to swing round under the boom when tacking. As you can imagine it leads to some spectacular displays.'

I will tell you about the spectacular displays. The only display you will find the Urban V enacting will be in the bar. It will most certainly not be on Loch Lomond on a canoe. It was not your man here who was swinging round any sort of boom while tacking.

In fact, on Sunday, it wasn't anybody at all, because the weather would have precluded the Urban Voltaire, Humphrey Bogart, Sir Francis Chichester, and Ferdinand Magellan, from venturing on to the loch, the weather was that bad.

The sailing was postponed quicker than an intervention in Sarajevo. Nothing like a spot of rain to make the Highlands make the Heilanman's Umbrella look civilised. We keep on coming back to umbrellas.

Wet as it was it didn't stop the lunatics who keep up this sport from being there. There were 58 entries and not just from Britain. Several oddballs hailed from Sweden (and they are likely to win the contest) and Germany, and even a competitor from the Cayman Islands, a country I had hitherto considered to be a postage stamp.

German Ernst Otte, from Hanover, was only a spectator and he told me there were seven Germans in the event. I saw the German entrants and had to explain what the word 'drookit' meant. They didn't know the word but they certainly knew the meaning of it.

The last world cup was, indeed, in Germany, and next year it will be in San Francisco. This will be, of course, expensive, but then it is an expensive sport. A sailing canoe will cost about five-and-a-half grand,

and that's cheap. Most of the boats are built by professional boatbuilders and at a cost to themselves at that.

Canoe sailing is expensive, though membership fees of the Clyde Club are actually quite slight. The Clyde Canoeing Club goes back more than 50 years and is not especially exclusive, though few women are members, and indeed few women have adopted the sport.

I suspect few women are daft enough. Any sport in which the participants wear crash hats, footballers' shin-pads, and extra padding for the bum, sounds strangely unattractive to weemenfolk. The bum gets awfy sore in canoe sailing. As a response to this fact there is even a boat, owned by the irrepressible Ian McPherson, called Rosie Cheeks. Canoe sailing is the equivalent of being spanked in a howling gale. It appeals to High Court Judges, no doubt. I withdraw that right now.

The origins of this sport are, as is the case with most ludicrous athletic activities, Victorian. It was about 1873 when the Clyde Canoe Club was first formed by, in fact, Warrington Baden Powell, brother of the famous fellow who was into Scouting For Boys.

Clyde Club has the second oldest canoeing club trophy in the world — the 1875 Challenge Cup. The oldest is the America's Cup. See the things I know. I wasn't dressed like Sir Thomas Lipton with a drink in him on Sunday for nothing.

Women don't go in for the sport, more's the pity, though world champion Steve Clark — a Yank at that — beat his sister Hannah by seconds in the 1981 World Cup. Children are much encouraged and there are junior and cadet sections, the former covering 16 to 21-year-olds, and the cadets go from five to 16. Adults go to any age at all, just as long as they are daft enough. Daft enough is right.

Did you know, for instance, that in canoe sailing, as in all sailing events, it is possible to be tried in court for mutiny? And that mutiny carries a death sentence? A dashed good idea. As a naval person once said to me of the RAF: 'The Air Force has no traditions: only habits.' Anything on water has tradition to the very fibres of its blue serge. The rule of canoeing which is the fundament is that one must prevent collision at sea. Loch Lomond is regarded as a sea. The more rules I heard about the more I was all at sea myself.

In fact, about the only person out on the loch was Peter the photog, because he was wanting snaps to illuminate this report. I saw the snaps. What Mr Rodger, the sports supremo of this blatt, was thinking of in assigning me to get drowned in any loch at all, I cannot imagine, but the moment I witnessed that flimsy little craft in the photie I knew that I was quite right to spend my time in the splendid little bar with Broon and his wife.

It is all right for young snappers, whipper or otherwise, to risk their lives; it is quite a different matter for a chap who is, today, 48 years of age. On Sunday I was a day away from my birthday. If it had been up to my bosses I would never have made it.

Today I am 48: yesterday I celebrated it in the company of grand folk. Some of them had a few bob. Said Andy: 'Sailing is like standing under a shower tearing up £5 notes.' But not a one was a snob. Nice people. As Flanagan and Allen would have put it.

TEUCHTERS' BIG DAY OUT

June 8, 1992

SHINTY is frae the Heilan's, (have I got that apostrophe right?), and today we are talkin' Heilan folk. There was a right wheen of them down here at Old Anniesland, where the Glasgow High School used to give chaps like me a right drubbing on the rugby field.

Mind you, this year's Camanachd Cup final struck off with the primary chiels giving it laldy at my own old school's playing fields in Bishopbriggs, where the Glen's lads used to destroy the boys in the brown and gold. Destroyed was what Fodderty primary from Strathpeffer did, beating the wee lads from Dunbeg/ Furnace 5-2.

This is by no means an unusual score in shinty: one expects high scores in a game as aff its heid as this. Sadly, it was a low score and — by the accounts of the 3000 teuchters I met — a poorish game in excitement, if splendid in the playing.

Fort William won by 1-0, scoring in the first 10 seconds. Myself, like most of the others, hardly had time to pour the dram down our throats than the scoreline was established.

It was good to see Fort William winning, all the same. Kingusssie are used, of course, to winning all the time, and Fort William were definitely the underdogs.

Kingussie sport red and blue jerseys and white shorts. They are, indeed, the Rangers of shinty, and in more ways than one. They have with them an arrogance which would do credit to an Ibrox when Bill Struth was in charge and an attitude of belief which would make Graeme Souness look a doubting apostle. Fort William could hardly have expected to win, but they did.

On the terracing I witnessed the Fort Williamites. There was young Sarah, ex-barmaid of Heraghty's and herself from that town, and in the company of her uncles, all of whom I know. I may say that she was in just about the most nefarious company which Glasgow ever sees.

Wee Sarah, thoroughly enjoying her team's victory, was looking lovelier than ever and I took her into the bar reserved for the press — claiming that she was my photographer, telling the decent man who was in charge of security that if he believed that he would believe anything. His reply was what you would expect from what turned out to be a Mull man.

'Och I know she's not a photographer, Mr McLean, but then,' he said, 'you're not exactly a sports reporter.' That's me telt.

Shinty is an occasion, not a game. There was Fraser Grigor there letting me buy him vodka and coke. 'I'm not drinking till later,' he said, and there was Billy from this paper's sports desk, who was wee-er than anyone, including the weans. There was the old doyen of shinty, Jack Richmond, calling me up to the balcony and demanding that I get served Glenmorangie by this gorgeously lissom girl, who represented the company which had sponsored, and has for some 16 years, the Camanachd Cup. There was Lesley Young of that company, who danced with me somewhat inexpertly, (her, no me, I say ungallantly) at the ceilidh later that night.

There was the Irvine Pipe Band with Dianne and Lorna dressed up in the full kilts and stuff. To my horror both the girls were wearing proper kilts with sporrans. To chauvinistic Mullochs like myself this is anathema. When I pointed out that lassies had no right to a sporran I was blithely informed that they used the sporrans to keep their make-up in. Is there no end to female incursions?

Lots more were in states of undress, for it was a hot day.

I spoke to the polis about this matter. There was, in fact, only one polis on duty, a very pretty 21-year-old policewoman called Audrey Brown. It is my guess that girls don't get into the polis unless they pass the prettiness test; a bit like casting chorus-girls for *42nd Street*. Audrey was smashing and dead nice.

Her boss was there with a big Highland polizei, both of them off-duty, to take a look around, he said (i.e. a wee drop of out of routine duty). 'How have you only one wee girl looking after this entire crowd?' I asked. 'What if fighting broke out?' The inspector and the big Highland gendarme looked at me. 'Och, they'd only be fighting amongst themselves. They're decent, Highland folk.' That's all right, then. And it is, of course. It was a smashing day.

Decent folk get to have a good time. At the end the Fort William boys and girls ran on to the pitch and celebrated more than somewhat. In fact, the yellow jerseys of the boys were damn near shredded with all that patting on the back. Och, the Kingussie lads got a wee hand as well. The throng stayed for half an hour, which must have been the only time they were not servicing their thoraxes with a libation.

Do not talk to me of libations at a Camanachd Cup final. I ended up at the ceilidh in the magnificent lounge of that school which had once rivalled Allan Glen's for intelligence.

I never knew my arthritis was that advanced till I woke up yesterday morning. It is the first time my body was sorer than my heid. Jane MacDonald, from Portree, is a nurse. After the Dashing White Sergeant with her it was a nurse I was needing.

Groundsman Graham Wilke told me later that you could dance on his grass as easy as you could on the dance floor. This morning I was that bad I could have danced on my grave, let alone the bed. That's shinty for you. See you all next year.

THE MOD KNOW HOW TO GIVE IT STICK

October 18, 1993

THE Mod at Airdrie now. The West End Bar was happy enough, for the Teuchters were out in force and will be all the week. There were bands out in the street, and Highlanders everywhere. Dancing, and theatre, and Gaelic. And to kick it off was the three together.

It is called shinty — played with a caman, a stick. The Irish have a similar game called hurling. Just two weeks back, the Irish lost to Scotland in the shinty-hurling international betwixt the two. This is never entirely fair in that Scotland's shinty is perhaps a little more complicated in the rules, and gives the dark blues a slight advantage.

The shinty on Saturday — the Mod Trophy donated this year by the Airdrie Civic Society — showed the most shocking advantage, for Mid-Argyll were well beaten. The scoreline was a classic, one known to generations of Old Firm supporters. It was, of course, seven-wan. Oh the ignominy.

Inveraray's Garry MacPherson scored five. A panel beater by trade, he beat everything in sight. It was sort of not fair in the first place. Inveraray had five internationalists in their team. Mid Argyll had perhaps too many Glaswegians, including, for heaven's sake, Martin English and Norman Campbell who live in the very terrace in which I reside myself. Nae wonder we lost.

And then again Robbie from Meadowburn, and Stuart frae Blanefield were both born and brought up in Glasgow of shinty parents, but it is not enough. Though both had been under-12s with Strathkelvin, (playing every second week at my old school's playing fields in Bishopbriggs), they were unable to stand up to the onslaught of Inveraray.

Even the referee agreed with me. He is a legendary figure. Jack Asher, from Glasgow. A retired teacher, Jack is a very young-looking 67-year-old, always terribly dapper. A bit more about Jack later.

'Mid Argyll were not tight enough and their defence was too light-weight,' Ashton reflected. 'And Inveraray were much quicker off the ball. That said, the Glasgow side showed more individual flair. But they will have to learn how to harness it.'

I suggested that such comments would be unacceptable coming from, say, a football referee. He gave me an answer which would never have come from such a footy person. Jack, incidentally, has only one sighted eye. This gives rise to good-humoured banter. 'He only sees one side,' said Murdo from Kyles, down here for the Mod.

Duncan Ferguson is the vice-president of the whole shebang, An Comunn Gaidhealach. 'This is a one-off game,' he told me. 'We kick off the Mod with it, really.' He is right at that, for the first thing is the shinty match for the under-14s.

This year it was Jordanhill College School against Blantyre High. Jorders won 5-4. It was an especially thrilling game. Blantyre High has had a fair input into shinty, as indeed has Airdrie Academy, whose grassy pitches the junior and senior games were played upon.

Blantyre in particular has been high on the list of shinty advocates with more than 12 years of the game being played there. And the only police presence on Saturday, Sergeant Murdo MacLeod — what else would he be called — told me his two boys are shinty daft. Ewan is 16 and Fraser 12, and both playing the game.

Murdo is from Lewis and a speaker of 'the tongue'. He tried very hard to stop himself, being the polis like, from supporting either team. It was clearly an effort. Next year the Mod — indeed the cup tournament itself — will be in Dunoon. Kyles v Strachur it is. The teams chosen are always the two nearest to the venue of the Mod. I shall be there next year, cheering on Strachur, doubtless with my clan leader and mentor, Sir Fitzroy MacLean, who lives in Strachur itself.

But despite the scoreline it has to be said that, as often happens in the specialist sports, it was a loser who was the winner really.

The man of the match had to be a chap on the losing side. Rory Fraser, a solicitor based in Glasgow, had a splendid game, and it was not due to him that his team lost by such a margin. I spoke to him after the game, when he had collected his losers' medal. He had a wonderfully sanguine response to my enquiry about the game. 'I enjoyed watching it,' he said with a glorious relish. This is a fellow who enjoys his sport. Nor could sub Ewan MacPherson be ashamed. Nor could any one of them. It was a long game on hard ground in cold weather.

Now I am not sure I should reveal this, but uncover it I will. One, well two, of the delights of covering the arcane sports I do, is that I will get to meet both girls and a small goldie. Thank you for meeting you, Anne McIntyre, and I hope your choirs do well this week.

Thank you, too, Ken, president, for a wee swifty of the amber in the Airdie Academy building where Strathclyde Region says you cannae have a drink at all and imposes a curfew where it cannot get weans into a school at all.

Anyone knowing Highlanders would know just how silly such an injunction would be.

HAPPY TO BE ON THE SLIDE

November 22, 1993

ALWAYS fancied skiing. Switzerland, chalets, Lady Di, a lot of aprés, Audrey Hepburn in a Fair Isle sweater; really I always fancied sliding down the piste. Yer Urban has undeniably been on the piste many a time and oft over the years. But it wisnae in Switzerland.

I have never stuck on the wooden runners, though I know the most surprising people who have. There was a time when there was a certain democracy about the most aristocratic of pastimes, a sort of winter version of polo. But only in Britain. Where the snow grows — in Scandinavia or France or Germany or Austria or anywhere in mid-Europe — skiing is rather like golf played in Scotland.

A few years back, ordinary Scots took themselves off to Aviemore and the like for the exhilaration of sliding down mountains on their own two feet. They go there rather less so now, but there are actually more people now doing the sliding. Let me explain.

Mike Westmacott, the PRO for Peat Marwick, accountants of this parish, who sponsor a lot of sport and a great deal of ski-ing, told me that there could be roughly 175,000 regular skiers in Scotland. I even believe him. Mike has, of course, a vested interest. I heard his entire family are keen on the sliding. Indeed his own daughter, Laura, 13 years of age and a prospect for the future, came in second in the British Schools championships on Sunday at the splendid Hillend Ski Centre, on the edge of Edinburgh.

She is an Edinburgh lass herself, at St George's, that bastion of lacrosse, fencing, and all-roundness. So good is St George's girls school that at the British Championships they were first placed in the team tournament.

Hillend, at 500 metres, is the largest artificial slope in Europe. The weekend had 200 races, 100 boys and 100 girls taking part, from Belfast, the far North of Scotland, the west of Wales and Torquay in the south-west.

English girl Jane Rawlings, of Folkestone School, was first, but it was still a good result for Scotland. Last year at Hemel Hempstead, the top Scot was fifth.

The Scots' boys did even better than the girls. Michal Pilarski from Graeme High in Falkirk, who had been second last year, took top place, and intends to go on to full-time skiing. He's also thinking of yooni. Stick with the skiing.

Ross Baxter of Boroughmuir High School — another state school — was third in his first year as a senior. It is quite important to write this because skiing is yet another casualty of the teachers' strike and the parsimony subsequently of the education services. Like many another specialist sport, skiing is no longer much of an option for ordinary youngsters.

It is certainly expensive, though affordable if local education authorities put their minds to it. There are a lot of sponsors, like Peat Marwick and property company KPMG, and even young Laura Westmacott has a personal sponsorship of nearly £1000 this year.

Yet the truth remains that those skis can start at as little as £150 and may last for years, top level skis go to £450 plus boots at £150, suits and other protective gear. Take travel, especially in Europe, and we are talking of an expensive sport.

I've a reservation about this. If parents are capable of spending the massive sums which they do on private education, then they reap the rewards of it. One of the rewards is the amazing cost of the enjoyable but recondite sports to which their progeny, unlike those of the less advantaged, are introduced. I just wish that all children had the same opportunities.

But there are still lots of people out there on the Hillend slope enjoying themselves no end. Karen, Dawn, and Gail, all from Lanarkshire, are having their second shot at skiing. They loved it, falling down as they did. Their day out was not expensive. A fiver for an hour's tuition, including the hire of skis, and all the rest of it. I met from Irvine three lordly toffs, I don't think. And thanks for your heart-warming dram, lads.

But I still won't slide down anybody's mountain.

SHOWING THE SIGNS OF A WELL-SPENT YOUTH

November 8, 1993

THE first time I realised that snooker was going to take off was when I came back to my house to discover that my mum had not made my tea and was instead lolling about on the sofa along with another old rip of a lady called Gail Dimeo, who also possessed a bachelor son staying at home. His tea had not been provided either.

The both of them were watching the splendours of the green baize and knew all the personalities. Hurricane Higgins was just starting out, Fred Davis was still alive, and Ray Reardon was the star of the show.

Reardon had been a miner before he joined the police. After having been buried in a minor pit disaster, he confided to the waiting reporters that he had spent the 36 hours underground not worrying, but making 600 maximum 147-breaks in his heid.

A lot of snooker is about thinking in your heid, which is probably the best place for such a process. The snooker players of that era were splendid fellows. They sported evening dress rather well and took no part in acrimonious disputes. Then came the young chaps.

First was Higgins, then Steve Davis, Tony Meo and Jimmy White, and lovely colonials. Incidentally I met Tony Meo at the Benson and Hedges tournament in Edinburgh on Saturday. He is expansive, friendly, full of patter, and would pass for a trader at the Barras. He likes Scotland, and particularly Edinburgh. 'It's better than Tooting Beck,' he said. 'But take a look at the Ebdon-O'Sullivan contest. If I've come a long way from Tooting, so has snooker.'

Peter Francisco is playing an Irish boy, Eugene Hughes. There really is a deathly hush in the close. It is 11am, and both players are clad in dress clothes. Francisco wears patent leather shoes. Like all the players in this game invented by Neville Chamberlain in a hill station in Poona in the 1880s (a 'snooker' was a young subaltern), there is elegance about Francisco.

He replaces his chalk in his waistcoat pocket like a regency elegante handling a lapis lazuli snuffbox. Says Peter, who doubles as a professional cyclist for Peugeot: 'This is a satellite tournament and the winner will get five grand, but importantly a wild card to the Wembley event.'

He also tells me that the table pockets are not standard size and not quite at professional standard. 'But it's a lovely club,' says Francisco about Edinburgh's JP Centre.

Jimmy Paterson, an ex-publican, owns it. It costs £15 a year for membership. There's bar food, executive suites, 35 tables and a 9am to 11pm licence.

And now I go down to what is regarded as the most exciting match of the day in some ways. Ronnie O'Sullivan is playing Peter Ebdon. It is a swift enough match. O'Sullivan is fast — some say faster than Alex Higgins in his heyday.

O'Sullivan is 17 years of age, for heaven's sake. His manager is the legendary Barry Hearn, who has included many of the biggest names in world snooker on his books. This prodigy has just beaten Ebdon again, this time to the tune of 5-4. 'A good result really,' says O'Sullivan, whom I eventually encountered in the hotel gymnasium. The days of pale mis-spent youth are long over.

Ronnie started at age nine on a full-size table, introduced by his father. It is rumoured that he will become the world's youngest-ever champion. His mum Maria is Italian and his dad of Irish background.

He might be ranked one of the best players in the world but he is, after all, still 17. I remember the days of Joe Davis, middle-aged men like him in their waistcoats and seals and fobs. It is young men now who are taking over the world of snooker — further emphasised with O'Sullivan's 5-1 defeat of Francisco yesterday.

Two out of the three top ranking players in the world are Scots — Stephen Hendry and Alan McManus, with Hendry the top player in the world and no messing. And more Scots are coming through. Not idle youths either. The modern young snooker players do well at school, (especially, I discover, at maths), don't drink or carouse, are quiet and well-behaved lads, and are going to be joined soon by a few young women.

'I started out a bit over-confident,' said Ronnie, 'but I learned quickly how much more experience the other players had.'

A very nice young man, O'Sullivan. Later still I meet Tony Knowles. He was worried about the Press for a minute and then discovered who I wrote for. That was all right then.

Some of these boys are earning as little as twenty thousand a year. Stephen Hendry probably spends a hundred grand on eccies. The chaps work very, very hard. And they are polite.

THE CENTRE OF ATTRACTION

March 18, 1991

WHEN I was a lad there were swimming pools (known to all Glaswegians as 'The Baths', for they doubled as facilities for the weekly ablutions). There were the 'recs', which consisted of red blaes pitches of uneven surface, and you dressed and undressed at the side of the pitch and went home covered in glaur and vain glory.

Badminton was played in church halls, bowling was confined to old men, tennis you played in the street without the benefit of nets, and gymnastics meant fighting up closes after the dancing. There was no such thing as a sports and leisure centre.

Eastern Europe and the Soviet Union had a plethora of such establishments, and it showed every time the Olympic Games came around. Sports and leisure complexes were essentially a feature of collective societies such as the Communist countries strove for.

In the USA, however, they became big business, starting out from humble ten-pin bowling alleys. The business of health became big in the States and the neurosis about the body gave rise to the development of huge hangars of health called sports centres. In the Britain of today no district worth the name will be without such emporiums of fun and games.

Expensive they are. The municipal sports centres make nothing, they are heavily subsidised. Such funding, at least in the minds of sports centre officials and employees, is now threatened by the process of privatisation which is to take place within the next year.

One thing is certain: no private company is going to run at a loss, and local authority sports centres, presently seen as a public amenity, will undergo a clear change in direction. Local authorities, especially the Labour-run ones, may well be loathe to subsidise some minority sports in such places if they think they are adding to the profitability of private firms.

But what are these leisure centres actually like? They vary enormously, as you might expect, and they do different things in different places. Glasgow's Easterhouse centre, for instance, caters for a local population which encounters levels of severe deprivation in some parts. As one young man put it to me: 'There are two types of young bloke in Easterhouse: sportsmen and drug addicts.'

The Easterhouse centre is an oasis of sense and decency among one of the most troubled areas of Europe. It is clean, well-run, free of vandalism, and has a very committed staff who know full well the benefits of sport in their local community.

The Allander Sports Centre in well-heeled suburban Milngavie could not be more different. Here the middle classes come to play. Opened a mere 13 years ago, it is in splendid condition. Swimming, indoor tennis, roller-skating, bowling, all go along with the ubiquitous five-a-side football and badminton (the two most popular sports in every sports centre; in fact, the Allander cannot cope with the demand for the above and frequently have to turn away would-be participants).

Duty manager Bob McKinnon is well aware of the centre's success. 'We are the luckiest sports centre in Scotland,' he boasts. 'Vandalism is virtually non-existent and our customers are a delight.'

The Allander is set among the rolling hills and pleasant bungalows of a contented, even fat-cat, community, though the centre attracts people from all over Glasgow and beyond. Caroline and Mary, from Kelvinside, were there the day I popped in — college students and well-spoken. They had taken three children, for whom they were babysitting, to the Allander. Characteristically, neither took any part in sport and had not done so since they left school. They admitted regret about this.

Another place, another time really. Bellahouston Sports Centre has the same problem in attracting female sports people (society's complacency concerning the lack of motivation in women's sport is a national disgrace for which both schools and local authorities, as well as male sporting institutions, have much to answer), but Bellahouston tries very hard to cater for its customers.

Boxing, under the watchful gaze of coach Billy Ward, a well known character in the boxing world, is popular, as are the martial arts, especially with children. Like the Allander, Bellahouston does have a difficulty in attracting not only women but, I was surprised to find, a lot of young people between 16 and 25. Apparently these are the fallow years, and it is children and over-25s who make most use of the complexes.

The sports centres in the inner cities have a problem in attracting women and young people; they have a problem in their marketing altogether. Outside in the small towns circumstances are different. Small towns are more homogenous and this is reflected in the very attitudes of the natives. In small towns any focus is a focus, and this is true of cinemas or theatres or — sports centres.

Take Blantyre, for instance. Blantyre is a village in some ways and possesses no real town centre. The people of Blantyre are the centre of the place. Situated sort of in and sort of out of a town which owns no heart to it, the Blantyre sports complex is well used and a major feature of community life for people of all ages.

The bar itself is regarded as a pub in it's way and is well supported. Housewives drop in for lunch at competitive prices many a restaurant would have difficulty in following. Blantyre folk like the place.

Irvine New Town, now. I was there the other week. The Magnum Centre in Irvine boasts a theatre, a cinema, a splendid bar and restaurant, ice-skating, swimming, and enough green bits outside to host the schools cross-country championship with 2000 entrants. In short, the Magnum Centre is damn near the perfect example of what a sports complex can and should be.

But is it? Is there not some disquiet about the obsession with sport and health which our society has thrown up in the last decade or so? There is with me.

When I was at the Magnum last I saw thousands of healthy and cheerful youngsters and their parents bouncing with health. Every cheek had a rubicund glow to it, every pair of sturdy legs was firm, every family looked the image of the American nuclear one in which 'the family that prays together, stays together'. The Magnum had an air of a Mormon convention; Salt Lake City by the Clyde. It was this which fuelled my doubts.

The Magnum has everything going for it and it is very popular. The children love it. The children, and their parents, are there in droves. Dressed in expensive shell suits and trainers costing 80 quid, they take readily to the consumer society with an almost religious adherence to health. No matter that they all swallow burgers and Coke in enormous quantities, and that the intellectual diet is of a similar nature.

In the very concept of sports and leisure centre there is no place for *mens sana in corpore sano*. The healthy mind has long since been disregarded in the search for the healthy body. In no sports and leisure centre will you find a library. Literature is confined to glossy brochures exhorting you to physical activity and no more.

The Sport For All campaign is harmless, but it is also mindless. And mindless it is meant to be. There is a disquieting, Orwellian aspect of the sports centres; a kind of athletic bromide for the less intelligent. We do not promote such athletic centres enough, of course, and we should, but we should be aware of the stilted intellectual content of such community resources.

A huge amount of increased funding in the schools is undeniably required for the health of our young people (not the least of such funding is the straightforward payment which should be made to physical education and other teachers to promote sport among young people).

But there is more than that. Sport really does have a purpose, and it is part of the mental health of the nation that it should be available to the people. But not at the expense of sense and intelligence. That would be costly indeed.

HIGH PRICE OF DRESSING UP

February 1, 1993

BUT a couple of years back, when Ally McCoist was still getting shards of wood into his backside on the Ibrox bench, he was asked if he would ever consider joining Celtic. 'I would have once,' he replied, 'but not now. Have you seen the state of their away strip?'

It was a classic Coistyism. But it had a wee dose of reality behind it. The then Bhoys' away strip looked as if Jackson Pollock had been sick over a bed-sheet. The aesthetics of the garment, however, did not deter small Bhoys from insisting on sporting it. Wee boys today don't play football: they just dress up.

Yet is is undeniable that football strips are not just big business for the sports companies: they are important business for the clubs themselves. Strips pull in an enormous amount, and not just for children. I have ever felt the notion of so-called grown-ups prancing about in team shirts as risible as tattoos.

Often such chaps have both. Teamed up with training shoes which have clearly been fried in chip fat, denims covered in superlager and kebab sauce, and a bum cleavage, you have the resistable Scottish male who could give lesbianism positive glamour, my dears.

But sport is big business. As part of the entertainment industry, it does well for the economy itself. And the spin-off of sporting clothes is not merely that: it is a multi-billion pound industry itself, going from sports clothes for sport, to sports clothes for everyday wear. The quite astonishing phenomenon of such gear for casual dress in the past few years has seen some dreadful developments. There is an entire generation of boys and girls — indeed men and women — who seem to live in sleep-suits.

But sportswear is not just trackies and trainers. Campbell's Girls Shop in Glasgow's Vicky Road does a strong line in riding clothes. Though their business is still mainly for little girls, they are edging into the adult market as well.

Riding clothes are, of course, expensive but still affordable. A pair of jodphurs will cost about £37, riding boots — made of vinyl, for leather boots are both incredibly expensive and impractical — go for £22, with adults boots reaching £100. Traditional tweed hacking jackets will set the fond mama and papa back £75, and the velvet-covered protective hats come in at £32.95.

It is a small price to pay considering the cost of riding lessons, stabling, let alone a horse itself. Campbells does more than riding wear: it also does sports clothes for schools.

You can play hockey in the full gear for less than eleven quid, with the boots costing a mere £5.99. When I was in Campbell's, a young mum was buying her daughter the full Brownies' uniform, recently re-vamped by top designer Jeff Banks — was it Sandie Shaw or Cathy McGowan who married the chap? The cost of the full outfit would have clad the entire Scotland football team, including the Ralph Slater blazers.

Greaves is the leading sportswear shop. Golf is a major part of their business with a set of Ping-Zing irons coming in at £900, but the clothes are a touch beyond your unemployed rabbit. Plus fours and twos are becoming increasingly fashionable. A Goretex waterproof suit is £90.

Tennis, too, sees expensive garments from Nike and Jordan and Lacoste. A shimmy shirt from the alligator label will cost thirty-five notes. Designer labels are getting wise to counterfeit sports goods and, indeed, Pringle of Scotland have a team of inspectors going round, well, inspecting. Fencing jackets are only £85, but a lady's ski suit can come in at as much as £1400.

But let us go to real toffs. Glasgow Gunmakers, in the Great Western Road, is the place to go if youse want to go out and kill things like big animals with horns, or wee birds with plumage, or quite innocuous clay pigeons.

Morton Cullen is in partnership with gunsmith Graham McKinlay. Unlike a lot of shops, Morton explained, they sell actual guns and service them too. 'Quite a lot of shops are just clothes shops,' he told me. 'We are in the business of enjoying the sport itself.'

And there is some splendid gear here too. If you should ever want a pair of proper corduroy trousers, this is the place to visit. Breeks (breeches) are the thing, and grand they are, too, in our own magnificent Scottish tweed. Haggarts of Aberfeldy do wonderful shooting suits and some estates will kit out all their keepers in the same tweed. That is costly, of course, but, surprisingly, the garments which Glasgow Gunmakers showed me were very reasonable indeed.

Rough shooting jackets are more than wearable for, say, a football match, and are warm and waterproof. Barbour has moved from the once ubiquitous waterproof into tweed shooting suits, which would be perfect for a country weekend. An Austrian company — Loden — are producing lovely jackets in Islay tweed made up by David Andrew of Manchester. What one wonders, are the chaps in Islay doing? Islay could do with the work, and their tweed, the colours of the heather, the burns and the whisky of that lovely island should make another industry.

Super Ally in a shooting suit? I shouldn't be surprised. But it'll no be in green and white. I will guarantee that.

HOW I REGAINED RESPECT FOR PING-PONG

March 9, 1992

PING-PONG. For some reason the two wee words have a risible feel to them but also a quintessentially 'Imperial' note to boot. One imagines British chaps taking the mickey out of the sort of orientals who actually play such a game.

As it happens, it was British imperialists who played such a game, and the reason why table-tennis should ever have been called ping-pong is that the silly little ball used in the game makes that sound as it pings and pongs on each side of the table. The silly little ball has afforded much amusement over many a year, not just to British Empire wallahs, but especially to the orientals themselves, to whom the game was originally introduced.

As it happens, the Chinese got very good at it indeed, and became leaders in the sport. Chairman Mao was extraordinarily enthusiastic because table-tennis was cheap, what he called 'space efficient', and led to an athletic grace which suited the Chinese race. At one time the only sport they practised was table-tennis. Now they do gymnastics, swimming, football, and rugby. The next thing you know they will be experimenting with democracy.

Table-tennis is healthy and nice, and good for the boys and girls and men and women who play it. When I was a little boy back in the 1950s there were table-tennis stars like Victor Barna and his sound-a-like Chester Barnes. I played table-tennis myself. In the house we fixed up a little net across the dining table. Every snooker hall had table-tennis rooms. That was in the days when table-tennis was part and parcel of Making Your Own Entertainment.

Today there are 1500 registered players in Scotland and more than 12,000 in the rest of the UK. Scottish coach Dave Firholm — ex-England coach, in fact, and bloody glad to be in Scotland now — says: 'England has gone a little down and Scotland has gone up. We (Scotland), came sixth in the Commonwealth Championships last April and we were the only ones who weren't professional. There is a Shetland table-tennis league and one in Wick. Joe Louis played table-tennis to keep his eye in and actress Susannah York was international class. Gregory Peck played for ...'

I stopped writing notes at Gregory Peck. I was afraid that Errol Flynn had played for Tasmania. But I take Dave's point.

I take his point especially when I met Susan Gray, a 19-year-old student teacher from Dundee whose dad, Jimmy, once fouled me horribly on a soccer pitch before he went on to glory at Leeds United. If you get to look like Susan does playing ping-pong as a Scottish junior internationalist, I cannot help but commend the sport. *(That's enough girls this week — Ed.)*

The Scottish Championships, held this weekend in Largs' rather splendid Inverclyde Sports Centre, attracted a lot of players from old and young, to mair able and less so. One of the benefits of what I took — before I went to the weekend's events — to be essentially a pastime is that table-tennis is ideal for the disabled.

This might be important for sport but it's damned important for the disabled, whose physical and other problems are so ignored by those fortunate to possess the smug facilities of the, too often, smug. It is also an injury-free sport, by and large, and one in which a lot of fun can be had without the neurosis of its bigger brother, tennis itself.

You will not find the manners of a McEnroe or a Connors at table-tennis. One of the well-mannered players was Stewart Crawford, who is 15 and a pupil at Graeme High in Falkirk. He is going off to the Euro Championships at Stuttgart. He made his senior international debut against Japan last October. He has the very look of a young man who could get off with Susan Gray. I should have stayed at the game.

SERVING UP SOME WIZARDRY

February 24, 1992

IT was a charming sight but awfully daft-looking. A young lassie some-how had attached the tennis ball to the back of the waistband of her tennis dress. It stuck there as she played, like some remarkable piece of legerdemain.

I asked an official about this piece of wizardry. 'Some of the girls want to play two-handed backhand returns,' he told me. 'Also, they don't want to keep the balls in their knickers ... I didn't say that,' said the (unnamed) official.

Charming or daft or even sexist; it doesn't matter. The two girls playing in this match in the weekend's Scottish Indoor Tennis Champi-onships were hitting so hard and so accurately that it took my breath away. Julie and Ailie are only 16 and about the height of Dudley Moore, though a lot more fleet-footed.

The championships were held this year at Gannochy National Ten-nis Centre, Stirling University, for the first time. A large well-designed hangar of a place, large and roomy with four smashing courts, it was opened only last year by the Princess of Wales in fact. (Raymond Miguel of the Sports Council, and late of Arthur Bell Distillers, introduced the SLTA members as being members of the Scottish Licensed Trade Assoc.)

These four indoor courts are the only ones Scotland possesses. There are a number of multi-purpose courts but these are hardly suitable for top-rank tennis. You cannot expect good tennis on courts which are awash with lines for volleyball and five-a-side. In the past Allander Sports Centre had been used but they have rather unsuitable surfaces.

The fact remains that Gannochy has the only indoor courts in Scot-land. There are 50 altogether in the UK, and Sweden, with a population of 8.5 million, has over 600 indoor courts. We have a population of 5.7 million and four courts. Not for the want of effort on the part of the Scottish Lawn Tennis Association. They are desperately trying to open another tennis centre at Bellahouston in Glasgow, an ideal spot one would have thought, but some local residents have objected on the grounds that it is open space. Privately, some of the officials believe that there is an ingrained belief that tennis is hoity-toity. Frankly, I don't see why that matters in the first place, but there is only one way to end such a notion and that is to open up the opportunities for this wonderful sport to all and to develop it to its highest levels. For that, we need tennis centres such as Gannochy.

There was a lot of high-level tennis going on at the weekend. The indoor championships include among its alumni of winners David Lloyd and Bob Howe, the Australian. The first winner in 1961 was Alan Mills, now a Wimbledon referee, and ladies winners include the indefatigable Judy Murray and Winnie Shaw.

Today's players look good too. No. 1 seed, 27-year-old Brent Parker, gives his all, as does 12-year-old Barry McColl, now playing junior and ranked UK No. 1 last year. In an open championship like the Scottish these little lads can find themselves playing against veterans, who can be any age after 45.

Tennis is an equal opportunities sport with perhaps the best record of any in getting both sexes to play. I spoke to young Yvonne Hutton, a pupil at Castlehead High, Paisley (why do pupils from this school figure so highly in so many sports?), who, sadly, had just been beaten by Alison Woods after a mammoth contest. Yvonne has represented Scotland at her age group and played for the senior county team, West District. She trains four times a week and plays every weekend. Such determination — and there are lots of other youngsters who display the same amount of grit — should be better rewarded. Every time you hear another dreary comment about why the Swedes or Germans do better at sport you should bear that in mind.

You cannot blame the SLTA who address their task cheerfully and courageously and often at financial loss to their members. International referee, one of only 63 in the world, Tom Kinloch admitted that it was only because he was a publican and had his own business that he could really get involved in this best of games. Frankly, I think he was being a wee bit modest there, but there is a truth in it all the same.

The work of people like council member Sheena Sim and the sheer enthusiasm they impart to the players is incalculable. True, there is a decent sponsorship from many bodies such as Scottish Brewers, The Royal Bank of Scotland, Vauxhall in the past, and this tournament's sponsors, Marshalls, of Chunky Chicken fame. But this, surely, is not enough. This is when all the grand promises of governments, of whatever hue, should be met. And that would be a wizardry, even more than a tennis ball at the waistband.

NO GREAT DIVIDE ACROSS THE CLYDE

July 26, 1993

DON'T give me any old oil about footy players being exhausted after having shuffled about a pitch twice in a week. I saw, as millions did, the hapless Jana Novotna lose in the women's singles at Wimbledon, and lose again on the same day in the doubles. That was damn near eight hours on court on one day.

And tennis clubs are practically aff their heids with decency. Which is why I took it into mine to jouk round a few tennis clubs and find out what goes on post-Wimbledon at such places.

Nothing would do but a visit to a very part of my youth, the august Newlands Tennis Club, just on the edge of one of the most splendid though doucest suburbs of Glasgow city, Newlands itself, and the other edge being the quietest and most desirable housing scheme in Europe, Merrylee.

I once thought of this club as the other side of the tracks. It is not so now.

Undeniably it is expensive to be a member, but not that much. Subs for seniors are £140 a year, for juniors £65. The intermediate members, players aged between 18 and 22, pay £92.

The bar convener, Alan Turnbull, admits the last group are a difficult area in that the intermediates are likely to be students and the most financially vulnerable of all, but there is sponsorship and a fair bit of fund-raising.

Cash over the bar helps a bit, but, like most tennis clubs, the reliance is on subs. There is no profit in this business if you don't count the smashing game itself.

Newlands' last annual report showed assets of £180,000, but resurfacing of the seven all-weather courts — Savannah surfaces, that is to say artificial grass and sand — cost 120 grand four years back, and resurfacing will come back as an expenditure again and again.

Needless to say this prime site in a prime area is worth millions of pounds. The remarkable Maxwell family left the ground to Newlands and legally bound it to be what it is, a leisure area.

The Newlands pro, Roy Grant, a Fifeshire chap who has travelled in many lands and been at the club for two years, charges a modest 12 quid per individual coaching session, but generally advises parents to send their weans on squad coaching sessions — 12 children at £2 an hour apiece makes him a little more, but it seems to me damned cheap at the price.

He told me he loves his job but not as much as the kids clearly love him. I watched him at work on Saturday, (he does seven days a week at 10 or more hours a day) and his patter is designed to make young weans want to be champions. Georgina, playing only a year, is advised not to worry about this ageing hack watching: 'There'll be thousands when you're playing your first Wimbledon.'

Partickhill is across the Clyde in Hyndland, and has a mere three blaise courts, for it is primarily a bowling club. Subs are £25 per annum for seniors and £15 for juniors. It is a modest little place with a lovely little clubhouse and the prospect is grand. Lesley and Dougie I meet in the shade of the bar. Both tell me how friendly the club is, but they need new members. There are only 55 seniors, where Newlands has more than 800. But is is a nice little club, and if there is undeniable rivalry among all the clubs in Scotland, there is a lot of fraternity too.

As at Sunday's vets' (over 55s) tournament betwixt Newlands and Berkshire as part of the run-up to the finals in Telford. Janette Coulter from traditional enemies of the south-side Glasgow Club, Whitecraigs, was there to overlook things. But she told me her rivals Newlands were also big in squash, and indeed they are.

Newlands has its squash team in Rotterdam in September in the international club championship, representing, if you like, Scotland. With three squash courts at the moment they have been able to grasp nearly £150,000 through the auspices of the Sports Council, and are rebuilding four courts with spectator facilities.

Sponsorship in both tennis and squash is not high — though all credit to Everest Double Glazing for its help over the years. Yet money is tight. Said professional Roy Grant: 'The Lawn Tennis Association is indeed elitist. That fact is stopping a real elite emerging.'

I wish there were more Roy Grants about Wimbledon during the mad fortnight. And more youngsters like Stuart and Jane and Gillian who blithely informed me that they play every day during the holidays. Sometimes you wish you had school holidays yourself.

MORE FUN THAN OLD BEER AND SKITTLES

March 25, 1991

THIRTY years ago — I swear it was 30 years ago — I was a teenage instructor at the Cathcart Bowling Alley. I got to wear an American-style hat, an American-style stripey shirt, and a pair of sneakers which would have suited Ricky Nelson. It was my job to explain the mysteries of five-pin bowling. Five-pin it was, for the Cathcart bowling was a very wee place, a former cinema and now a Kingdom Hall for the Jehovah's Witnesses. The American influence is quite strong in Cathcart after all.

Later there was a huge ten-pin outlet opened right opposite Hampden Park. The crowds came in their droves. A night out for the family it was and you got hotdogs and hamburgers with onion and ketchup. The craze lasted no more than five years.

But crazes come back and in fact crazes are never very far away. Look at yo-yos. Or hula-hoops. Or skateboarding, if it comes to that. And the latest phenomenon to hit the leisure industry is what I once did a spot of youth mis-spending over — ten-pin bowling. The lower orders have taken to it in a big way and not just the lower orders; people with what one assumed was more sense are now regulars at this cornucopia of mindlessness.

Hotdogs and hamburgers; bowls and bathos. Nothing would do but your UrbanVoltaire had to investigate this farrago of false consciousness. A busy night at Glasgow's own Hollywood Bowl. I will tell you about the mindlessness. It is mindless and so was I the other day, for I enjoyed it immensely.

There is something about chucking a bloody great lump of resin down an alley and knocking over bits of wood; it has the sort of satisfaction one might feel if one were to skelp one's sports editor with a bottle from behind and to hell with the threepence back. Knocking bits of wood over is undeniably therapeutic; a bit like breaking windows out of badness. Ten-pin bowling is, of course, nothing other than skittles, a game of great antiquity, and the beer goes with it.

The Hollywood Bowl in Glasgow is one of 13 similar establishments throughout the UK but this one in the Finnieston district of Scotland's real capital does as good business as anywhere in Chicago or Dallas or elsewhere in the home of the sport. Sport? You could hardly call it that. It is not even a game. It is, as they say in the leisure trade, 'a good night out'. Not a cheap night out but not too expensive either. A game costs two quid per person and you get a couple of hours out of that.

Bowling makes a lot of money all the same. The Hollywood employs nearly 50 workers and takes in 50 grand a week. This is not hay.

On the other hand, it must be expensive to maintain a place like this. There are 32 lanes and the woodwork itself must have been a considerable investment. The well-appointed bar and restaurant and the ready staff will take a gloss off the profits. The above are important to the business for this is a night out and the punters make the most of the experience.

A major factor is that you can take children. Bowling is enjoyable for everybody and kids love it. The advent of computers which give the scores attracts the weans anyway. Even wee ones. Louise, aged eight, was there the other day with her uncle and aunt and looking forward to chucking the bowls. The family had come all the way from East Kilbride.

The customers come from all over and from every social and age strata. Stewart Lever turns up every Thursday with his niece, nephew, and daughter. He is an optician. I wish he'd have got me a set of specs the way I was playing. Debbie and Dawn represented a younger generation, both 18 and working as clerkesses. They like the place because you get a bit of fun and it keeps them out of smokey pubs and the like.

In some ways the new-found popularity of bowling alleys is like the old days — the alleys are healthy and sensible places for teenagers to go. Since the demise of the cafe and coffee bar there has been a lack in this area for the young who are too old for toys and too young for boys.

Talking of boys, I went off to the Hollywood Bowl in tow with a right collection of boys, albeit ageing ones. Wullie and Bernie the Bolt and Georgio from Heraghty's and Rocky off the rigs and myself were giving it big licks with the bowls. Well, not myself admittedly. It was astonishing how involved I got, though. I mean, this entire enterprise is nothing but a waste of time. There is absolutely no point to it. What skill is involved is so meagre it makes tiddlywinks look like contract bridge. Manager Tommy Cusack admitted much the same himself but got it right too. 'Look at yourself,' he said. 'You're having a great time with your pals. That's what this is all about. And I'm here to make sure that you and everybody else enjoys the night.' He was right at that and clearly young Mr Cusack likes watching others have a good time. I have rarely seen a business operation with employees who like their jobs so much.

But it is business and not sport. This will doubtless be denied by some of the people in the trade. Next weekend, for instance, sees the Ten High Bourbon British Classic at the Hollywood sister centre in Stirling with a prize fund which goes into five figures. (The winning male will take £2000 and the top female gets £500: make of that what you will). But money maketh not the man anyway. Or the sport.

A silly business throwing balls about is, no matter what the reason. Fun though.

THE LONG AND THE TALL

March 29, 1993

A VOLLEYBALL match takes as long as it takes, and when you get two splendidly matched teams, it takes as long as the likes of myself to drink up after the last bell.

How these women can manage the stamina of three hours at a game which is always played at breakneck speed, and with a pressure on them unknown to your average rugger chap, is beyond my comprehension.

The men's final this year featured two teams who have never reached that stage — Su Ragazzi (who Su is, I can only conjecture), and the Jets club from Edinburgh.

Both teams have a surprising number of international players at Scottish and British level, including captain Iain Grubb, who is married to the captain of women's finalists, TCB, at that. The development of the men's game has been rapid in the past three years since Haitian coach Ralph Hippolyte took over the Scottish men's coaching. It was not the men's squad I had come to see.

Always determined to advance women's sport, I regard the fact that men's volleyball taking the final bow as a bit of an insult to the women. Why should the men be deemed the most important and last, even? Volleyball is an ideal sport for women in that it involves tactical and spatial skills, and no, or little physical contact.

Not that this isn't a very physically demanding sport. Apart from the stamina required, and the mental agility as well as athletic, these floors are bloody hard, and the lady stoics I saw perform at Meadowbank hit them without demur. I was wincing every time they performed with a courage last seen at Stalingrad. Glasgow's Powerhouse team started with the suspicion of an advantage — well, they won last year when I reported it then. They enjoyed the advantage over Whitburn's Team Components Bureau in having slightly taller players over all, and younger players, too, though Powerhouse captain, Morag Brown, is 36 and has been playing for 23 years, which is damn near as long as the sport has been going on in Scotland.

Morag is a PE teacher, but increasingly large numbers of players are drawn from all walks of life, (in men's volleyball, many come from the police and fire services).

The Scottish Volleyball Association have been developing the younger players. Still a young sport in this country, they are very conscious of the divide betwixt themselves and European sides, and are trying hard to create a new approach with younger and taller players.

While some of the girls are most certainly taller than me, (frankly most of them), they are simply not tall enough to compete with continentals. Jenny Ellis, at 17, is nearly six foot tall. It showed in yesterday's match just what height can do. She played superbly for Powerhouse. Chiropodist Morag Malcolm also had a splendid game for TCB. But then, they all had good games, each and every.

It was hard fought, with Powerhouse taking the first two sets. TCB came back with a fighting game and won the next two sets mainly due to a frightening capacity to set up their spike with winners.

A spike is the one who belts the ball right into the field, like Ally McCoist on a good day. A setter is the one who sets it up, and TCB looked horribly competent in this. Powerhouse had the advantage in defence and perhaps more balanced, if less exciting, play. And, yet, it somehow seemed inevitable that the Whitburn girls should win by claiming the last set.

They seemed more direct and adventurous. Morag Brown, Powerhouse captain, was not really that disappointed. She is a former player for the rival club. This is common in volleyball, much to my surprise. Players come and go from club to club. The Jet's men's team are even trying to sign up a Newcastle lad, Gavin Yates, who will be travelling from Wor Jacky country every week, just to play for a better club. There is a lot of commitment in this sport. There is a good reason for it.

It is not a much played sport in this country, but it should be. Volleyball is splendid for youngsters in particular. So said two young ladies from Falkirk, Linda Mitchell and Claire Thomson, 13 and 14 respectively. 'It's very hard work and you have to train a lot,' said Claire, 'but that's the fun really.'

But if that is the fun for the players, there is more than that for the spectators. It really is a marvellous game, with the most nail-biting rallies you ever saw. The sponsors of these teams think so. The Royal Bank puts thousands into this and the bank officials were out in force, enjoying every minute of the two finals. Myself, as one would have guessed, preferred the women's final. There is something about the sheer delight of watching female athleticism and smiles afterwards.

Sweet Lord, I was smiling myself, despite losing on the bet on my own city's team.

PLAY UP AND PLAY THE GAME

October 12, 1992

TODAY you should be reading about badminton, but you are not. This is because I am, instead, in the Emerald Isle once again, where the only sport I expect to witness will be at a family wedding, and maybe in the bar as well.

This weekend I have missed the badminton. This is a pity, because I was looking forward to yesterday's West of Scotland Open, at which a lot of excellent players would have given me the pleasure of watching a sport I used to take a lot of pleasure out of playing.

Badminton, long thought of as a game enjoyed largely by church-going chaps and chapettes, is in fact a marvellous game, and quite bereft of the kind of appalling sportsmanship associated with another racket game, tennis. You will not find badminton players claiming that the world 'cannot be serious'.

Sportsmanship now. What is sport if it is not sportsman/woman-like. Play up and play the game may not make much sense in professional sports, but I do remember when the very word sportsmanship meant doing just that and playing for pleasure.

Today the word has become confused with gamesmanship; a very different matter entirely. And another thing: what is a sport and what isn't seems dependant on whether it is going to be televised or not, or on whether the Olympics have recognised the game as a sport at all. Sometimes the lines drawn are quite bizarre.

I have covered synchronised swimming, which I much enjoyed, partly because the girls are delightful and pretty and partly — well, mainly really, in common with almost all the world — because it is so hilariously ludicrous. Yet synchronised swimming is an Olympic sport.

Every time I encounter yet another minority sport I am informed by the officials that their particular lunacy 'is soon to be an Olympic sport'. As if playing games were made the more serious to the expression of mankind's existence on this earth by getting a blazered orotundity to acknowledge its legitmitacy with a gaudy medal and a lot of freebies for the officials and their partners.

What is a sport? My editor has sent my out twice to chess because he claims it is a sport for the mind. When I covered chess I had to agree with him. I was exhausted myself after writing up about the splendid competitiveness of the players.

On the other hand, my sports desk colleagues tell me that ice dancing, for instance, is not a sport at all. I cannot grasp why they should hold this opinion, but suspect it is a ploy to keep me away from any game which has girls in short skirts.

What is true of the both above is that you will find sportsmanship.

I have found it in most of the minority sports. When wee girls on skates lose out to another wee girl they might cry a little, but they always go across and congratulate the winner. When chess players win they don't leap into the air punching God's right hand, but shake their opponent's mitts instead.

When I covered Gaelic football in Dublin the fortnight back the players demonstrated their ecstasy by patting a back and giving a nice wee decent wave to the crowd. When badminton players lose a point they exclaim to their opponents that it was a damned good rally.

Sadly, sport often finds itself yet regarded as good for delinquent adolescents to run off their vibrancy or as some kind of cold bath for their spontaneous combustion. Sport, in short, can be merely part of the entertainments industry, no more enervating than a Bruce Forsyth show, and no more elevating than *Winner Takes All.*

What is less than enervating is this constant lobbying for whatever silly game you can think up being considered a sport at all, especially an Olympic one. It reminds one of art students giving themselves degree status when not one single art critic, let alone buyer, is bothered with the qualification but only with the paintings.

A sport or game is only either because people play it and enjoy themselves.

I have covered lacrosse, a wonderful, alive game, which is virtually impossible to televise because it is that fast. Unfortunately, it is played almost entirely by the daughters of the rather well-off, but that does not have to be.

How about boxing. Is that a sport? Well, it is, but I would ban it: despite my pleasure in it, how can you call brutality like that a sport?

Rugby is both a sport and a game, but if the increasing professionalism brings about the sort of money which soccer does, scores of players will be killed every year and therefore rugby, too, should be banned if it goes that far.

I will not be at the hockey this week, though I most assuredly will be in November when the Scottish Open takes place at Glasgow's Kelvin Hall. All the silly games and all the major sports and all the pastimes with which we amuse, divert, and sometimes exalt, ourselves are sport — but only if we are actually at the game in presence, in participation, in thought, and in deed.

As the late Solly Sanderson used to say: 'Were you at the game yourself?' This weekend, in Ireland, I suppose I am. In spirit.